Vancouver Ltd.

Vancouver Ltd.

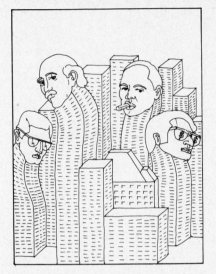  

  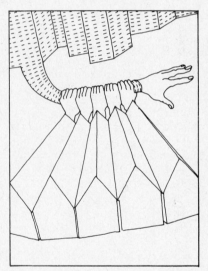

DONALD GUTSTEIN

James Lorimer & Company, Publishers Toronto 1975

ISBN: 0-88862-081-0 paper
0-88862-082-9 cloth

James Lorimer & Company, Publishers
35 Britain Street
Toronto

Printed and bound in Canada

Canadian Shared Cataloguing in Publication Data

Gutstein, Donald
    Vancouver Ltd. / Donald Gutstein. —

1. Vancouver — Politics and government.
2. Vancouver — Economic conditions.
I. Title.

JS1791.G8   320.9'711'33
ISBN: 0-88862-082-9; 0-88862-081-0 (pbk)

Cover photo: George Allen Aerial Photos
Original drawings: Eric Metcalfe & Barbara Shapiro

Contents

Preface

Far too quickly Vancouver has reached a watershed in its short 90-year history. The choice is clear: to continue on the mindless drive toward a high-density prestige 'executive city' — a Manhattan with mountains; or to redirect itself toward providing adequate housing and a decent environment for all classes of people. The first route is being promoted by those who currently control Vancouver's development. The second route will require drastic changes in the priorities of the decision-makers.

I was more hopeful when I started work on this book four years ago than I am now. Somewhere during those years we seem to have passed a point of no return and embarked on that disastrous journey toward developer city. Yet I may be wrong. The course of Vancouver's future could be redirected, given the collective will to do so. This book is my contribution to such an enterprise. I hope to show who does control our city, what is the structure of that control, and why decisions are being made that lead to the steady deterioration of the urban environment. I also present some ideas for discussion about what we need to do to get us going in that other direction.

This book is not about the grand abstractions of planners and geographers. I do not talk about *pressures* for redevelopment, market *forces,* location *theories.* In our society development is not caused by pressures. It is caused by individuals and corporations searching for profitable ventures. Neither is this book a biographical account of the lives and loves of those nasty developers. Individuals do appear throughout the book, but by virtue of the *roles* they occupy — the mayor of the city, or the president of the corporation. To understand these roles we need to look at both the formal prerogatives of the role — the mayor has the legal power to appoint aldermen to committees — but just as important is the informal culture surrounding the role — most recent Vancouver mayors have been millionaires or developers or both.

Many people have helped in the research for this book. Much material was gathered by students in the school of architecture, University of British Columbia from 1971-74. In 1972, with the aid of a local initiatives grant, the Vancouver Urban Research Group produced a booklet, *Forever Deceiving You,* that in many ways is a precursor of this book. Specific contributions were made by: Ken Bartesko, Peter Chataway, Robert Chodos, Richard Fedoruk, Andrew Gruft, Charles Haynes, Bill Henderson, Barry Holmes, Nathan Idelson, Rob Kleyn, Michael Kluckner, Don Manning, Leslie Morgan, Nette Pereboom, Sidney Portner, Greg Richardson, Evelyn Roth, Howie Smith, Craig Strand, Mel Tobias, Haren Vakil, Dave Whetter and Ed Witzke. To all of them I am deeply grateful.

Murray James of the Vancouver city clerk's office was very helpful at an early stage in the research. I must particularly thank Peter Beaudin for his perceptive comments and Jim Lorimer for his careful reading of the manuscript and his many suggestions, but of course any errors are solely my responsibility. My special thanks to Nathan Karmel and to members of the West Broadway Citizens Committee who helped me to understand what was happening to our community and I would like to dedicate this book to them.

1 Introduction: Just what is happening to Vancouver?

And certainly, when I stand downtown in Vancouver on a spring day in 1974, it takes an effort to envisage the city at which we arrived on that late April day in 1949. But it is hard now to reconstruct the total feeling of a city where there were perhaps three highrise buildings instead of a forest of them covering the whole West End and quickly occupying the centre, where the West End itself consisted almost entirely of wooden houses ... and where along Georgia Street the best and most elaborate of those houses still stood, mansions almost, with their deep verandahs and their strange Gothic turrets. In the middle of it all, a red brick cadaver, on the site that the black tower of the Pacific Centre now occupies, stood the shell of the old Vancouver Hotel, no longer in use, its doorways haunted by human derelicts and full of windblown litter. Perhaps, however, that shell of a building had a kind of prophetic function, for its destruction marked the beginning of the end of the early Vancouver it symbolized, the growing invasion of the bulldozers, till all that really remains west of Granville of the Vancouver I first saw is Stanley Park.
(George Woodcock in *Saturday Night*, May 1974).

George Woodcock's words echo something we all feel: that over the past 25 years Vancouver has been going steadily downhill. Fine old buildings are demolished, high-rises sprout up everywhere, familiar landmarks disappear overnight, whole blocks of perfectly good houses are torn down and replaced with unsightly three-storey walkup apartments. And the change seems to be occurring at an ever-increasing pace. To the average bewildered citizen, the whole process seems to have gotten out of control.

Why is this happening to Vancouver? And is there anything that we can do? These two questions form the basis of this book. I believe that both questions have relatively simple answers. Vancouver's environment has deteriorated so rapidly because its development has been in the hands of people and corporations who look upon the city as a real estate operation. Developers, speculators, and their political allies have systematically despoiled the urban landscape in their search for profiable ventures. Vancouver was blessed with one of the most beautiful settings in the world. The wasteland it is becoming is all the more striking in contrast.

What can we do about it, if anything? As it stands now, in most cases we don't even know what decisions have been made, let alone being able to influence them. Yet Vancouver's residents are concerned. This has been demonstrated time and time again by the numerous protests, pickets, and petitions against development proposals. Their protests have been successful on occasion, defeating many of the more outrageous proposals put forward by the developers and politicians. But being excluded from the centres of decision-making power, they can do little that is positive, such as propose basic alternatives for the city's future. Urban decision-making is under the thumb of those who have a vested interest in continued growth and expansion of the city. These include:

1 *Investors in property:* such as the Hong Kong interests who invest in Vancouver because of the safe political climate; the doctors and dentists who used to invest in real estate as a tax shelter; and the speculators who reap the rewards of other people's efforts;

2 *Developers:* local, such as Ben Wosk, the Bentall family, Block Bros.; the big eastern developers such as Cemp Investments (the Bronfman family), Marathon Realty Co. (CPR); and the foreign developers such as the Guinness family (British Pacific Properties, the Guinness Tower), and Grosvenor-Laing (Project 200).

3 *Financiers:* the banks, trust and loan companies, life insurance companies, and pension funds who lend the bulk of mortgage money and who build large corporate palaces themselves.

4 *Real estate agents, property insurance agents,* and *real estate lawyers* who service the developers and financiers.

5 *Utilities:* the gas, telephone, electricity, and cable TV companies who have a stake in the continued expansion of their services.

6 *Construction companies, construction unions, and building material suppliers* who can only work when buildings are being built.

7 *Architects, engineers, and surveyors* who have a vested interest in continued and expanding construction.

8 *Government departments and agencies* who own land themselves, who develop their own property, or who lend money for real estate development. This includes politicians as well as civil servants.

It is a very diverse list, but they all have one thing in common. They all make their living out of building and development and so have a vital interest in the continued growth and expansion of cities. For them, the city is simply a place to make money.

First we turn to the question of how these groups operate in Vancouver. Vancouver's growth has radiated out from the downtown core which, as the centre of business and industry, more and more has come to dominate the region politically and economically. During the fifties when the downtown was stagnating, the suburbs experienced rapid growth

Vancouver, 1919. This was the view up Georgia St. to the old CPR hotel at Georgia and Granville Streets. The photograph is the first aerial shot taken of Vancouver. *B.C. Provincial Archives*

and the establishment of regional shopping centres but downtown was able to reassert itself during the sixties to become the dominant power in the region. Large multi-national corporations and the international banks have increasingly recognized Vancouver as the administrative centre for Pacific Basin trade. This has led to rapid downtown growth and further solidified downtown's position as the primary power in the region. The overall picture, then, is grim indeed. But it is even worse than that, for Vancouver has always been in the grip of promoters and speculators. Its history has been a succession of real estate booms and busts. The majority of its local politicians have always been associated with the real estate industry in some form or other. With the exception of the very recent past, the provincial politicians have always been noted for their desire to give away British Columbia's resources, whether timber, minerals, or land to groups of promoters and entrepreneurs. At the federal level, one party, the Liberals, have been in power for so long that they have come to be completely intermeshed with the local and national business establishments and to protect and promote the interests of the property

industry. Part I thus is a study of downtown development, as that is crucial to an understanding of all that is happening in Vancouver.

Downtown development and the promise of more and more such development has led to a spilling over of downtown's influence into the areas adjacent to downtown. Harbour activities are being forced out of a significant part of the waterfront (Main St. to Stanley Park) and being replaced by the same old downtown activities — offices, shopping, tourism. The same is happening in the False Creek area. A new wrinkle in both of these areas is the introduction of large amounts of rental accommodation for the numberless clerical workers and junior executives required to man the downtown office buildings. Part II studies these areas as the next in line for redevelopment.

Downtown's domination goes further. It is primarily responsible for the blockbusting and redevelopment of the older residential neighbourhoods which are close to downtown: Fairview, Mount Pleasant, Grandview, Kitsilano. These areas all had lives of their own, but they are being killed by the pressures from downtown. This trend is far advanced in one area — the West End — where over 40,000 people have been crammed together to provide for the continued dominance of downtown retail and office

Vancouver, 1973. This photo is taken from almost exactly the same position as the 1919 photo on the left. Several important patterns in downtown development are to be seen here: first, the high-density core on Georgia St. from the Pacific Centre at Granville to the Royal Centre/MacMillan Bloedel building west of Burrard St.; second, the string of towers along the waterfront — the Marine Building, Guinness Tower and Columbia Centre; third, standing on top of the railway tracks by the waterfront, the CPR's Project 200 with the potential for more towers alongside it; fourth, in the foreground on the left, the Bayshore Inn development and other waterfront land awaiting profitable redevelopment; and fifth, the West End on the right with its high-rise apartment towers accommodating downtown office workers. *George Allen Aerial Photos*

functions.

Downtown influences us in other ways too. Because so much of our financial resources are pumped into the profitable downtown ventures, little is left for housing. Fifty million dollars that is put into the Royal Centre is $50 million that does not go into housing. We are in the midst of our worst housing crisis ever, and yet new downtown office towers are going up every day. Clearly, private enterprise will only involve itself wherever the profit is greatest. This means primarily office and other commercial accommodation. Private developers step into the housing field only when it is profitable enough for them to do so. This means a critical lack of housing for those who most need it. Governments at all levels have been reluctant indeed to step in and fill the gap. This would mean stepping on the toes of private enterprise, something that governments are loathe to do.

Part III deals with the housing problem by examing its effect on various areas of the city: the West End, an area substantially redeveloped; **Kitsilano**, an area in the process of redevelopment; Richmond, an area of suburban growth. It also pinpoints some of the people, corporations and government institutions who play their part in leading to the current situation.

Part IV focuses in on city government in Van-
couver, as the institution that most directly affects the course of city events. An examination of the two major political parties vying for municipal power — The Elector's Action Movement (TEAM) and the Non-Partisan Association (NPA). The question here is who really does control the city and whose interests are the politicians really promoting? The evidence overwhelmingly re-inforces the view that both civic parties support the developers and other business interests that look upon Vancouver as nothing more than a real estate operation. One reason why developers have had an almost free hand is because they have always dominated city government.

Is there anything to be done, given this rather hope-

When the demolition of the Birks Building in downtown Vancouver was finally allowed, citizens demonstrated their concern with a procession and funeral ceremony. In many other development issues, people have been more successful in stopping destructive projects.

less-looking situation? I believe there is. Vancouver's residents, time and time again, have demonstrated their concern for the wanton destruction of their environment. Some of the classic examples are described in Part V to show how citizens have participated — the Chinatown freeway, the Third crossing, Strathcona urban renewal, the Four Seasons site. Each of these highly destructive projects has been stopped, or severely modified to make it more acceptable to the citizenry. So we can influence the decision-makers. But these are all one-issue actions. Once the problem was solved, the organized citizenry dissipated. If citizens are to play a more positive role in the development of Vancouver, they must build up stronger organizations and take the initiative for development into their own hands. Part VI discusses what average citizens have done in the past and can do in a more direct way. A rich area for further effort lies in co-operative enterprises, owned neither by public agency nor by private developer, but by the people who own or make use of it. Co-operative housing projects and credit unions are two examples of such enterprise at work. Credit unions in particular are becoming a potent force in B.C.

But even these efforts may be compromised by the established powers that be. Citizens must take further actions to get adequate control over the development process. These could involve building up strong citizen organizations in many parts of the city and occupying vacant land and buildings throughout the city by people who now lack satisfactory housing. Finally, the possibilities of political action are explored: can citizens get control over city government and make it more accountable to the citizens' real needs?

2 Vancouver: Brought to you courtesy of the Canadian Pacific Railway

CPR land at the foot of Burrard St.

Statistically speaking, Vancouver is Canada's third largest urban area. In fact, Vancouver is nothing but an overblown company town. The company, of course, is the CPR. Vancouver was a creation of the CPR and its fate has always been intimately tied to the railway company. At one time most of the area of Vancouver belonged to the CPR. Even the name of the place, Vancouver, was given to it by a CPR official to improve the CPR's business. Many areas of Vancouver and downtown streets bear the names of CPR luminaries: Shaughnessy, Strathcona, Marpole; Beatty, Hamilton, Cambie, and Abbott streets. The whole shape of the city is the result of the decisions made by those CPR officials to suit the CPR's needs.

Vancouver's future as well will be indelibly stamped by the CPR. The redevelopment of the False Creek basin is perhaps the greatest single issue facing Vancouver over the next few years. The way False Creek is developed will determine, to a large extent, the way Vancouver as a whole will develop. If the CPR has its way, False Creek will become a high-density high-rise playground for the thousands of affluent young executives who will be working in all those downtown high-rise office towers.

For 80 years False Creek was a heavy industrial area controlled by the CPR who leased the land to those industries that generated the most traffic for the railway. During the mid-sixties, however, the CPR decided it would be more profitable to develop some of its extensive inner urban land holdings in Vancouver — first Project 200, then False Creek — for high-density residential and commercial accommodation. The city, following its long-standing policy of giving the CPR everything it wanted, designated the whole False Creek area for residential-commercial-recreational uses. Finally, in mid-1974, the city gave the green light for the CPR to proceed with its massive development, and to pocket the windfall profits picked up by the rezoning of the land from industrial to comprehensive development.

This give-away is nothing new in Vancouver's history. The CPR has always had its way. Vancouver might have remained a small logging town if the CPR had not decided to make it the western terminus of the transcontinental railway. Beginning in 1871, when the province of British Columbia joined the Dominion of Canada, a bitter struggle was waged between Vancouver Island and lower mainland interests for the location of the west coast terminus of the railroad. It was not until 1884, when the railroad was almost complete, that Burrard Inlet on the mainland was made the official terminus of the transcontinental railroad. And the specific place on Burrard Inlet was to be Port Moody, at the head of the inlet.

Land speculation was rampant at Port Moody as construction neared completion in the Fraser canyon. But even before the first train pulled into Port Moody in 1886, secret negotiations were underway between the provincial government and the CPR to extend the line to Coal Harbour. On its side, the recently-elected government of William Smithe had enacted a policy of the most reckless give-away of provincial lands and resources to private interests to undertake the most meagre development. It was no rarity to give away hundreds of thousands of acres of land to companies for the construction of the shortest of railway lines.

The CPR, on its side, didn't like Port Moody as the site for the terminus. The publicly-stated reason for this was that the Second Narrows of Burrard Inlet might present a hazard to shipping; but it was awfully late in the game to be making that discovery. There was another reason. The CPR was aware that the construction of a railway depot increases the value of the land around the depot enormously. Aside from the terminus site itself, the CPR didn't own any land in Port Moody. That had all been taken up by the speculators and promoters. If another site could be found, one where the CPR owned all the surrounding land as well, how much more desirable (and profitable) it would be.

Following such reasoning, the CPR would have extended its line past Port Moody even if it had to buy every piece of property along the way. But the CPR and the Smithe government made a deal. For extending its railway line a measly 12 miles, the CPR got 6,000 acres of valuable Coal Harbour property — all of DL. (district lot) 541 (downtown Vancouver), all of DL. 526 (much of present-day Vancouver from

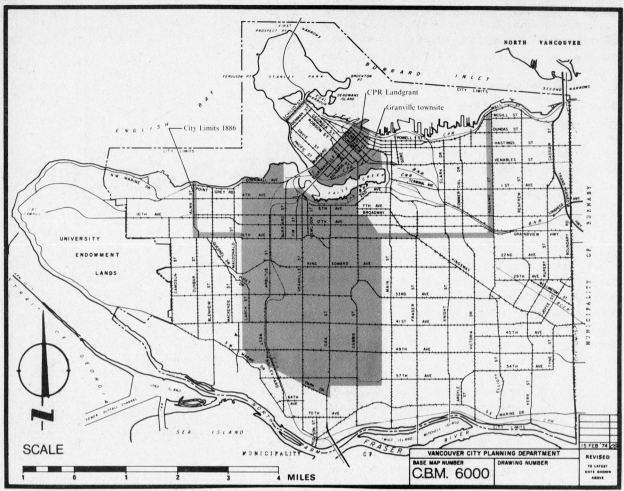

The shaded area is the land grant received by the CPR for extending its line to Vancouver. Vancouver's 1886 city limits are also indicated.

Trafalgar St. on the west to Ontario St. on the east), all lots in the Granville townsite not yet taken up by others, a right-of-way from Port Moody to the terminus site, one-half mile west of Granville, and most of the waterfront from Gore St. to Stanley Park. Further, all large private landowners had to give up one-third of the lots in each block they owned (since they were going to benefit from the coming of the terminus). Thus the CPR acquired one-third of the West End, and one-third of all the lots from Carrall to Nanaimo streets.

The CPR set to work immediately surveying and laying out the streets on its new property. The work was supervised by CPR's land commissioner Lauchlan A. Hamilton, who named the downtown streets after CPR officials (starting with himself), and provincial dignitaries such as his friends Smithe and Robson. Running out of names, he finally turned to the British Admiralty charts for the rest — Nelson, Denman, et al.

That same year Granville was unofficially renamed Vancouver by William Van Horne, the CPR's general manager. We can imagine Van Horne standing by the unpolluted waters of Burrard Inlet, top hat in hand, gazing off into the dense underbrush. Beside him, his faithful associate Hamilton with his blueprints tucked under his arm. Van Horne speaks. 'Hamilton, this eventually is destined to become a great city in Canada. We must see that it has a name that will designate its place on the map of Canada. Vancouver it shall be, if I have the ultimate decision.' Presumably, Van Horne did have the ultimate decision. The name Vancouver was a good one for the CPR. The CPR, with its eye never wandering from the tourist trade, wanted a name that people could identify easily. The name Vancouver Island was already well-known throughout the British Empire.

The CPR continued to clear the land, grade the streets, and sell the lots. In 1887, DL. 185 — the West End — was put on the market, and CPR executives and other wealthy Vancouverites began to build their large houses on the bluffs overlooking Burrard Inlet. One of the first houses was built by Henry Abbott, the CPR's western general superintendent, and many others followed suit.

Granville St. was laid out all the way from Burrard Inlet to False Creek and the first Granville St. bridge built over the creek. The CPR railyards and engine house were built on the north side of the creek, and a railway trestle was built across the creek to Kitsilano, which was to be the site of the terminus. However, this trestle cut off shipping access to False Creek. The federal government passed the Navigation Waters Protection Act which put False Creek under federal regulation and protected it from any structure which would obstruct navigation. The trestle bridge was never used and 13 years later a new bridge was built (the present one) with a swing span in the middle to allow ships to pass into the creek. The CPR also gave up its idea of building a deep-sea terminal at Kitsilano and put it instead on Burrard Inlet at the foot of Howe St.

Vancouver's first suburb, Yaletown, was opened in connection with the CPR yards on False Creek, where CPR work gangs and their dwellings were moved from Yale, in the Fraser canyon, after completing work on the railway.

Mid-way between the CPR depot at the foot of Howe St. and the CPR yards on False Creek, the CPR began the construction of a 100-room luxury hotel, 'away out on a hill' at Georgia and Granville streets with its wonderful view of the harbour. The hotel was intended as the stopping place for the first-class tourist trade who transferred in Vancouver from CPR Pacific liner (the Empress ships) to CPR transcontinental railway. Sitting on the spacious verandah of the luxury hotel, after an elegant dinner, the weary traveller would have a commanding view of the harbour, as the sun never set on the British Empire.

The plaque at the corner of Hamilton and Hastings Streets at the point from which CPR land commissioner Hamilton began laying out the streets of downtown Vancouver. He began by naming the first street after himself.

Vancouver's first CPR depot, built at the foot of Howe St. in 1887. The houses on the bluffs above belonged to CPR officials. *B.C. Provincial Archives*

Richard Marpole's house, at the north-west corner of Hastings and Howe Streets, about 1903. *B.C. Provincial Archives*

Richard Marpole, general superintendent of the Pacific division of the CPR. *B.C. Provincial Archives*

The CPR purposely built its hotel away from what was then the city's centre at Carrall and Cordova streets, since it owned *all* the land around the hotel site, and only one-third of the land in the Granville townsite. Several years after the opening of the hotel, the CPR built the Vancouver Opera House next door to the hotel (renamed the Lyric Theatre in 1937 and demolished in 1969 for the Pacific Centre). The following year, the Hudson's Bay Co. store moved to a location kitty-corner to the hotel, planning to cater to the luxury tourist trade. A few years later, the Bay was joined by Henry Birks and Son, and gradually Granville and Georgia streets became the centre of downtown development.

The West End soon became filled with the homes of the wealthy, and in 1910, at the height of Vancouver's greatest building boom, the CPR opened up its exclusive Shaughnessy Heights residential district, which was protected by a special act of the Provincial Legislature. Spreading out from its centre on The Crescent, with its broad avenues and stately stone mansions. Shaughnessy rapidly became the symbol for all that was grand and luxurious in high society.

It was commonly said that 'everything in Vancouver is CPR from the big hotel downwards.' The Bank of Montreal was the first eastern bank to open a

The CPR's first Vancouver hotel, built in 1887 at the corner of Granville and Georgia Streets. *B.C. Provincial Archives*

branch in Vancouver in 1891. The CPR's Abbott was intimate friends with the bank manager. Of course it was no accident that the Bank of Montreal was the first bank to come to Vancouver, since it had been intimately tied to the CPR right from its very beginning.

It was also said in Vancouver that 'the CPR's the government here.' CPR man Hamilton was elected to the first city council and appointed chairman of the board of works. The first mayor's brother-in-law, A.W. Ross, MP for Lisgar, Manitoba, was so intimately connected with the railway company that he was commonly known as 'the member from CPR' in Ottawa. For years, the CPR had an unofficial representative on city council. This practice has continued right up to the present time. When CPR was planning to build a huge regional shopping centre on its Arbutus property, alderman Ed Sweeney, whose family owned property adjacent to the CPR on the north side of False Creek, strongly represented CPR interests in city council.

One of the consequences of this power is that the CPR has been consistently undertaxed by city council, at the expense of the ordinary home owner or tenant. The railway originally secured a 20-year exemption from taxes by offering to build the railway yards and

engine house on the north, rather than the south, side of the creek. This pattern has continued up to the recent past. In 1957, CPR property between 41st and 45th avenues, east of Oak St., was assessed at $1,480 per acre (for the land only; there were no buildings on it). Home owners' land in the same area was assessed at $1,470 for a 33-by-100-foot lot, or roughly $19,400 per acre, more than ten times the CPR assessment. CPR sold 35.5 acres of the land to Woodward Stores for the Oakridge Shopping Centre. The assessment then shot up to $13,600 per acre. In 1962, city council submitted a money by-law to the voters to buy the Old Shaughnessy Golf Course from the CPR for $2,250,00. The voters turned it down. The following year, when assessments were rated at 50% of value, the land was assessed at $463,270. Was the city offering too much for the land, or had the CPR been outrageously underassessed, or both?

By the mid-fifties, the CPR had sold off the bulk of its Vancouver property although it still retained substantial chunks. It still had the land required for its transportation activities — the False Creek and waterfront marshalling yards, and terminus; three large pieces — 60-acre Old Shaughnessy Golf Course,

The CPR's second Vancouver hotel. *B.C. Provincial Archives*

The CPR's second Vancouver depot, at the foot of Granville Street. *B.C. Provincial Archives*

The CPR's close connection with the banks was less hidden in the 1880s than it is now. *B.C. Provincial Archives*

160-acre Langara Golf Course, and 65 remaining acres of the Quilchena Golf Course; plus an additional 250 acres between Oak and Cambie streets and 37th and 57th avenues.

About this time a change occurred in the company's attitude toward its land holdings. Although it still continued to sell some of its land — such as the property for the Oakridge Shopping Centre, and the adjacent residential developments — the company became interested in doing its own developing. This changing attitude, which has had the severest consequences for Vancouver's development, reflected a change in the structure of the CPR itself.

Twenty years ago, the CPR was a railroad with extensive holdings in other resource industries. However, the federal government allowed the CPR to separate the railway operations from all the other assets. A separate subsidiary was set up for each holding, and then they were all united together in Canadian Pacific Investments: 56%-owned Cominco is a subsidiary of CP Investments, as is 100%-owned Marathon Realty Co. set up in 1962 to develop all the land not required for the operation of the railway. It took about ten years to build Marathon up to the point where it could undertake its own projects. During the interval, some of the properties were developed through joint ventures with other developers. CPR teamed up with Alvin Narod to develop the Langara Gardens project — a medium-to-high-density high-rise and garden apartment development at 57th and Cambie streets; and the Arbutus Village development at Arbutus St. and King Edward Ave. In the early phase of the massive Project 200 development for the CPR's waterfront lands, English-controlled Grosvenor-Laing was brought in as the developer, along with Simpson-Sears and Woodward's who were both going to operate department stores in the development.

In the new phase, Marathon will be doing the developing for the CPR so that more of the profits will remain within the company. Project 200 was the first step in the CPR's long-range plans for Vancouver. CPR doesn't own any land in the downtown core itself, the area which is currently experienceing the greatest growth. But it does own substantial land immediately adjacent to the downtown — its False Creek and waterfront holdings. If the downtown boom in building continues, it will not be long before the downtown is totally redeveloped, especially since the city council downzoned the downtown area, forcing development to spread out more. Then the CPR can

Oakridge Shopping Centre. When the CPR sold 35.5 acres of under-assessed land to Woodward's, the surrounding land which the CPR still owned shot up in value...

...The CPR was able to sell it at a much higher price than it would otherwise have been worth for high-density residential development.

take over and intensively redevelop its lands. In the meantime, the CPR merely plays a waiting game, and watches its $200 million worth of Vancouver real estate appreciate in value.

Part I Downtown

3 Who is downtown for?

You cannot go downtown in Vancouver these days without seeing at least five high-rise office buildings under construction. When completed, each one will add another 3,000 to 4,000 office workers to the downtown daytime population; it will add to the growing congestion and pollution in the downtown peninsula; it will further destroy the natural amenities of view and sunlight; it will further contribute to the monotony and anonymity of the architecture; it will produce another barren windswept plaza; it will point out clearly the lack of public open space, the lack of civic focus, the concentration on private high-cost luxury development at the expense of the ordinary citizen.

Just who is downtown for anyway?

Is it for the banks and the national and multi-national corporations who want a concentrated node of prestigious high-rise office towers to oversee the exploitation of British Columbia's natural resources? Or is it for Vancouver's citizens who want an open, pleasant, liveable downtown full of activity and public amenities?

The answer is all too evident. The multi-national corporations have designated Vancouver as an administrative centre for the Pacific Basin trading-block — Japan, the U.S.A., southeast Asia, Latin America, Canada. Trade among these countries is destined to grow enormously during the 1970s and 1980s. Consequently there will be a growing demand for prestige office space to house the headquarters of the companies engaged in Pacific Basin trade, along with the bankers, trust and insurance companies, investment dealers, law firms, chartered accountants, engineering and architectural firms — all of those organizations that serve the large corporations.

The corporate planners are well-prepared for the coming boom. Most of the major banks have already established regional and international headquarters in the downtown core of Vancouver. Many of the larger national and international real estate companies have descended on Vancouver in anticipation of the coming building boom.

This flood of office buildings is shocking compared to the meagre amount of moderate-income housing being provided by those same developers, even though there is an enormous demand for such accommodation. But office buildings are much more profitable, even if half-empty, so that developers will continue to build those and ignore our housing needs.

Developers will build wherever the profit potential is greatest. In large downtown commercial develop-

ments there are no ungrateful tenants organizing rent strikes, there are no militant citizens' groups opposing the assembly of land and the destruction of the existing buildings, there are no rent freezes being imposed by a hostile provincial government. There are only stable, predictable corporate tenants who like to cluster together in prestigious surroundings and who don't mind high rents because they can pass on the cost to their clients or customers.

Developers cannot build what the money men — the banks, trust and insurance companies — will not fund. Large commercial developments such as the $50 million Royal Centre, and large developers such as the $600 million Trizec Corp., are much more attractive to the financial sources than small home-builders and single-family homes. For one thing large commercial mortgages are a more secure investment than a small mortgage on a single-family house. For another, one large $50 million mortgage is much cheaper to service for the bank than 1,000 mortgages for $50,000 each. And finally the financiers can take an ownership position in the development, and hence share in the profits and appreciation of the land, as well as receive the interest payments on the mortgage. One example was Great West Life Assurance Co.'s involvement in the Bentall Centre. Consequently, a company like Trizec has a much easier time getting $50 million for a downtown high-rise than you or I have in getting $50,000 for a house.

Each new downtown high-rise increases the land values in the surrounding blocks, and since property owners like to see their property increase in value, they are all for more high-rises. Over the past eight years land values in the downtown core have increased at a compound rate of 20% per year. Therefore, owners of downtown property can only applaud whenever a new high-rise is announced.

Even the utility companies — B.C. Hydro & Power Authority (a publicly-owned company) and B.C. Telephone Co. (a privately-owned company) — like to see high-density, high-rise buildings, because their operating expenses are reduced substantially compared to the servicing of more spread out residential property; consequently, their profits are increased.

Once a developer has assembled property for a development, he has to line up a major tenant before he can finalize the financing. In many cases, the financing institution itself can become the major tenant; in others, companies associated with the developer take space in the building. In still others, the federal and provincial governments, using public funds, lease space in private developments; this enhances the value of private property, increases the pressure for more downtown high-rises, and plays its part in the increasing downtown congestion and the deterior-

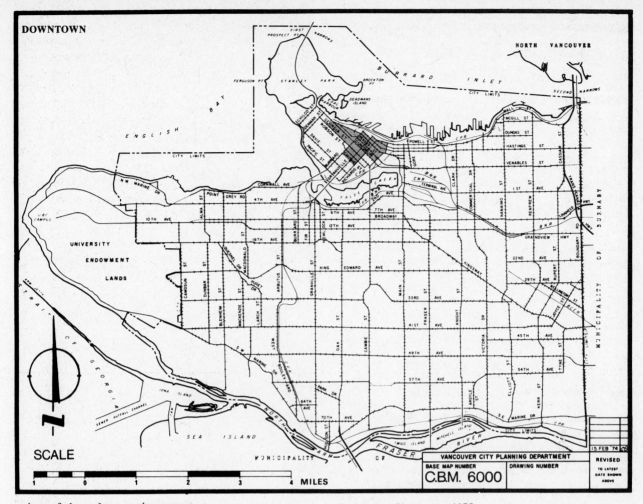

DOWNTOWN

NORTH VANCOUVER

VANCOUVER CITY PLANNING DEPARTMENT

BASE MAP NUMBER	DRAWING NUMBER

C.B.M. 6000

15 FEB '74

REVISED
TO LATEST
DATE SHOWN
ABOVE

SCALE

1 0 1 2 3 4 MILES

Downtown Vancouver 1975.

ation of the urban environment.

If the past actions of city council are any indication, the developers and multi-national corporations will continue to set our building priorities. It seems that developers make their plans to suit their own corporate needs. City council then comes out with policies that turn out to be remarkably similar to what the developers wanted in the first place.

Schemes such as The Elector's Action Movement (TEAM)-inspired Granville Mall seem like attempts to divert public attention from the harsh reality of downtown — that the developers own it. In spite of such efforts, developers carry on much the same as before TEAM. The only difference between the TEAM-dominated city council and the Non-Partisan Association (NPA) city council that preceded it is that NPA gave the developers *even more than* they wanted, whereas TEAM gives them *slightly less than* they ask for.

Over the years, the city planning department has made a great show of planning for downtown. Numerous reports have been produced. But the assumption of continued and increasing growth was never questioned seriously. The city planning department busied itself with the details — a few more

buildings here, a few less there, a little taller, a little shorter, but the basic question was never asked: what do the people of Vancouver want from their downtown ?

At least it was never asked of the vast majority of the public. The only groups involved in the process of determining what downtown should be were the usual business and professional groups and a few ratepayer groups from the more affluent parts of the city.

Few people actually live in the downtown core, so it is a relatively easy matter for developers to assemble property, to get the development permits, to get relaxations of the zoning by-law to permit denser developments, to tear down the buildings that were there before without a big public outcry, and to get the building up with a minimum of delay.

By the time the public does find out about the development, it is far too late to do anything about it. The decisions have been made, probably years before, in the corporate boardrooms of Tokyo or New York, that have led to the destruction of fine old downtown buildings and their replacements by the sleek, shiny towers that continue to populate the downtown core.

Downtown subway system essential, aldermen advised by city planners

By RANDY GLOVER

A subway system is absolutely essential to handle the growth of downtown Vancouver, city council was told Tuesday.

This was the joint recommendation of city planner Bill Curtis and planning director Ray Spaxman.

Without the subway, and a new system of roads for the downtown peninsula, Curtis said, the goals of the planning department's downtown study team could not be achieved.

These goals, released in a report last fall, were to encourage residential living downtown close to employment, to de-emphasize cars and emphasize transit, and to "pedestrianize" the core.

At the same time, he said, recommendations in the report that certain areas of the downtown become "pedestrianized," with a de-emphasis on cars, would need the development of other street routes to handle traffic.

The report suggests development of a "ring road" around the pedestrian areas

and major routes along the Burrard Inlet waterfront and the north shore of False Creek.

Curtis said that the transit system should be improved before street capacity is reduced by putting more emphasis on the pedestrian.

He quoted figures from the study team's report which predict a doubling of the downtown population by the year 2000.

The projection is based on what the study report calls "a middle ground" between a no-growth policy and unlimited growth with only minimal controls.

It also predicts the employee population in the downtown peninsula would increase to 180,000 in the year 2000 from about 100,000 this year. The residential population is projected to rise to 105,000, from the present 47,000.

"Our only hope is a subway system," Curtis said.

The site of the former Marwell Building, built in 1950 and designed by architects Harold Semmens and Douglas Simpson. It was the first winner of the Massey Gold Medal, awarded for excellence in architectural design. The building and two others less than 25 years old were demolished by Crown Life Insurance Co. to make way for a new 20-storey office tower.

Why is a downtown subway system 'essential'? Because it would make the limited supply of downtown land even more valuable than it now is, and permit developers to continue the present pattern of concentrating as much growth as possible in the downtown.

Business interests and city politicians keep telling us how necessary all this development is for our own good, but there is one question that we should keep in mind at all times: *what does downtown development cost us?* Will all the proposed developments generate enough tax revenues to pay for the required public services and amenities that have become necessary because of the new developments? The roads, rapid transit and buses, the sewers, sidewalks, and fire protection, the parks and open spaces? Or will the home owner through his taxes and the tenant through his rent have to foot the bill and subsidize the big out-of-town developers?

In spite of what city council tells us — that the big downtown developments are paying their own way — the answer is not all that clear. A study done in San

Francisco showed that it cost more to run the downtown than the downtown brought in revenues: downtown contributed $62.9 million in local revenues, but cost $67.7 million to run. Does the same hold true for Vancouver? Are the ordinary taxpayers and tenants bailing out the developers? Vancouver has never conducted the comprehensive research which would provide the answer to this question. If taxpayers are subsidizing this redevelopment, the situation is indeed appalling. Not only do the large multi-national corporations have almost carte blanche to come in and develop downtown as they wish while continuing to destroy Vancouver's natural amenities, but the people of Vancouver are subsidizing them to do it.

There is a hierarchy of decision-making affecting downtown development. At the top level, the large multi-national corporations are making broad overall policy decisions about the growth of the Pacific Basin and national trade and commerce. The consequences of these decisions are felt in Canada through the

Downtown Vancouver from Stanley Park. Virtually every high-rise tower in the photograph — with the exception of the pyramid-shaped Marine Building in the centre — has been built since 1965.

Downtown development has reduced the spectacular view of harbour and mountains to an ever-decreasing slit.

```
┌─────────────────────────────────────────────┐
│ Downtown Vancouver Decision-Making Hierarchy │
│                      |                        │
│               Multinational                   │
│               Corporations                    │
│                      |                        │
│                 Canadian                      │
│              Chartered Banks                  │
│                      |                        │
│                Local bank                     │
│                 directors                     │
│                      |                        │
│              Local business                   │
│               establishment                   │
│    Corporations - law firms - old families - clubs │
│                      |                        │
│               Local political                 │
│                  parties                      │
│          Liberals - Socreds -TEAM- NPA        │
│                      |                        │
│          Developers - planners - architects   │
└─────────────────────────────────────────────┘
```

chartered banks who provide the necessary funds and who are the centres of power in the country.

Control flows through the banks, via the local directors of the banks, into the local business establishment — the corporations (such as MacMillan Bloedel, Cominco, and B.C. Telephone), the law firms (such as Davis & Co.; Farris, Vaughan, Wills & Murphy; Ladner, Downs), the old families (such as Bell-Irving, Killam, Reifel, MacMillan), the clubs and associations (Vancouver Club, Board of Trade). From the local business establishment the decision-making chain leads into the local political structure — the federal Liberals, the provincial Liberals and Social Credit, and the municipal parties, the Non-Partisan Association and The Elector's Action Movement.

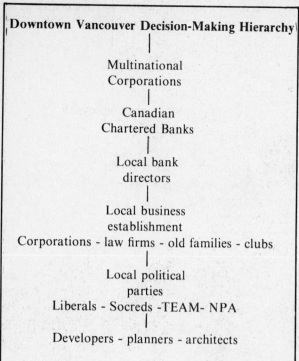

Downtown developers, left to their own devices, have been obliterating street level activity. This is the face presented to the street by the Eaton's store in the Pacific Centre development.

4 Downtown decision-makers I: The multi-nationals

Big business has big things in store for Vancouver during the 1970s and 1980s. The growth of trade with Japan, the opening up of the vast mainland Chinese market, and the continuing alienation of British Columbia's natural resources — all of these mean an enormous boom for Vancouver.

The Pacific Basin Economic Council (PBEC) — a group that likes to keep well in the background — is actively involved in determining what kind of a city Vancouver is likely to become. Formed in 1966, PBEC is an informal organization of senior business executives representing the major multi-national corporations engaged in business in the Pacific Basin countries — Japan, the U.S.A., Canada, Australia, New Zealand. The group also includes observers from other Pacific Basin countries in southeast Asia and Latin America.

PBEC represents over 300 major multi-national corporations and financial institutions; American-based concerns like the Bank of America, the Bank of Hawaii, Caterpillar Tractor Co., American Airlines and Dillingham Corp.; Japanese-based concerns like Mitsubishi Corp., Japan Air Lines Co., the Fuji Bank, Toyota Motor Co.; Australian- and New Zealand-based concerns like the National Bank of New Zealand, the Colonial Sugar Refining Co., Commonwealth Steel Co; and Canadian-based concerns like INCO, Royal Bank of Canada, and Canadian National Railways.

The group's basic interest is the exploitation and development of the earth's resources regardless of what country these resources happen to lie within. Mr. Hiro Hiyama, president of the Japanese-based Marubeni Corp. says that 'international co-operation is indispensable in the development of natural resources.' For B.C. this means exporting our natural resources — our minerals, fisheries and forestry products — to Japan on Japanese ships, and importing Japanese-made cars and TV sets on Japanese ships.

In fact, the members of the group are strongly hostile to the idea that the people of a country should have some say in how the country's resources should be developed. Charles W. Robinson, chairman of the U.S.-based Marcona Corp., representing the U.S. national committee for PBEC, has been quoted as saying that nationalism was a threat to the multi-national corporation. Said Robinson: 'An expanding multi-nationalism is locked in *mortal combat* with the forces of nationalism.' Translated into real terms the

Two pages from an advertising supplement for the Pacific Basin Economic Council in *Fortune,* September 1972.

Pacific conference told

Foreign money welcomed

Canadian Press

WASHINGTON — Business executives from countries bordering the Pacific Basin were told Monday that Canada is "one of the most open countries in the world for making new investments."

In a paper prepared for the 7th general meeting of the Pacific Basin Economic Council, John D. Wilson, of Vancouver, senior vice-president of Canada Trust Co., reported on Canada's Froeign Investment Review Act that came into force last April.

He said the act should not be interpreted as a deterrent to foreign investment.

Wilson's paper was one of a number prepared for council committtees by chairmen of Canadian sub-committees.

Wilson, chairman for Canada on the council's international investments committee, said the act "is certainly not new on the international scene and is perhaps overdue in Canada when one considers that a major percentage of Canadian manufacturing, Canadian petroleum products and Canadian mining is already under foreign control."

"Under these circumstances, the Canadian government has taken steps to assure that Canada will have a measure of control over future investments."

Wilson said that to avoid discouraging foreign firms from providing needed capital venture to Canadian business, "the act permits a takeover as long as the foreign firm divests itself of any type of control and reduces its ownership within a certain time, up to a maximum investment of $10 million per Canadian business.

"Certainly there has been a change in the Canadian political arena in recent years and such legislation as the Foreign Investment Review Act presents a new set of rules to be followed. However, let us recognize that the Canadian investment climate continues to be healthy and foreign investors should still consider Canada as one of the most open countries in the world for making new investments."

In a report to the committee on transportation, R. A. Hubber-Richard, of Vancouver, president of White Pass and Yukon Corp., Ltd., reviewed some projects undertaken by Canadian consulting and engineering service companies in transportation planning in the Pacific rim.

He listed 48 projects carried out in 15 rim countries by three major consulting firms "as an indicator of the variety of talent available in Canada."

They ranged from earthquake rehabilitation in Managua, Nicaragua, to an inter-island ferry study in Hawaii.

"The projects have been financed in a variety of ways." Hubbard-Richard said, "some of a purely normal, private-enterprise, commercial basis, some from funds derived through aid programs provided by the Canadian government, and some . . . paid for by governments of the countries who requested the work.

"There are a number of agencies with aid funds available in Canada for such work, and developing countries would have access to these agencies for specific projects."

Long-term strategy and flexibility to cope with change are essential in planning for lasting tourism, a report to the tourism committee said.

The report was prepared after a study of the tourist industry in Barbados by Prof. George Doxey of York University, Toronto, and submitted to the council by Duncan Laing, of Vancouver, vice-president western region, Air Canada.

It said the most important priority in tourism development is the need to decide from the outset the type which best suits an environment, both from the human and physical point of view, and to plan consistently as a result.

"Planning for a lasting tourism to ensure that it is maintained intact involves not only long-term strategy for growth but also flexibility to cope with change in the important areas of marketing and supply and within the most decisive area of the destination environment."

R. W. MacLaren, of Toronto, director, public relations, Massey-Ferguson Ltd., reporting to the human resources development committee, said a permanent secretariat or outside consultants are needed if further progress is expected in human resources development projects.

The principal areas with which the committee was concerned were annual seminars, assistance in management training for the developing countries of the Pacific area and unemployment and labor-intensive industry. These were tasks which could not be satisfactorily assigned to PBEC volunteers, emphasizing the need for permanent assistance.

---

question is: who is going to decide how B.C. should develop her natural resources — British Columbians or the Nippon Steel Corp.? Who will decide how downtown Vancouver should grow — the citizens of Vancouver or the Bank of America? Since Canadian corporations have been enthusiastic participants in the PBEC, the answer to these questions has been only too clear. So far, the multi-national corporations have absolute control over the way Vancouver is to develop. Canada's participation in the Pacific Basin Economic Council, representing the major multi-national corporations and financial institutions, was co-sponsored by the Canadian Chamber of Commerce and the Canadian Manufacturers' Association in 1968. For several years, the Vancouver business establishment resisted participation in PBEC but by the early 1970s saw the wisdom of becoming involved and joined in with a vengeance. The annual meeting was held in Vancouver in 1971 and will be held here again in 1976. Membership in the organization changes, but a few names reappear from year to year. The most prominent of these are:

Kenneth H.J. Clarke: Toronto; international pre-

The CPR is a Canadian-based multi-national conglomerate with a vital stake in increasing Pacific Basin trade from its Vancouver-based operations: Cominco and Fording Coal, CP Air Lines, CP Rail, CP Hotels, CP Ships.

---

sident PBEC, 1972-74; president, Canadian marketing division and director, international sales, INCO. Canada's fourth largest corporation, exploiting our nickel and copper resources, controlled by an alliance of Rockefeller and Morgan interests in the U.S.A. Clarke is chairman, commercial intelligence committee, Canadian Manufacturers' Association.

J. Hugh Stevens: Toronto; chairman of the Canadian delegation, PBEC; president and chief executive officer, Canada Wire and Cable Co., a subsidiary of Noranda Mines, Canada's tenth largest corporation, who got to be that size through its brutal opposition to the organization of its workers. Stevens is also a director of numerous Mexican, South American and New Zealand subsidiaries of Noranda Mines, a member of the executive council, Canadian Manufacturers' Association and a governor, Canadian Association for Latin America. According to Stevens, 'We are trying to create an atmosphere or image of

Fording coal flow started to Japan

A trial shipment of 5,670 tons of coking coal destined for Japan arived at Roberts Bank bulk loading facility Friday.

The movement marked the start of a 30 - million - ton - a - year trade in coking coal from the east Kootenay strip mine of Fording Coal Ltd.

Fording has a 15-year contract which calls for the export to Japan of 45 million tons of fuel. It will come from a mine 18 miles north of the new community of Elkford.

The mine is an $80 million venture and CP Rail has spent $30 million on laying a 34-mile spur line into the mine site and on acquiring locomotives and rolling stock.

New equipment comprises two dozen 3,000 h.p. diesel - electric locomotives, bought from General Motors, and 330 105 - ton gondola cars built by Hawker Siddeley, of Trenton, N.S.

The first train is made up of only 54 cars. When the operation is in full swing CP Rail will be operating consists of up to 104 cars, laden with up to 11,000 tons of fuel going to feed Japanese blast furnaces.

Fording's operation is managed by Cominco Ltd., which with Canadian Pacific Investments Ltd., owns the mine.

welcoming capital in Canada.''

Arnold F.C. Hean: Burnaby; senior partner, Hean, Wylie & Co., solicitors for over 200 companies including more than 30 in the real estate and development field. Hean is president of the 'Majority Movement,' an abortive attempt to unite the 'anti-socialist' elements in B.C. in one party to oppose the New Democratic Party in the next provincial election; a former Burnaby alderman for four years; and a senator and governor, Simon Fraser University.

Alexander H. Hart: senior vice-president, Canadian National Railway Co.; president Canalog Consultants. As chairman of the transportation committee of PBEC, Hart is probably most concerned with the problem of moving Canada's resources to the west coast ports for shipment to Japan and other Pacific Basin countries.

Pacific Basin trade means basically five things to the Canadian corporate world. It means first promoting tourism and air travel, and both Air Canada and CP Air Lines are members of PBEC. Next it means financing the foreign acquisition of Canadian resources, and Montreal Trust Co., Canada Trust Co., the Royal Bank of Canada and the Bank of Montreal are members of PBEC. Third, it means exporting those resources, and B.C. Packers, Placer Development, Crown Zellerbach Canada, Bethlehem Copper Corp., Cominco and MacMillan Bloedel are members of PBEC. It means transporting those resources to Pacific coast ports for shipment, and CNR and White Pass and Yukon Corp. are members of PBEC. Finally it means servicing all the other activities, and law firms

The Royal Bank of Canada competes with the Bank of Montreal to see who can erect the tallest corporate tower.

such as Hean, Wylie & Co. and Davis & Co. are members, auditors such as Riddell, Stead & Co., and engineering consultants such as Sandwell & Co. are members.

Each one of these companies and firms has a strong Vancouver presence and every one of them has a vested interest in seeing Vancouver continue to grow into an 'executive city' and major centre of Pacific Basin trade.

5 Downtown decision-makers II: The banks

Why does the Royal Bank of Canada need a $50 million 37-storey high-rise office tower in downtown Vancouver? Does the Bank of Nova Scotia really need a new 36-storey office building so badly that it is prepared to tear down the beautiful irreplaceable Birks Building? Why does the Toronto Dominion Bank find it necessary to populate every major city in Canada with Towers of Darkness? Why is it the banks who are spearheading this mad rush into the sky? They really don't *need* any of these buildings to operate from — many other existing buildings (such as the Birks Building) would do just as well.

Quite simply, the banks are building monuments to themselves, to promote their corporate image, as well as making a lot of money. Allen Lambert, head of the Toronto Dominion Bank, and chief perpetrator of those Towers of Darkness, was quite frank about their purpose:

Of the big five, we were the smallest bank. Certainly large enough to do anything we wanted, but what was important is that we appeared to be the smallest. Since the building opened, it's given our people a tremendous lift, an opportunity to attract the brightest young recruits, and to establish relationships with many major new accounts.

What a complete lack of social responsibility is shown in Lambert's remarks. The sole reason for building these huge tombstones is that they are good for business. But are they good for the average citizens of Canada? The banks have taken hundreds of millions of dollars — the savings of countless Canadians — and tied them up in concrete and glass, instead of investing the money in something really needed by those same Canadians such as low-cost housing. The banks themselves are the ones who tell us we must have foreign capital if we are to develop Canada's resources, and yet they will use Canadian money to build their own corporate monuments. Although the banks appear to be competing for the prestige of having the tallest building, they still all like to cluster together, because it is convenient for businesses to be close to one another.

Banking interests, with the Royal in the vanguard, have turned the area around Georgia and Burrard streets into what developers call the 'hottest corner in Canada'. The 'superblock' (as it's called) — Georgia St. to Pender St., Burrard St. to Thurlow St. — has been turned into the most densely populated part of the downtown core. Including the MacMillan Bloedel

Building, the Royal Centre, and the three towers of the Bentall Centre, over 20,000 workers are crammed into that block.

Who decided that the corner of Georgia and Burrard streets should become the hottest corner in Canada? Was it the citizens of Vancouver? Civic politicians? The city planning department? Or the banks and developers? Of course it was the banks and their developer allies. They saw that there was a great deal of scope for further redevelopment in that tiny area — and the city went along with their plans.

However, when you cram together so many people into one tiny area, you create some serious problems. How do all those 20,000 people get to work and home again? Mainly by car, of course. The downtown streets are now choked with cars at all hours of the day, not just during rush hours as used to be the case. Where do 20,000 people go on their lunch-hour? There is almost no parkland or open space in the downtown core. Of course, it's not up to the banks to solve these problems, even though they did create them.

It all began in 1957, in Montreal, when American real estate tycoon William Zeckendorf was arranging financing for the $100 million Place Ville Marie, his first Canadian project. Place Ville Marie became the prototype for all that is happening in downtown Canada — huge skyscrapers, vast bleak plazas, underground parking lots, and underground shopping malls.

Zeckendorf was able to convince Jim Muir, head of the Royal Bank of Canada, to move into Place Ville Marie as the prime tenant, after which Zeckendorf was able to arrange the rest of his financing.

No sooner had plans for Place Ville Marie been announced than the Canadian Imperial Bank of Commerce acquired property across the street and began planning an even higher skyscraper. There was no visible response from the Royal. Zeckendorf just waited until the Commerce's plans had been finalized, then added three extra floors to make Place Ville Marie the tallest building in the Commonwealth at that time. The commerce retaliated by putting a TV antenna on top of its building so that it stuck up a few feet higher.

The scene then shifted to Toronto, where the Toronto Dominion Bank led off with the $160 million Toronto-Dominion Centre. This surpassed Place Ville Marie as the tallest building in the Commonwealth until the Canadian Imperial Bank of Commerce completed its 57-storey Commerce Court in 1971. Both the Royal and the Bank of Montreal then jumped in with their own $100 million developments. As of this moment, it appears that the Bank of Montreal will

This glamorous architect's sketch shows the 36-storey tower which is to go up on the site of the former Birks Building. It will provide the Bank of Nova Scotia with a new Vancouver head-quarters.

finish first with a 72-storey skyscraper.

The banks engaged in some smaller skirmishes in the prairie cities — Winnipeg, Calgary, Edmonton — but the next big battle shaped up in Vancouver. The Toronto Dominion Bank, still fresh after its Toronto venture, was first off the starting block with its 30-storey tower in the $100 million Pacific Centre. Like the Toronto Toronto Dominion development, it was a shining black tower, hence the name Tower of Darkness. The Royal Bank of Canada was close behind with the 37-storey Royal Centre, the current leader in the tallest building race. The Bank of Montreal took control of the 30-storey Tower Three in the Bentall Centre. The Bank of Nova Scotia, delayed because of public opposition to the destruction of the Birks Building, will be fourth with a 36-storey tower across the

street from the Toronto Dominion. That leaves the Canadian Imperial Bank of Commerce, probably waiting in the wings until the dust has cleared so that they can come in with the tallest of all.

Why are the banks able to get away with such irresponsible activities? Few people realize the enormous power that they wield. There are only five large chartered banks in Canada, and they control a vast portion of the Canadian economy. They direct how our savings are used; they own billions of dollars in securities; through their affiliated trust, insurance, and investment companies they control other billions of dollars; they exert strong influence over all levels of government in Canada; they maintain links with banks, corporations, and governments in most countries of the world; they finance foreign take-overs of Canadian corporations.

The largest chartered banks are the centres of financial power in Canada. Around them are arrayed the other financial institutions and the major resource and manufacturing companies to form distinct centres of economic and political power. Although large parts of the Canadian economy are owned by American and other foreign interests, the banks still play a central role here. American multi-national corporations finance their take-overs of Canadian companies, and their expansion of business in Canada, using Canadian money provided by the banks.

Altogether, there are ten banks in Canada: three very large ones — the Royal Bank of Canada, the Canadian Imperial Bank of Commerce, the Bank of Montreal; two medium-sized banks — the Bank of Nova Scotia and the Toronto Dominion Bank; two small Quebec-based banks — Banque Canadien Nationale and Provincial Bank of Canada; and three junior-sized banks — the American-controlled Mercantile Bank of Canada, the Bank of British Columbia, and the recently-opened Unity Bank of Canada. But the five largest, the Royal, the Commerce, the Montreal, the Scotia, and Toronto Dominion hold among them over 91% of the banks' total assets, some $77.2 *billion* as of mid-1974. The Royal led the way with $20.5 billion.

There used to be many more banks than now. In 1900, for example, there were 36 banks in Canada, compared to the ten banks in 1974 (two of which were formed in the past few years). Although several of the smaller banks have failed over the years, the vast majority disappeared by being gobbled up by larger banks. This trend toward monopoly and concentration has been actively encouraged by the federal government over the years, especially by the minister of finance, who has to approve each merger application personally. In comparison, there are over 13,500 banks in the United States.

At the time of Confederation, the Bank of Montreal was the largest bank by far in the fledgling country. It got an enormous boost after Confederation because it was intimately tied in with the Canadian Pacific Railway capitalists who were using money supplied by the Canadian government, British capitalists and Canadian citizens, to turn themselves a handsome profit and, incidentally, build a cross-Canada railway.

The Royal Bank of Canada originated in 1869 as the Merchants Bank of Halifax (the name was changed in 1901). The Royal increased in size rapidly over the years from 1900 to 1930 through a series of mergers, and after a sustained effort surpassed the Bank of Montreal in size during the 1950s. In 1960 the Canadian Bank of Commerce and the Imperial Bank merged to present a threat to the Royal's dominance, but the Royal successfully fought off this challenge through very aggressive policies. Because of the degree of concentration in the Canadian banking system, the Royal is one of the largest banks in the world.

The ten Canadian chartered banks have roughly 300 directors among them who make the decisions about what to do with the banks' billions. The directors are not ordinary people. They represent the cream of the Canadian business elite and the 300 of them hold over 3,000 corporate directorships representing over $700 billion in assets. R.G.D. Lafferty, a Montreal investment dealer, has described the Canadian banking system as 'a highly concentrated, monolithic structure, with interlocking interests that employ restrictive practices to prevent new initiative and enterprise from challenging its dominant position.'

The banks, enjoying a monopoly position, are very conservative institutions, set up on a very rigid hierarchy. Only those who have made banking their career can hope to achieve a top-level position in their bank. The upwardly-mobile bank executive must resign himself to continual shifting from location to location. One year he might be working in Vancouver. The next year might find him in Winnipeg or Toronto. Then perhaps a stint in the international division, in London or the West Indies. Finally, if he is lucky and waits long enough, he might be transferred to head office in Montreal. The bank executive, therefore, does

The inviting plaza provided by the Royal Bank for the 4000 workers in the Royal Centre and the general public.

not identify with any of the places he has been posted; his loyalty remains solely with the bank.

The employee on the way up has to go through a series of well-defined hoops. After years at a junior level he might finally make it to become manager at a local branch. After that, he may become manager of the regional main branch. Then to supervisor, then to assistant general manager, then district general manager (or deputy general manager if it's a head office position). Then if he's fortunate enough, it's vice-president, and finally, chief general manager, deputy chairman, or executive vice-president. By the time he's made it this far, he's probably been working for the bank for 30 to 40 years; it's the only job he's ever had, the only company he's ever worked for. He probably left high school at age 16 to go right into the bank. Over those 30 to 40 years all innovation has been weeded out; the bank demands total dedication to it and to its aims; banking must be your life. These are the kind of people who make it to the top positions in the banks — Canada's most powerful institutions.

Most bank directors, in contrast, have not come up through the bank, but are brought in from outside corporations. The most important bank directors hold directorships in the big trust companies (or did so until 1967, at which time it became illegal to be a director of both a bank and a trust company), in the life insurance companies, in the important investment trusts. They appear on the boards of mining and industrial enterprises, transportation companies, utilities, and department store chains; they are members of the boards of governors of the universities; many of them are members of the Senate; they own radio and TV stations and newspapers; sit on the boards of charitable foundations; and they help administer the funds of churches. They pass into and out of public service, either as politicians or as appointed officials. They include managers and corporation lawyers, invest-

Increasing emphasis on international banking business means that Vancouver will become more important as a centre for Pacific Basin trade.

ment dealers and accountants; they include representatives of the most wealthy and powerful families. 'They are highly skilled people, even though most of their skills have no social value. Among them are experts in refinancing, in mergers, in take-overs, in the minimizing of tax liability, in the management of other people's money.'

No one can dispute that the banks and their allied corporations have a stranglehold on the Canadian economy and can direct the growth of Canada as a whole, and Vancouver in particular, as suits their interests. And one of the major interests of all the banks is to transform Vancouver into the corporate headquarters for Pacific Basin trade.

The Royal Bank of Canada was a founding member of Orion Multinational Services together with the Chase-Manhattan Bank (U.S.A.), the National Westminster Bank (U.K.), and the Westdeutsche Landesbank Girocentrale (West Germany). Orion was set up in 1970 to finance multi-national ventures in Europe. In 1973 the group set up a new company in Hong Kong — Orion Pacific — to provide banking

services for major multi-national corporations. Among the services to be provided is assistance in mergers and acquisitions, and advice on investments. At the same time the Royal set up an international banking division in its new regional headquarters in the Royal Centre.

Rowland C. Frazee, chief general manager for the Royal Bank of Canada, expects a major part of future growth to come from ventures such as Orion Multi-national Services and Orion Pacific. The Royal, at the present time, has foreign assets representing 31% of its total assets, and clearly intends to increase this ratio.

The Toronto Dominion Bank joined a number of other banks — Commercial Bank of Australia, Euro-Pacific Finance Corp., Fuji Bank, United California Bank, European Asian Bank, and Trustees Executors and Agency Co., in forming the Commercial Pacific Trust Co., based in Port Vila, New Hebrides, a tax haven in the south Pacific. The year previous, Toronto Dominion had set up an international banking division in its regional headquarters in the Pacific Centre, as well as opening up a branch office on Taiwan.

With these grandiose plans for expansion, is it any wonder all the banks are building those office towers in downtown Vancouver?

6 The Royal Bank: Portrait of a Canadian chartered bank

The Royal Bank of Canada may well be the most powerful organization in Canada. With its assets of $20.5 billion, and its loans to countless individuals and corporations, its substantial investments in stocks and bonds, its real estate investments, and its mortgage loans, it can exert a strong influence on the economy of the country.

But its influence extends far beyond its own financial muscle. It has intimate connections with many other financial institutions — trust companies who manage the vast estates of the old-time robber barons and railway magnates and who control the billions of dollars in trust and pension funds; insurance companies who invest their billions in mortgages, real estate, and stocks and bonds; and the investment trusts, many of them foreign-owned, who exert substantial control over many large Canadian corporations.

The Royal has very intimate connections with Power Corp. of Canada, the $5.5 billion financial, industrial, and communications empire; and through Power Corp. to the Liberal party and the federal cabinet. The Royal has strong connections with many of the other largest corporations in Canada. It has increased its influence in the Canadian Pacific Railway conglomerate to the point where it rivals the Bank of Montreal for control.

The directors of the Royal are members of the Senate, trustees and governors of universities and hospitals, and directors of charitable foundations and government policy councils. The Royal is also one of the largest advertisers in the country, and 'Mary of the Royal Bank' is well-known across the country, although there is not one woman either on the 46-person board of directors or among the senior management of the bank.

The Royal does not own the companies in which it has influence, neither do those companies have a controlling interest in the bank. But they work together for a common purpose. For example, the president of American-owned Imperial Oil, no matter who he is, always sits on the board of the bank. Now suppose that the Royal owned debentures of Imperial Oil, thus giving the bank a vested interest in the profitability of Imperial Oil. Clearly, Imperial Oil might find less difficulty in getting financing from the Royal than other financial institutions.

Who owns the Royal Bank of Canada? One of the largest blocks of Royal shares is held by the Investors

The Royal Bank of Canada's presence in downtown Vancouver.

Group, a mutual and pension fund empire based in Winnipeg. Investors owns just under 1,000,000 shares of the Royal, or about 3% of the outstanding shares. But Investors is owned by Power Corp. of Canada which has three interlocking directorships with the bank. Thus we see how the Investors' block of shares could be used to support the existing management of the Royal. Investors controls Montreal Trust Co. which owns a further 200,000 shares of the bank and probably manages countless other Royal shares for its customers. The Royal and Montreal Trust have always had the closest of relationships. To further link the companies, Investors owns 500,000 shares of Imperial Oil, and Montreal Trust another 100,000. In this way an established centre of power is structured so that, using the pension and mutual funds provided by the savings of ordinary Canadians, it can maintain and promote its own interests.

For many years the banks and trust companies have been closely linked to each other. The trust companies perform a number of important functions in the financial structure of the country. They act as trustees for other people's property. They are transfer agents for the big corporations, keeping records of stock ownership. They have under administration billions of dollars of assets belonging to their clients; these assets include stockholdings in all important corporations, huge property holdings, and billions of dollars in mortgage loans.

The two largest trust companies are the Royal Trust Co. and the Montreal Trust Co., the first linked to the Bank of Montreal, the second to the Royal Bank of Canada. Montreal Trust has over $600 million on deposit in its branches. It also has $5 billion in assets under administration. The large amounts of stock included in its portfolios have voting rights the same as all shares, and these voting rights would be exercised by the trust company. Suppose that clients of Montreal Trust hold a large number of shares in Westcoast Transmission Co., the Vancouver-based oil and gas pipeline company. Montreal Trust would normally vote the shares in support of the existing management of Westcoast. In fact we see a merging of interests since there are three interlocking directorships between the Royal Bank and Westcoast, and another between Montreal Trust and Westcoast.

Up to 1967, there were innumerable interlocking directorships between the banks and trust companies. For example, the Bank of Montreal and Royal Trust Co. had 14 directors in common; Montreal Trust Co. and the Royal Bank of Canada shared 15 directors. The Canadian Imperial Bank of Commerce shared nine directors with National Trust Co. and four with Canada Trust Co. But in 1967, amendments to the Bank Act prohibited interlocking directorships between the banks and trust companies, to break the monopoly position of the existing institutions. The banks got around this requirement handily. They merely spread the interlocking around a little. Before 1967, Royal Bank's principal law firm, Ogilvy, Cope, Porteous, Hansard, Marler, Montgomery & Renaud, was represented on both the Royal Bank and Montreal Trust boards in the person of senior partner J. Angus Ogilvy. After the new requirement came into effect, Ogilvy retained the Royal Bank directorship (becoming a vice-president in the process) and another partner, Matthew S. Hannon, was appointed a director of Montreal Trust, and chairman of the executive committee. There are many other examples which show the structure of control:

STEWART, MACKEEN & COVERT: *Royal Bank's law firm in Halifax: partner Frank M. Covert is a director of the Royal Bank; partner J. William Mingo is a director of Montreal Trust.*
POWER CORP. OF CANADA: *vice-chairman Peter Nesbitt Thomson is a director of the Royal Bank; chairman Paul Desmarais is a director of Montreal Trust.*

DUQUET, MACKAY, WELDON, BRONSTETTER & JOHNSTON: *another Royal Bank law firm in Montreal: partner J.E.L. Duquet is a director of the Royal Bank; partner R. de Wolfe MacKay is a director of Montreal Trust.*
CANADIAN PACIFIC INVESTMENTS: *Duff Roblin, former premier of Manitoba and former president of CPI is a director of Montreal Trust; Ian Sinclair, chairman of CPR and chairman of CPI is a director and vice-president of the Royal Bank.*
SIMPSON-SEARS: *Douglas J. Peacher, president of Simpson-Sears, is a director of Montreal Trust; G. Allan Burton, chairman of Robert Simpson Co. and a director of Simpson-Sears, is a director of the Royal Bank;*
STANDARD BRANDS: *G.T. Morrissette, chairman of American-owned Standard Brands, is a director of Montreal Trust; W. Earle McLaughlin, chairman of the Royal Bank, is a director of Standard Brands;*
DOMINION BRIDGE CO.: *MacKenzie McMurray, president of Dominion Bridge, is a director of Montreal Trust; J. Angus Ogilvy, already mentioned as a vice-president of the Royal Bank, is also a vice-president of Dominion Bridge.*

Thus we see an amazing degree of interlocking of interests among the dominant financial institutions and corporations. No one is ever appointed to the board of directors of a major bank by accident. Each person has a precise role to play and represents a specific power group. To give two related examples:

DENNIS YORATH, *vice-chairman of the American conglomerate IU International Corp., which owns the Edmonton-based company, Canadian Utilities, is a director of Montreal Trust. Yorath is also a director of Canadian Utilities. Sitting with Yorath on the board of Canadian Utilities is* PETER L.P. MACDONNELL, *Q.C., a partner in the Edmonton law firm of Milner and Steer, who specialize in the pipeline and utilities business. Macdonnell is a director of the Royal Bank, having been appointed in 1968. Another partner, H.R.* MILNER, *had been a director of the Royal Bank before Macdonnell (from 1947-1965), and a director of Montreal Trust. Macdonnell thus continued the representation of the law firm on the bank board. But Macdonnell has another reason for being on the board. His sister Katharine had married R.W. Lawson, now deputy-governor of the Bank of Canada, the government agency that controls banking in Canada.* GRAHAM TOWERS *had been the governor of the Bank of Canada up to 1956. When he left his government position he was quickly appointed to the board of the Royal Bank, stepping down in 1966. Macdonnell helps continue the close connection between the bank and the government institution.*

The board of the Royal Bank of Canada has always been rich in corporate lawyers. With their highly-specialized training in corporation law, they act as advisers to the industrialists, to the financial groups, and to the banks:

Their fund of experience on what is legally possible, their technical understanding of how to manoeuvre through and around the Companies Act and Combines Investigation Act, on how to minimize tax liability and extract capital gains, are of great value to the financial groups. Corporation lawyers often do the negotiating behind the scenes with the politicians on behalf of the monopolies.

One law firm in particular, the Montreal law factory of Ogilvy, Cope, Porteous, Hansard, Marler, Montgomery & Renaud, has played an important role in the Royal's drive for dominance in all spheres of Canadian life. J. Angus Ogilvy, senior partner in the firm, has already been mentioned as a Royal vice-president. Over the years, the firm has provided three more vice-presidents to the bank, three Quebec judges (one of them a chief justice), a senator, an ambassador, and a member of parliament, as well as numerous corporate connections. As of 1974, the 58 Ogilvy, Cope lawyers were directors of the following companies (the company's ranking in the top 100 Canadian corporations is given in brackets):

Domtar (18)
Northern Electric Co. (20)
Genstar (26)
Hiram Walker-Gooderham Worts (31)
Dominion Bridge Co. (48)
Canada Steamship Lines (58)
Price Co. (62)
Canron (63)
Reed Paper Group (66)
Standard Brands Canada (78)
Jannock Corp. (83)

They also sit on the boards of Canadian International Paper Co.; Canadian Vickers; Cadbury Schweppes Powell, the English food conglomerate; Ciba-Geigy Canada, the Swiss pharmaceutical giant; Avis Transport of Canada; Canadian Marconi Co.; and Trizec Corp., Canada's second largest developer. They have ties with other financial institutions: Montreal Trust Co., Beneficial Finance Co. of Canada, Imperial Life Assurance Co. of Canada, Manufacturers Life Assurance Co. of Canda, the Morgan Trust Co., and Roymor. Twenty of the firm's lawyers are Q.C.'s. Ogilvy, Cope's close association with the Royal Bank of Canada gives all these corporations an association with the Royal.

Another important area where the bank exerts

On the left, Paul Desmarais, Chairman and Chief Executive Officer of Power Corp., and on the right Peter D. Curry, President and Chief Operating Officer. Desmarais is the dominant figure in Power, which in turn exercises enormous economic and political influence in Canada through the many corporations it controls or is linked with.

influence is through the investment trusts. One trust with strong Royal influence is United Corporations, with over $100 million invested in stocks and bonds. Sitting on the United Corps. board is: Kenneth S. Howard from Ogilvy, Cope; Jock K. Finlayson, deputy chairman of the Royal; Ian Barclay, Vancouver-based chairman of B.C. Forest Products, and Royal director; and until his death in 1973, T. Norbert Beaupre, chairman and president of Domtar, and Royal director.

But the most important link the Royal Bank of Canada has with investment trusts is with Power Corp. of Canada. Power Corp. is a holding company established in 1925 by the Nesbitt Thomson & Co. stock-brokerage firm to invest in Canadian utility companies. By the late 1950s Power Corp. had gained control of a number of utilities in Quebec and British Columbia, including B.C. Power Corp. (Dal Grauer, president of B.C. Power, was a director of the Royal). In the next few years, a number of the Power Corp. subsidiaries were nationalized. This left the company with a treasury brimful of cash, and Power Corp. began to invest in other companies. With so much cash lying about Power Corp. became ripe for take-over and this was accomplished a few years later by Paul Desmarais, the 'Howard Hughes of Canada' who forced the Nesbitt Thomson interests into a secondary role (Desmarais is now chairman, and Peter Nesbitt Thomson, formerly chairman, is vice-chairman). The

Royal Bank of Canada chairman and president W. Earle McLaughlin, whose directorships demonstrate major corporate ties to the bank. He is a director of: Genstar, Power Corp., Standard Brands, Metropolitan Life Insurance Co., Algoma Steel Co., Canadian Pacific Railways, and General Motors Corp. (Detroit).

Power Corp. and the Royal share three directors: Thomson, who is also a director of many Power Corp. subsidiaries; Earle McLaughlin, the Royal president; and Claude Pratte, a leading figure in Quebec City media, and a director of the CPR.

Power Corp. of Canada under Desmarais, has built up an enormous financial and industrial empire (see Royal Bank of Canada diagram for major Power Corp. interests). One of the major reasons for Power Corp.'s success, beyond the indisputable business acumen of Desmarais, is its unusually close connections to the Liberal party. Some of these are listed below.

PETER NESBITT THOMSON *was treasurer of the Quebec Liberal Party when he was chairman of Power Corp.*
CLAUDE FRENNETTE, *one-time executive assistant to Quebec Forestry Minister* MAURICE SAUVE *(now a vice-president of Power Corp.-controlled Quebec*

Louis Desmarais, Chairman and Chief Executive Officer of Canada Steamship Lines, Limited, a Power Corp. subsidiary. Illustrating the Power Corp.-Liberal Party connection, Louis Desmarais was appointed vice-chairman of the government-controlled Canada Development Corp. by Pierre Elliot Trudeau.

forestry giant Consolidated-Bathurst), was a Power Corp. vice-president, head of the Quebec wing of the federal Liberal party, and was instrumental in promoting PIERRE ELLIOTT TRUDEAU *in his sweep to power in 1968.*
PAUL DESMARAIS *and Quebec Premier* ROBERT BOURASSA *have been friends for many years.*
ARTHUR SIMARD, *father-in-law of* ROBERT BOURASSA, *and chairman of Marine Industries, was a director of Power Corp.*
PAUL MARTIN JR., *son of senator and Liberal party power Paul Martin, is a Power Corp. vice-president.*
MAURICE STRONG, *was Power Corp. president in 1966. The Liberal government offered him a job as head of Canada's foreign aid program. He refused preferring to become involved as Canada's leader in the U.N. World Environment Conference in Sweden in 1972.*
ANTHONY HAMPSON, *former Power Corp. vice-president, was appointed chairman of the Canada Development Corp. by* TRUDEAU.,
LOUIS DESMARAIS, *Paul's brother, and president of the Power Corp.-controlled Canada Steamship Lines, was appointed vice-chairman of the Canada Development Corp. by* TRUDEAU.
JEAN LUC PEPIN, *former minister of trade, industry and commerce, after his defeat in the 1972 election was appointed to the board of directors of Power Corp. While he was minister, Power Corp. subsidiaries received substantial grants from his department.*

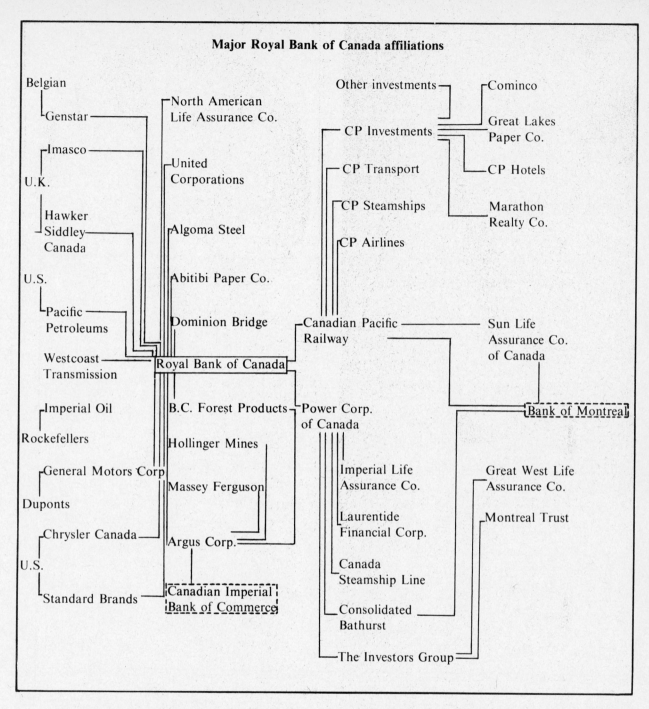

Major Royal Bank of Canada affiliations

Belgian

└ Genstar ──── North American Life Assurance Co.

┌ Imasco ────

U.K.   United Corporations

└ Hawker Siddley ──── Algoma Steel
Canada

U.S.   Abitibi Paper Co.

└ Pacific ──── Dominion Bridge
Petroleums

Westcoast ──── Royal Bank of Canada
Transmission

┌ Imperial Oil   B.C. Forest Products ┐

Rockefellers   Power Corp. of Canada

┌ General Motors Corp   Hollinger Mines

Duponts   Massey Ferguson

└ Chrysler Canada ──── Argus Corp.

U.S.

└ Standard Brands ──── Canadian Imperial Bank of Commerce

Other investments ┐ ┌ Cominco
                  │ │
CP Investments ═══╪═╪═ Great Lakes Paper Co.
                  │ └ CP Hotels
CP Transport   │
                  Marathon Realty Co.
CP Steamships

CP Airlines

Canadian Pacific Railway ──── Sun Life Assurance Co. of Canada

Bank of Montreal

Imperial Life Assurance Co.   Great West Life Assurance Co.

Laurentide Financial Corp.   Montreal Trust

Canada Steamship Line

Consolidated Bathurst

The Investors Group

BRYCE MACKASEY, former minister of labour, an especially important ministry for Power Corp. with its 50,000 employees, quit his government post after the poor showing of the Liberals in the 1972 election. He was then hired by Canada Steamship Lines as a 'consultant.'

Another key to the Royal Bank of Canada's power is its recent success in building links to the vast CPR empire. Ever since work began on the transcontinental railroad in 1880, the CPR has been intimately connected with the Bank of Montreal, at that time Canada's largest bank. Donald Smith (later Lord Strathcona and Mount Royal), the chief promoter of the railroad, was appointed president of the Bank of Montreal the year following the completion of the railroad. The president of the bank has always been a director of the railroad company. But there is now a difference. The Royal has been increasing its influence in the CPR to the point where now Ian Sinclair, chairman of the CPR, is a director and vice-president of the Royal, and Earle McLaughlin, president of the Royal, is a director of the CPR. The above table, listing the number of interlocking directorships between the banks and the CPR in 1958 and 1973 tells the story.

INTERLOCKING DIRECTORSHIPS, MAJOR BANKS AND THE CPR, 1958 AND 1973.

	ROYAL BANK OF CANADA	CANADIAN IMPERIAL BANK OF COMMERCE	BANK OF MONTREAL	TORONTO DOMINION BANK	BANK OF NOVA SCOTIA
1958	1	2	9	2	0
1973	4	2	5	1	1

The Royal Bank of Canada has always played a strong role in the petroleum industry. The president of Imperial Oil is always a director of the bank: George L. Stewart (1949 - 56), John R. White (1956 - 60), William O. Twaits (1961-74), and John A. Armstrong (1974-). The Royal has three directors in Trans Canada Pipe Lines, sharing its influence with the Canadian Imperial Bank of Commerce and the Toronto Dominion Bank. At Westcoast Transmission Co., the Royal predominates with three directors. There are two Royal directors at Pacific Petroleums, and one at Texaco Canada. The Royal was the dominant bank with Petrofina Canada, but the Bank of Montreal seems to be increasing its influence there.

The forest products industry is another area of strong Royal Bank of Canada influence. There are two interlocks between the Royal and MacMillan Bloedel: Ian Sinclair, representing the CPR's controlling interest, and Arthur Christopher, a local businessman. The Royal shares its influence in MacMillan Bloedel with the Canadian Imperial Bank of Commerce. There are two interlocks between the Royal and Domtar, the second largest forest products company; the Royal shares three directors with Abitibi Paper Co., two with Consolidated-Bathurst, and one with B.C. Forest Products.

The Royal is perhaps weakest in the mining industry (which traditionally has been under the control of the Canadian Imperial Bank of Commerce): in INCO, Alcan, Noranda, Falconbridge, Rio Algom mines it has no influence at all; in Cominco it has some interest through Ian Sinclair, CPR chairman.

The Royal Bank of Canada has also been weak in the utilities. It used to be very influential in Bell Telephone Co., but now influence in Bell is shared among Bank of Montreal, Canadian Imperial Bank of Commerce, and Toronto Dominion Bank. Influence in B.C. Telephone Co. is shared between the Commerce and the Bank of Nova Scotia. Other companies within the Royal sphere include Massey-Ferguson (which it shares with the Commerce), Algoma Steel (strong), General Motors of Canada (Earle McLaughlin on GMC Board), Chrysler Canada (two interlocks), Genstar (has always been strong in this Belgian-controlled conglomerate), Canada Steamship Lines (controlled by Power Corp. of Canada), Imasco (the English-controlled tobacco empire), Hawker Siddely (the English aircraft manufacturer taken over recently by the Canadian govermment), Standard Brands of Canada (American-owned food empire), Dominion Bridge Co. (Canadian-controlled). The Royal Bank of Canada perhaps illustrates better than any other example the vertical mosaic of power in Canada.

When John Armstrong succeeded William Twaits as chairman of the board of Imperial Oil, Exxon's Canadian subsidiary, he automatically took over Twaits' directorship in the Royal Bank. Twaits was then made a vice-president of the Royal.

The appointment of a Royal Bank vice-president as president of Canadian Pacific Investments illustrates the Royal's growing influence in the CPR empire. CPR chairman Ian D. Sinclair is also a Royal vice-president.

7 Downtown decision-makers III: Vancouver's business establishment

The major banks are, of course, based in eastern Canada — the Royal Bank of Canada and the Bank of Montreal in Montreal; the Canadian Imperial Bank of Commerce, the Toronto Dominion Bank, and the Bank of Nova Scotia in Toronto. It is in these centres that the Canadian economy is integrated into the international economy and the activities of the multinational corporations. It is also in these centres that the regional economies of Canada are tied together.

At the same time, each region has developed its own economy and its own structure of control. Vancouver has emerged as the centre of the British Columbia regional economy and at the same time a local business establishment has developed. The B.C. economy has been mainly an extractive one — forest products, mining, fishing; in fact, eight of the ten largest companies in B.C. are based on the exploitation of B.C.'s resources. This economy, together with the law firms that serve it, and the old landed families that founded many of the corporations, is the basis for the local business establishment. It is thoroughly tied in with the major centres of financial power in eastern Canada. Local interests provide the knowledge of markets and business conditions. Through the local business establishment, local capital — that is, the savings of B.C.'s residents — is integrated into the national and international systems

The specific links between the local business establishment and the major centres of business power are the Vancouver-based directors of the major banks. This group of 20 men provides interlocking directorships with virtually every major company in British Columbia. They provide 26 interlocks between the five banks and the ten largest companies. The Vancouver bank directors tie together many other major corporations active in B.C. They interlock with Canada Cement Lafarge and Ocean Cement, Gulf Oil Canada and Panarctic Oils, Alcan, John Labatt, Hudson's Bay Co. and CPR, of course, Sun Life Assurance Co. of Canada and Royal General Insurance Co. and Canada Life Assurance Co., Canada Trust Co. and National Trust, Pacific Press and B.C. Television Broadcasting System, Daon Development Corp., British Pacific Properties, Dominion Construction Co. and Grosvenor International Holdings, in fact, there are few large companies that they do not influence.

Many of the old Vancouver families are

Where it all happens — in the Vancouver Club, 915 West Hastings St. in the heart of the downtown office district.

Budge Bell-Irving heads Board of Trade

Vancouver-born H.P. (Budge) Bell-Irving, DSO, OBE, member of a Vancouver pioneer family, is president-elect of the Vancouver Board of Trade.

He will be elected by acclamation at the Board's annual meeting, with other officers, on Jan. 21. Directors will be chosen by ballot.

Chairman and president of A.E. LePage Western Ltd., Budge Bell-Irving was first vice-president of the Board of Trade in 1973. His former company, Bell-Irving Realty Ltd., a family real estate brokerage business which has been in existence in Vancouver since 1894, amalgamated with A.E. LePage in 1972. In 1972 he was also president of the Canadian Real Estate Association.

represented on the boards of the five banks — Bentall, Rogers, Prentice, Dawson, Woodward and (formerly) Farris. They all belong to the same clubs — the Vancouver Club, the Shaughnessy and Capilano golf and country clubs, and the Royal Vancouver Yacht Club. They live near each other. Of the 20, nine huddle together in Shaughnessy, and five more are strung along S.W. Marine Dr.

They also associate together through the old established law firms that handle the corporate

One of the most important Vancouver marriages was this one in 1929 at the height of the building boom of the 1920s when the Marpole (CPR) and the Bell-Irving (fishing, real estate) families united. *Vancouver Public Library*

business of the old family trust funds. Rarely do the lawyers themselves appear on the bank boards. The one recent exception was John Lauchlin Farris who was a director of the Toronto Dominion Bank as had been his father before him. Legal representation on the bank boards is usually provided by the large Toronto and Montreal law factories.

The Vancouver bank directors tie in to the political parties: James Sinclair, ex-Liberal cabinet minister is a director of the Bank of Montreal; Charles Namby Wynn Woodward, while not a politician himself, comes from a family which included a Liberal MLA and a lieutenant-governor of B.C. Many of the

directors, especially those associated with the Bank of Nova Scotia have been important figures in the Non-Partisan Association.

Although there is a commonality of interests, there is also rivalry. As pointed out previously, each bank represents a separate centre of power. An analysis of the Vancouver-based directors shows that there are local mini-centres of power which mirror the major centres in Toronto and Montreal.

VANCOUVER-BASED DIRECTORS OF THE MAJOR BANKS.

ROYAL BANK OF CANADA:

1 Charles Namby Wynn Woodward: chairman, Woodward Stores; president, Douglas Lake Cattle Co.; director, Westcoast Transmission Co. and B.C. Molybdenum; member, Vancouver Board of Trade; home: 3513 Point Grey Rd. (Kitsilano).

2 Percy Ritchie Sandwell: chairman and chief executive officer, Sandwell & Co.; director, Athabasca Columbia Resources, Placer Development, British Columbia Medical Research Council, Pacific Basin Economic Council (Canadian executive committee); former director, Export Development Corp. of Canada; former member, British Columbia Research Council, National Research Council of Canada, Science Council of Canada; home: 1389 The Crescent (Shaughnessy).

3 Arthur B. Christopher: president, Montrose Development; director, MacMillan Bloedel, Rivtow Straits, Hayes Manufacturing; home: 2585 Point Grey Rd. (Kitsilano).

4 Ian A. Barclay: president and chief executive officer, B.C. Forest Products; director, United Corporations, B.C. Lions Football Club, Boys Club of Canada; home: 5925 Chancellor Blvd. (West Point Grey).

5 Frank McMahon: retired to Bahamas; chairman emeritus, Westcoast Transmission Co.; former director, Ocean Cement and Supplies, Weldwood of Canada, The Jockey Club; home: 2010 S.W. Marine Dr. (S.W. Marine).

CANADIAN IMPERIAL BANK OF COMMERCE:

1 J. Ernest Richardson: vice-president of the bank; chairman, president and chief executive officer, B.C. Telephone Co.; director, MacMillan Bloedel, Placer Development, Halifax Insurance Co., Canada Cement Lafarge, and Westcoast Transmission Co.; home: 6138 Southlands Pl. (S.W. Marine).

2 Dennis W. Timmis: president and chief executive officer, MacMillan Bloedel; director, Canadian Pacific Railway Co.; home: 1310 33rd Ave. (Shaughnessy).

3 Thomas H. McClelland: president and chief executive officer, Placer Development; president, Canadian Exploration, Gibraltar Mines and Mattagami Lake Mines; director, Craigmont Mines; chairman of board of governors, Employers' Council of B.C.; home: 1716 Drummond (West Point Grey).

4 Robert G. Rogers: president and chief executive officer, Crown Zellerbach; director, Ocean Cement and Supplies, Royal General Insurance Co. of Canada, Gulf Oil Canada, and Hilton Canada; past

chairman, Council of the Forest Industries of B.C.; member Canadian committee, Pacific Basin Economic Council; honorary vice-president, National Council Boy Scouts of Canada; member board of governors, B.C. Lions Football Club; home: 1691 W. 40th Ave. (Shaughnessy).

BANK OF MONTREAL:

1 Graham R. Dawson: president, Dawson Construction; chairman, Daon Development Corp.; vice-chairman, Kaiser Resources; director, Ancore International (Canada), Zeller's, Andres Wines, Harbour Park Developments, Hayes Manufacturing; member of advisory board, National Trust Co.; member, Vancouver Police Commission, Vancouver Board of Trade (past president), Young Presidents Organization; governor, Employers' Council of B.C.; convocation member, University of B.C. and Simon Fraser University; home: 3838 Cypress St. (Shaughnessy).

2 John G. Prentice: chairman, Canadian Forest Products; vice-president, West Coast Woollen Mills; director Intercontinental Pulp Co. and Prince George Pulp and Paper; member Vancouver advisory board, Royal Trust Co.; member British Columbia Research Council, Canadian Chamber of Commerce and Vancouver Board of Trade; chairman, Canada Council; honorary life president, Playhouse Theatre Company; convocation founder, Simon Fraser University; home: 1537 Matthews Ave. (Shaughnessy).

3 Forrest Rogers: chairman, president and managing director, B.C. Sugar Refining Co.; director, Belkin Packaging and Weldwood of Canada; home: 2680 W. 50th Ave. (S.W. Marine).

4 A. John Ellis: vice-chairman of the bank; member, Vancouver advisory board, Royal Trust Co.; retired Senate member, Simon Fraser University; honorary vice-president, Vancouver Art Gallery; member Canadian committee, Pacific Basin Economic Council; past president, Canadian Chamber of Commerce; home: 3851 Marguerite Ave. (Shaughnessy).

5 Hon. James Sinclair: deputy-chairman, Canada Cement Lafarge; director, Columbia Cellulose, Sun Life Assurance Co. of Canada, Canadian Industries, Cominco, and Alcan; former Liberal member of parliament; home: 3435 Capilano Rd. (North Vancouver).

6 H. Richard Whittall: partner, Richardson Securities of Canada; chairman, Grosvenor International Holdings; deputy-chairman, Canada Cement Lafarge; director, Anvil Mining Corp., B.C. Sugar Refining Co., B.C. Television Broadcasting System, Brenda Mines, Dynasty Explorations, Inland Natural Gas Co., Placer Development, and Weldwood of Canada; home: 3410 Marpole St. (Shaughnessy).

BANK OF NOVA SCOTIA:

1 Gerald H.D. Hobbs: president, Cominco; director, B.C. Telephone Co., Okanagan Helicopters, Pacific Coast Terminals Co., MacMillan Bloedel, Pacific Press, Western Canada Steel, Royal General Insurance Co. of Canada, and White Pass and Yukon Corp.; home: 3974 Angus Dr. (Shaughnessy).

2 Allan M. McGavin: chairman, McGavin Toastmaster; director, B.C. Telephone Co., B.C. Forest Products, British Pacific Properties, John Labatt, Hudson's Bay Co., Hudson's Bay Oil and Gas Co., Park Royal Shopping Centre, and Trans Mountain Pipe Line Co.; chairman board of governors and chancellor emeritus, University of B.C.; vice-president, Canadian Olympic Association; home: 1608 Avondale (Shaughnessy).

TORONTO DOMINION BANK:

1 H. Clark Bentall: president, Dominion Construction Co. and its subsidiaries; director, Scott Paper, Finning Tractor & Equipment Co., and Cominco; member advisory board, Canada Trust Co.; member Vancouver Board of Trade; home: 2194 S. W. Marine Dr. (S.W. Marine).

2 Frederick E. Burnet: chairman and chief executive officer, Cominco; director, Panarctic Oils, West Kootenay Power Co., and Pine Point Mines; home: 4232 Staulo Cres. (S.W. Marine).

3 W.M. Young: chairman and president, Finning Tractor & Equipment Co.; director, Pine Point Mines, Northern Electric Co., and Royal General Insurance Co. of Canada; home: 2376 S.W. Marine Dr. (S.W. Marine).

SOURCE: *Financial Post Survey of Industrials, 1974. Financial Post Directory of Directors, 1973-74.*

PP May 26/73

ANNOUNCEMENT
CANADA CEMENT LAFARGE LTD.

HON. JAMES SINCLAIR   H. RICHARD WHITTALL

Canada Cement Lafarge Ltd. announces the retirement of the Hon. James Sinclair as Deputy Chairman of the company. He will continue as a Director and member of the Executive Committee and as Chairman of Lafarge Canada Ltd.

Mr. H. Richard Whittall of Vancouver succeeds the Hon. James Sinclair as Deputy Chairman. He is a Director and member of the Executive Committee of the company and has been associated with the Lafarge Group since 1961.

Mr. Whittall is a Partner of Richardson Securities of Canada and a Director of B.C. Sugar Refinery Limited, B.C. Television Broadcasting System Ltd., Inland Natural Gas Co. Ltd., Placer Development Ltd., Weldwood of Canada Ltd. and of other Canadian companies.

The Vancouver business establishment is well enough organized to allow for the succession to positions of power. As James Sinclair, father-in-law to Pierre Trudeau, is phased out, many of his corporate positions are being assumed by Richard Whittall, partner in Richardson Securities.

8 The Royal's Vancouver directors: Integrating the local business establishment

Five of the 46 directors of the Royal Bank of Canada are resident in Vancouver: Charles Namby Wynn Woodward, Arthur B. Christopher, Frank McMahon, Ian A. Barclay and Percy Ritchie Sandwell. As a group they are strong where the Royal is strong — in the oil and gas industry and in the forest products industry. They are weak where the Royal is weak — in utilities and mining. They represent other aspects of Vancouver's business life as well: Woodward in merchandising, Christopher, general business conditions, and Sandwell, engineering. These five men provide one of the links between the international economy and the local business establishment; Sandwell, for example, is a member of the Canadian executive committee of the Pacific Basin Economic Council, a group we have already met. They thus play a key role in determining what kind of a place Vancouver will become. Also as a group they are very strong in the real estate and development industry. Both Westcoast Transmission Co. (McMahon) and B.C. Forest Products (Barclay) have recently completed new head office buildings in downtown Vancouver. Woodward was one of the motivating forces behind the gargantuan Project 200 development. And both Sandwell and Christopher are actively engaged in real estate development on a smaller scale. Let us now look a little closer at each one in turn.

Charles Namby Wynn Woodward, 50 years old, was appointed a Royal director in 1961, succeeding his father who had held the same position from 1939 to 1957. Woodward, like his father and grandfather before him, is head of Woodward Stores. His grandfather, the founder of the department store, was a Liberal MLA during the 1920s, and his father was lieutenant-governor of B.C. from 1941 to 1946.

Woodward Stores is the largest Vancouver-based chain of department stores and shopping centres, with 1973 sales of $430 million. Woodward Stores is very actively involved in developing its own properties, such as Oakridge Shopping Centre; the company is a partner in Project 200 on Vancouver's waterfront.

Charles Woodward holds several other directorships. He is a director of B.C. Molybdenum, a wholly-owned subsidiary of the giant American Kennecott Copper Corp., which owns a mine near Alice Arm, B.C. (Kennecott Copper was one of the corporations involved in plotting the violent overthrow of the Allende government in Chile). Woodward is a director of the Douglas Lake Cattle Co., one of the largest ranches in Canada, which was built up by his maternal grandfather. Woodward is a director of Westcoast Transmission Co., where he reinforces the Royal's influence exerted through Frank McMahon and Kelly H. Gibson (Calgary-based president of Westcoast and another Royal director).

Thus Woodward has very powerful business and political connections. But his family connections to the centres of power are even stronger. One cousin married the daughter of Aeneas McB. Bell-Irving, Non-Partisan Association alderman on city council during the 1960s. Woodward's father-in-law, Arthur E. Jukes, was a prominent stockbroker, manager of the Imperial Bank (before it merged with the Canadian Bank of Commerce), and one-time president of the B.C. Conservative Association.

But Woodward's most interesting family connection is through his cousin Shirley, who married *A.E. Dal Grauer,* also a Royal director until his death in 1961. Grauer was one of Vancouver's most influential figures during the 1940s and 1950s. He was president of B.C. Power Corp. of Canada, one of the utilities owned by Power Corp. of Canada in Montreal. Grauer himself was responsible for one of the first post-war high-rises in the downtown core, the B.C. Hydro Building built on the highest ground in the downtown peninsula.

With his important position came appointments to many of the largest corporations: director of Montreal

Royal Bank Director *Charles Namby Wynn Woodward:* his Vancouver store, his Clearbrook B.C. shopping centre, and his residence (until recently), a luxury 2-storey penthouse apartment in Vancouver's West End overlooking English Bay.

Trust Co., Sun Life Assurance Co. of Canada, MacMillan Bloedel, Webb & Knapp (Canada), Dominion Bridge Co., and Ford Motor Co. of Canada, and chancellor of the University of British Columbia. Grauer was originally a professor of economics and was a member of the Gordon Commission on Canada's economic prospects where he met Jack Davis, also a bright young economist, whom he brought into B.C. Electric Co. Grauer died in 1961, Bennett nationalized the power utility, and Davis ran for parliament as a Liberal, was elected in 1962, and eventually became minister of the environment in the Trudeau cabinet.

Mrs. Woodward Grauer kept all the right connections when in 1973 she remarried, this time to *Walter Stewart Owen,* who like her first husband had been on the board of directors of Webb & Knapp, and who, like her uncle William Culham Woodward, had been appointed lieutenant governor of B.C. Owen received this reward for his work as a Liberal party organizer and his position as a law partner of Ralph Campney, also a former Liberal cabinet minister during the 1950s.

Arthur Christopher, appointed to the Royal board in 1964, was an oddity in these circles. He was a self-made man who had none of the connections to the old families. Christopher dropped out of school at the age of 12. He bought Nelson's Laundries in 1939 and built it into Canada's largest laundry chain before selling out to the Steiner American Corp. in 1968. Christopher is a director of MacMillan Bloedel, and Rivtow Straits, and in the past has been on the boards of Montreal Trust Co. and Jim Pattison's Neonex International. Through his holding company Montrose Development, Christopher buys and sells real estate, especially in the Richmond and Delta suburban areas.

Seventy-two-year-old *Frank McMahon* retains his Royal directorship even though he has virtually retired from business to his tax-exempt estate in the Bahamas. (He does still maintain another house on S.W. Marine Dr. in Vancouver). McMahon was the driving force behind Westcoast Transmission Co. and Pacific Petroleums, both of which he founded, having got his start oil drilling with his two brothers in 1928. Westcoast owns and operates the gas pipeline from the Peace River/Fort Nelson area of B.C. to the B.C. border, where it connects up with the pipeline of El Paso Natural Gas. Naturally enough most of the output from the gas fields ends up in the United States. El Paso owned 13.5% of Westcoast, but this share was bought by the B.C. government in 1974. Another 22.4% of Westcoast is owned by Pacific Petroleums,

Royal Bank director *Frank McMahon:* his sparkling office building on West Georgia St.

the lower mainland. B.C. Hydro is now a crown corporation, but before it was nationalized, it belonged to Power Corp. of Canada, and B.C. Power Corp. president Dal Grauer, Westcoast's customer, sat on the board of the Royal Bank of Canada along with McMahon.

Kelly Gibson, who succeeded McMahon as chairman and chief executive officer of both Westcoas Transmission Co. and Pacific Petroleums, was recently appointed a director of the Royal Bank of Canada, thus preparing for the day that McMahon steps down.

The forestry industry is represented on the Royal Bank of Canada Board through *Ian Barclay,* president and chief executive officer of B.C. Forest Products (and Christopher who sits on the board of MacMillan Bloedel). B.C. Forest Products ownership is shared between Noranda Mines, Canada's large mining and lumber conglomerate, and the American-owned Mead Corp. Barclay is a director of United Corps., a $100 million investment trust dominated by the Royal. He is also a member of the Economic Council of Canada, an advisory group of top-level bureaucrats and businessmen strongly tied to the Liberal administration in Ottawa.

The fifth member of the Royal Bank of Canada board resident in Vancouver is 62-year-old *Percy Ritchie Sandwell,* chairman and chief executive officer of Sandwell & Co., world-wide engineering consultants to the forestry and mining industries. Ownership of Sandwell & Co. is shared by Sandwell himself with Swedish and Swiss interests. Sandwell & Co., in turn, owns 40% of Swan Wooster Engineering Co. another world-wide firm of engineering consultants.

Sandwell, who lives in a large Shaughnessy mansion, is a director of Placer Development (controlled, as is B.C. Forest Products, by Noranda Mines), a $200 million corporation which owns the Endako Mine near Burns Lake (open-pit molybdenum mine) and ships the total output to Japan, Placer controls Gibraltar Mines, an open-pit copper-molybdenum mine near Williams Lake, which, as well, sells its total output to Japan. Placer also controls Craigmont Mines, a copper mine near Merritt, B.C., which sells its total output to the U.S.A. and Japan. Sandwell thus has a vested interest in the continued export of B.C.'s resources, and his membership on the Pacific Basin Economic Council reflects this interest.

Sandwell, with one daughter married into the multi-millionaire Killam family, is chairman of Athabasca Columbia Resources, a mini-conglomerate active in real estate development in Mexico and Hawaii; hotels in Vernon, Duncan and Victoria, B.C.; mining and petroleum exploration; and trucking services to industry. Athabasca has a major interest in the trans-Alaska pipeline project, and hence a vested interest in

which in turn is controlled by the American oil giant Phillips Petroleum.

Westcoast Transmission Co. also sells gas to Inland Natural Gas Co. which distributes it in the Cariboo, Okanagan, and West Kootenay districts of B.C. Frank's brother John is president of Inland. Another portion of Westcoast's output is sold to B.C. Hydro & Power Authority for distribution through the shipment of oil down the coast of B.C. to the Washington state refineries.

Until 1971, Sandwell was a director of the Export Development Corp. (EDC), a crown corporation which lends public money to foreign corporations and companies in order to buy goods and services made in Canada. Because it is a crown corporation, it can approve loans without cabinet endorsement; in 1973, loans made totalled almost $500 million. This leaves enormous discretionary power in the hands of the directors of the EDC. During the decade 1961 to 1971 most of the money went to firms in eastern Canada. But two firms in B.C. received substantial credits. One of these two firms was Sandwell & Co. Sandwell is no longer on the board of the EDC; his place was taken by I.S. Ross, president of Swan Wooster Engineering Co., (as we have noted, 40%-owned by Sandwell).

The business interests of four of the five Royal Bank of Canada directors are further tied together through the old establishment law firm of Lawson, Lundell, Lawson & McIntosh. Senior partner D.A. Lawson is the secretary and a director of Charles Woodward's Douglas Lake Cattle Co. Lawson is also secretary of Sandwell & Co. Oscar Lundell, former president of the Canadian Bar Association, is a director of B.C. Forest Products where he meets with Ian Barclay; surprisingly Lundell is also a director of Crown Zellerbach, a major competitor. John G. Trueman, another Lawson lawyer, is a shareholder in Montrose Development, Art Christopher's real estate company.

For its official bank business the Royal uses another old establishment law firm, Bull, Houser and Tupper. When the Royal moved to its new offices in the Royal Centre, the lawyers followed right behind to remain close to their clients. The Bull, Houser and Tupper lawyers do not have many important corporate connections. They have, however, essayed into the political arena, one partner running as the Liberal candidate in Vancouver Quadra (West Point Grey) in the 1974 federal election, and another partner as a Non-Partisan Association candidate in the 1974 municipal election. Both were unsuccessful.

The five Royal Bank of Canada directors thus illustrate, in a microcosm, the structure of the Vancouver ruling class — the interlocking directorships, the intermarriages, the political connections, the government handouts, the role of the big law firms, the smooth relationships with the dominant American corporations, the selling out of Canadian resources. The corporate connections of the five directors also illustrate the role of the national and multi-national corporations in determining what kind of a city Vancouver is to become. Westcoast Transmission Co. opened its new corporate headquarters in downtown Vancouver several years ago. In 1973 B.C. Forest

Royal Bank director *Ian Barclay,* and his Vancouver home near the University of British Columbia.

Products opened its new corporate headquarters in downtown Vancouver. Woodward was an active promoter and shareholder in Project 200, which was relying on and pushing for a waterfront freeway for its economic viability. And they all get together in their corporate headquarters in the Royal Centre.

9 Downtown decision-makers IV: The developers

Knowing what business interests have in store for Vancouver, developers of every sort have been only too glad to lend a helping hand, at the same time making sizeable profits. Many downtown developers are foreign-controlled, and the majority of these, British in origin. There are two reasons for this. First is the long-standing friendship between the mother country and its colony. Many people feel that British developers just cannot be as bad as, say, the Arabs, who are threatening to swoop down on the Canadian real estate market in a big way. This, of course, is sheer myth. The second reason for the strong British presence in Canada is the tight real estate market at home. Competition is rough in Britain, and the profits to be made rather small. In Canada, on the other hand, the real estate game is still wide open — at least for the large corporation — and the profits to be made are enormous. Therefore many British firms have moved into Canadian real estate, either by setting up Canadian subsidiaries, or by buying out existing companies.

The most longstanding British presence in Vancouver has been the Guinness family interests: British Properties, the Lions Gate Bridge, the Marine Building, more recently the Guinness Tower on the waterfront, and soon a mate for the Guinness Tower.

Another strong British presence is Trizec Corp., owners of the Royal Centre (see following chapter). Other companies, although large in Britain, are relative newcomers to the Vancouver scene. Hammerson Properties is one example. A British-based company with world-wide assets of $700 million, Hammerson has been busy building office and commercial projects in Toronto and Calgary. In Vancouver it has recently completed twin office towers in the heart of the financial district, on Pender St.

Hammerson is also active in downtown development through its wholly-owned subsidiary, aptly-named Grander Developments. In 1973 Grander acquired the block bounded by Burrard-Dunsmuir-Hornby-Georgia (with the exception of the Christchurch Cathedral property) from Hong Kong-owned Ark Investments, for $9 million, or roughly $180 per square foot, at that time an unprecedented price for downtown real estate. To justify such a high price Grander needs an extremely high density development. Grander achieved its aim by working out a deal with neighbouring Christchurch Cathedral, which was starved for money to stay in operation. Grander gave

ANNOUNCEMENT

FIRST CITY FINANCIAL CORPORATION LTD.

R. C. BAXTER

Samuel Belzberg, president, is pleased to announce the appointment of R. C. Baxter, B.Comm., to the Board of Directors of First City Financial Corporation Ltd.

Mr. Baxter is president of R. C. Baxter Ltd., the managing company in a group of property development and investment firms which owns over $70 million worth of income-producing real estate in Canada. Mr. Baxter, a graduate of the University of Manitoba, holds a number of other directorships and is also a Fellow of the Real Estate Institute and vice-president of the International Council of Shopping Centres.

First City is listed on Toronto and Vancouver Stock Exchanges and its two major subsidiaries are City Savings & Trust Company and Pacific Leasing Corporation Ltd.

The downtown developers: when Dick Baxter arrived in Vancouver from Winnipeg he looked at the waterfront and said, 'This is the most fantastic stretch of real estate in Canada.' He proceeded to build the Columbia Centre.

the church the money it needed. In return, Grander will be able to include the church property when the calculations are made as to the density of development Grander will be allowed on its property.

A second group of downtown developers are the family-controlled corporations based in eastern Canada. One of these is Cemp Investments Co., controlled by the Bronfman family of Montreal. Cemp owns a substantial quantity of Distillers Corp.-Seagrams stock, and it uses the dividends from that stock as its development equity (the name comes from the first letters of four Bronfman children: Charles, Edgar, Minnie, Phyllis). Cemp, in alliance with Eaton's and the Toronto Dominion Bank, was the developer of the Pacific Centre, Blocks 42-52.

Across the street from the Pacific Centre, another eastern-Canadian family-controlled project is underway. The family, the Birks jewellery merchants from Montreal, have allied themselves with the Bank of Nova Scotia and Famous Players Theatres to tear down the old Birks Building and put up the monstrous Vancouver Centre development. Locally-based developers make up the third group active in downtown development. Through its development company, Dominion Construction Co., the Bentall family has been active in Vancouver construction for over 60 years. At one time, they dealt almost exclusively with industrial development, but during the 1960s moved into the profitable downtown commercial market. Bentall Centre Tower One was the first

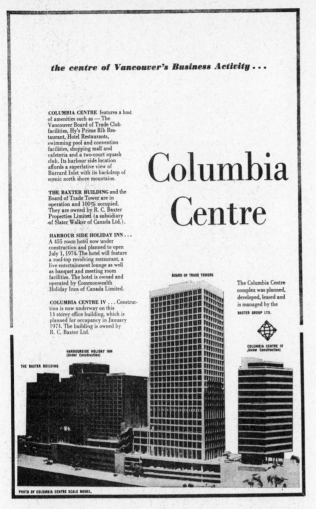

the centre of Vancouver's Business Activity...

COLUMBIA CENTRE features a host of amenities such as — The Vancouver Board of Trade Club facilities, Hy's Prime Rib Restaurant, Hotel Restaurants, swimming pool and convention facilities, shopping mall and cafeteria and a two-court squash club. Its harbour side location affords a superlative view of Burrard Inlet with its backdrop of scenic north shore mountains.

THE BAXTER BUILDING and the Board of Trade Tower are in operation and 100% occupied. They are owned by R. C. Baxter Properties Limited (a subsidiary of Slater Walker of Canada Ltd.).

HARBOUR SIDE HOLIDAY INN... A 455 room hotel now under construction and planned to open July 1, 1974. The hotel will feature a roof-top revolving restaurant, a live entertainment lounge as well as banquet and meeting room facilities. The hotel is owned and operated by Commonwealth Holiday Inns of Canada Limited.

COLUMBIA CENTRE IV ... Construction is now underway on this 14 storey office building, which is planned for occupancy in January 1974. The building is owned by R. C. Baxter Ltd.

Columbia Centre

The Columbia Centre complex was planned, developed, leased and is managed by the BAXTER GROUP LTD.

BOARD OF TRADE TOWERS

COLUMBIA CENTRE IV (Under Construction)

HARBOURSIDE HOLIDAY INN (Under Construction)

THE BAXTER BUILDING

PHOTO OF COLUMBIA CENTRE SCALE MODEL.

office building completed during the present building boom. It has been followed with two more in the Bentall Centre complex, and a fourth is on the drawing boards.

Originally from Winnipeg, developer Dick Baxter moved to Vancouver in the late 1960s, when the NDP came to power in Manitoba, and it was clear that Vancouver was the place where all the action was to occur. Baxter began by developing the Columbia Centre on the Vancouver waterfront, just down from the Guinness activities. Containing the Board of Trade Building and the Baxter Building and a recently completed Holiday Inn, there are plans for a fourth building in the complex.

The large corporations themselves who build their own corporate monuments in downtown comprise a fourth group of developers. Beginning with MacMillan Bloedel's prestige headquarters in 1967, the large corporations have continued to construct a substantial number of all downtown office buildings including the Westcoast Transmission and Crown Life Insurance Co. buildings.

Provincial and federal governments make up a fifth group of downtown developers. The federal govern-

Central federal office blocks for major cities

As part of its plans to decentralize administration, the federal government is planning construction of a $25-million building in Toronto.

J. E. Dubé, minister of Public Works, said it is part of the government's intentions "to provide a visible presence of our a c t i v i t y across the country and to meet the growing needs of the increasingly decentralized federal services across Canada."

Similar b u i l d i n g s are "now under way or in the planning stage" in Halifax, Montreal, London, Calgary and Vancouver, although u n t i l now the Montreal building is the only project that has been officially announced.

Dubé said he did not know which federal departments would eventually occupy the building, but the 660,000 square feet of office space would accommodate 3,200 public servants. Completion is scheduled for 1978.

Currently, the f e d e r a l government leases a b o u t 580,000 square feet of office space in Toronto. However, several major leases expire in 1977 and 1978 so there will be sizeable requirements for additional office space, Dubé said.

The lower levels will be turned over to commercial use.

ment sparked the post-World War II building boom with its Unemployment Insurance Commission and Income Tax buildings. It has continued to play a dominant role in downtown, first with its massive post office building — a Centennial year project — and lately with the equally massive CBC building kitty-corner to the post office. The federal government plans to top its present building campaign with a yet more massive federal office structure.

Vancouver has been just as unfortunate with the provincial government. For years Socred premier Wacky Bennett threatened to unload his 55-storey provincial government tower on downtown. With the passing of Bennett came the hope of a more responsible provincial presence in Vancouver. Whether the totally redesigned project is an improvement over Bennett's 55-storey tower must await the completion of construction.

A sixth and final group of downtown developers are the hotel men. Four large hotels are being added to Vancouver by the big international chains for whom it is indifferent whether a hotel is located in Vancouver or Tokyo — they design them the same in either place. The four are the Hyatt Regency in the Royal Centre, the Holiday Inn in the Columbia Centre, the Four Seasons Hotel in the Pacific Centre, and the CP hotel planned for Granville Square on the waterfront. Once it had become clear that Vancouver was to be an important regional and international centre, there was a rush to construct large expensive hotels to house the executives and managers who fly around the world from one branch office to another, and who congregate at endless conventions.

Although they come from diverse sources, developers have one thing in common — they all see downtown in terms of its high and increasing land

The downtown developers: Morris Wosk owns the Blue Horizon Hotel, the high-rise tower on the right. His brother Ben Wosk then out-did Morris with the Sheraton Landmark Hotel, the high-rise tower on the left.

values and its opportunities for highly profitable development. One result of this continuing inflation in land values and the consequent necessity to build larger and larger projects is that building projects are becoming more and more costly. Even the simplest office buildings these days will cost $10 million, many of the larger projects can cost $50 million (e.g., Royal Centre) to $100 million or more (e.g., Pacific Centre).

The primary requirement for the successful developer is guaranteed access to this kind of money. Thus the fastest growing development companies, and the most profitable, are the ones who can get at large pools of money, either by interlocking interests with financial institutions or by direct corporate connections. At the same time, development corporations have exhibited a rapid increase in size, either by concerted efforts to grow quickly or by take-overs and mergers. During the 1940s and 1950s many developers that started up were family concerns: Block Bros., Wall & Redekop Corp. (cousins), the older Dominion Construction Co. (Bentall family). Gradually these types of operations have increased in size until they have become large-scale development corporations.

The largest development company in Canada is probably Marathon Realty Co. which has acquired all of the non-transportation land holdings of the CPR.

The downtown developers: the Vancouver family firm of Block Bros. owned 1700 apartment suites as of 1974, a reduction from a peak of 2,300 reached several years earlier, at the same time as the B.C. government imposed rent controls on residential properties. Block's 1974 declared after-tax profits were $4.1 million, a sharp increase from the 1973 figure of $1.7 million.

Marathon's assets are probably in excess of $1 billion.

The second largest company, Cadillac-Fairview, is a newly formed company resulting from the merger of the Bronfman family-owned Fairview Corp. (a subsidiary of Cemp Investments) and the Toronto-based Cadillac Development Corp., with stated assets of $754 million. There were many reasons for the merger, one of the most interesting being that Fairview had been most active in building shopping centres from coast to coast. In most locations Fairview still owned substantial property around each shopping centre. Cadillac was a highly experienced apartment builder and could surround Fairview's shopping centres with a ring of high-rise apartment buildings, thus making the shopping centres that much more valuable. Also such a large company would have more political muscle with governments at all levels in getting legislation favourable to the development industry.

Close behind Cadillac-Fairview is Trizec Corp.

The directors of the Canadian Institute of Public Real Estate Companies (CIPREC), representing the largest real estate companies in Canada. CIPREC directors meet to discuss common industry problems and to lobby governments at all levels.

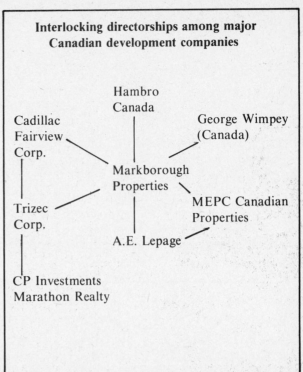

Interlocking directorships among major Canadian development companies

This diagram indicates some of the interlocking directorships between companies competing with each other in the Canadian real estate market.

with assets of $679 million, still digesting its two takeovers in 1971 of Great West International Equities and Cummings Properties. (See separate chapter on Trizec).

Two years ago, there was no such company as Abbey Glen Property Corp. Today it is the fifth largest real estate company in Canada with assets of $296 million. It got that way by taking over two large Canadian companies: Vancouver-based Western Realty Projects, and Toronto-based Great Northern Capital Corp. Abbey Glen, of course, is British-owned. Western Realty Projects had been owned by the Belzberg family of Calgary operating mainly in the three major western centres, Calgary, Edmonton, and Vancouver. Over years of aggressive operation it had built up assets of over $120 million and a huge land bank of over 11,000 acres. In fact Western Realty is one of the largest landowners in the Vancouver region. The Belzberg family sold out to British interests for a cool $75 million. But the Belzbergs were by no means retired. The family still owned City Savings & Trust Co., a rapidly growing trust company with 1973 assets of $157 million. The Belzbergs set up First City Financial Corp. to own their shares of City Trust and to wheel and deal in other financial affairs. In late 1974

they announced their next move — a merger with Block Bros. Industries, Vancouver's second largest real estate company. The merged company would be the largest real estate-financial conglomerate in western Canada, and possibly the sixth largest real estate company in Canada. However for unknown reasons the deal was called off at the last minute

Theoretically developers compete amongst themselves to assemble land, get financing and tenants, and undertake developments. Yet many of the developers do congregate together in industry associations such as the Urban Development Institute (UDI) and the Canadian Institute of Public Real Estate Companies (CIPREC). This latter association contains every major developer in Canada — Marathon, Cadillac-Fairview, Trizec, Daon, and Abbey Glen. Its purpose is to lobby governments at provincial and federal levels to get legislation favourable to the real estate industry. CIPREC produces its own glossy yearly report presumably to build up its public image.

However, there are much closer connections between these supposedly competing companies. The above chart illustrates some of the more direct interlocking connections and directorships between companies in the same real estate market. As well there are numerous indirect connections through law firms, banks, trust companies, and other financial

Trizec Corp. owns a string of 20 'retirement homes' across Canada. This one is at 1645 W 14 Ave in the South Granville apartment area of Vancouver. They are one of Trizec's big money earners.

institutions. Another form of connection among the companies is the pattern of forming joint ventures amongst two or more of them to undertake specific projects. If all these interrelationships were known and were traced out completely, the big developers would look much more like one big happy extended family of brothers, sisters, cousins, and aunts than an industry of bitter independent rivals fiercely competing with each other.

10 Trizec: Portrait of a downtown developer

Suppose you were standing at the corner of Georgia and Burrard streets in downtown Vancouver, and suddenly you were instantaneously transported to the corner of King and Bay streets in downtown Toronto. Could you tell that you had moved? And then from there you were whisked to the corner of Dorchester and Mansfield in downtown Montreal. Could you notice any difference? Probably not!

The fact is that every city in Canada is beginning to look like every other city in Canada, regardless of strong local and cultural differences. Every city is getting its Tower of Darkness. Every downtown is being bombarded by a host of sterile standardized office towers and hotels, designed according to the same criteria — maximum profitability, catering to the same standardized corporate interests.

One of the companies pushing most vigorously for *Developer City, Canada,* is Trizec Corp. No one really knows which is the largest real estate company in Canada. It may be the CPR's Marathon Realty Co. Or it may be the largest public company — the newly merged Cadillac-Fairview Corp., with stated assets of $754 million at the end of 1973. Right behind Cadillac is Trizec with assets of $679 million as of October 31, 1973. But this is book value only — what the properties were worth when they were built or acquired. The true value must be well over $1 billion. Trizec has properties in all major Canadian cities, and in Vancouver its presence is particularly strong. Trizec owns the Lougheed Mall and Brentwood Shopping Centres in Burnaby, a retirement lodge on W. 14th Ave., the Hyatt Airport Marine Hotel at Vancouver International Airport and the Hyatt Regency Hotel in downtown Vancouver, and the 37-storey office building — the tallest building in Vancouver — which together with the Hyatt Regency forms the Royal Centre. Prime tenant in the Royal Centre is the Royal Bank of Canada, which leases eight storeys and operates a three-storey high 'banking pavillion.'

Trizec has teamed up with the Royal Bank of Canada in other cities. In Calgary, the Royal is the prime tenant in Trizec's 24-storey Royal Bank building. In Montreal, Place Ville Marie, the 'flagship' of the Trizec fleet, has the Royal as one of the prime tenants. The connection between Trizec Corp. and the Royal Bank of Canada is not accidental. There are four distinct interlocks between the real estate firm and the bank. Frank M. Covert, a partner in the Halifax establishment law firm of Stewart, MacKeen &

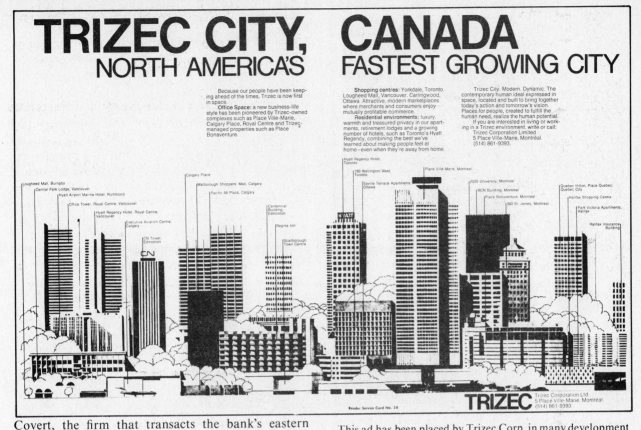
Covert, the firm that transacts the bank's eastern business, is a director of both Trizec and the Royal. In Montreal the two are linked through the Phillips, Vineberg law firm: Hon. Lazarus Phillips, the father, is a director of Trizec. Neil Phillips, the son, is a director of the Royal having succeeded his father in that position in 1971. The developer and the bank are also connected through the Royal's principal law firm in Montreal, Ogilvy, Cope, Porteous Hansard, Marler, Montgomery & Renaud. J. Angus Ogilvy is a vice-president and director of the Royal; Frank B. Common is a director of Trizec. The fourth interlock is less direct but nevertheless acts to tie the two groups together. Sir Charles E.M. Hardie, a partner in a prestigious firm of English accountants is a director of the Royal, and a director of the Hill, Samuel group, one of the founding partners of Trizec, and London's second largest merchant bank.

Trizec Corp. has always been intimately connected to the Royal Bank of Canada. In 1956 American real estate tycoon William Zeckendorf had come to Canada to develop the site where the Place Ville Marie complex now stands. Through an introduction to James Muir, then head of the Royal, Zeckendorf was able to assemble a blue-ribbon board of directors for his Canadian subsidiary, Webb & Knapp (Canada). For the sake of public relations a majority of the board had to be Canadian, even though Zeckendorf's American company owned more than 50% of the shares. This was a move designed to allay the fears of

the ultra-conservative Canadian financial community about Zeckendorf's reputation as a wheeler-dealer. Six of the original board members, including Vancouver's Dal Grauer, were Royal directors.

When Zeckendorf ran into trouble finding a prime tenant for Place Ville Marie, Muir came to the rescue by moving the Royal Bank of Canada headquarters into the project. Zeckendorf still had further trouble in completing the financial arrangements for the $100 million project. He was able to convince British interests to take a share of the action. It was just around the time that many British real estate companies were moving into the lucrative North American market because competition was getting exceedingly tough at home.

These U.S. and British interests formed Trizec Corp. in 1960 to own Place Ville Marie. The name comes from *TRI* plus *Z*(eckendorf), *E*(agle Star Insurance), and *C*(ovent Garden Properties). Wheeler-dealer Zeckendorf indeed soon over-extended himself and had to pull out of Canada, selling out his interests to the British group. Trizec is currently 65% owned by Star (Great Britain) Holdings, a large British real estate firm controlled by the two original partners: Eagle Star Insurance (Sir Brian Mountain) and the Phillip Hill Investment Trust (Kenneth Keith) in London.

53

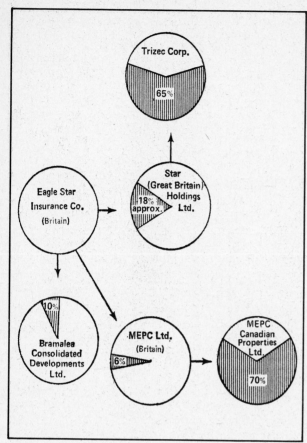

Trizec Corp. is controlled by Star (Great Britain) Holdings, which owns 65% of all outstanding Trizec shares. Star is related to Eagle Star Insurance Co., a British-owned firm, which has other real estate interests in Canada through its 10% interest in Toronto-based Bramalea Consolidated Developments Ltd. and its 6% holdings in MEPC Ltd. in Britain.

Trizec Corp. took over Zeckendorf's other ventures, major shopping centres in Toronto, Halifax, London (Ontario) and Brentwood in Vancouver. Trizec lost money for a number of years while it tried to unravel Zeckendorf's convoluted financial arrangements. The turnaround came in 1967 when Trizec made a modest profit, and Trizec hasn't looked back since. In 1972, profits were over $4 million.

In 1968, Trizec bought out a chain of 'retirement lodges' — Central Park Lodges of Canada — which owns and operates 20 buildings across the country, many of them high-rise. One of these is in Vancouver, a low-rise in the south Granville St. apartment area (1645 W. 14th Ave.).

In 1970, Trizec Corp. bought out two large Calgary-based development corporations to expand its base of operations outside of Quebec. One of Trizec's acquisitions, Great-West International Equities, had built itself up rapidly through an amalgamation of the development skills of Calgarian Sam Hashman and the substantial cash resources of Bronfman family interests (Distillers Corp.-

Seagrams). Great-West was planning Vancouver's Royal Centre at the time of the take-over, and continued the operation as a wholly-owned subsidiary of Trizec. Another subsidiary, Hashman Construction, actually undertook construction of the project.

The other developer which Trizec Corp. took over, Cummings Properties, also of Calgary, had been built up by the Cummings family who still controlled the company. Most of its assets were concentrated in Alberta. By taking over Cummings and Great-West International Equities, Trizec received a bonus. Cummings owned 55% of the massive Calgary Place project in Calgary; Great-West owned the other 45%. Trizec thus acquired 100% control.

One of Trizec Corp.'s main areas of expansion is in the United States through another subsidiary, Tristar Developments. Projects are currently under way in New York and Chicago.

In mid-1974 Trizec Corp. announced another deal, this time involving German investors. Trizec planned to invest in commercial projects in Canada and the United States using funds from a number of German banks. Other funds were to come from French and Swiss banks. Most of the money would probably be seeking a safe haven in Canada. The amount of funds was sizeable, being estimated at about $100 million. Most of it would go for acquistion of projects in the United States, particularly through Tristar South Inc. another subsidiary set up in Atlanta, Georgia.

This latest move illustrates Trizec's unhappiness with current conditions in Canada where the company is faced with a scarcity of serviced land, project delays, and a generally anti-development climate. The move was also part of Trizec's goal to double its assets in three to five years (in mid-1974 around the $850 million mark, including the assets of all subsidiaries). This venture seems a good way of doing it for Trizec although how it helps the severe housing situtation is not as obvious.

Presumably, Trizec Corp. competes with other developers in its business. But somehow this does not prevent the companies from having interlocking directorships. Trizec has three important ones: Markborough Properties, a large nation-wide real estate and development company; Canadian Pacific Investments, owners of Marathon Realty Co.; and Cemp Investments, developers of the Pacific Centre and many other projects.

Watch for Trizec Corp. to take over other major real estate companies in the next few years as British money continues to escape from the tight economic conditions in the U.K. and to find a welcome haven in the lucrative Canadian market. And watch for the Royal Bank of Canada to continue to lend a helping hand in the continuing alienation of one of Canada's most valuable resources — its urban land.

11 Downtown decision-makers
V: Foreign property investors

The Sheik of Kuwait — is he one of the largest landowners in downtown Vancouver? Given the secrecy surrounding the ownership of land, no one will ever know for certain, probably not even the Sheik himself.

It is known, though, that the enormously oil-rich Arabian sheiks have been pumping some American dollars into North American real estate, collecting shopping centres and office buildings. Some of those dollars probably found their way onto the lucrative Vancouver market through untraceable holding companies and trust accounts.

In fact, the Sheik of Kuwait has been to Canada — the August 18, 1973, edition of the *Financial Post* reported the hush-hush stay in Toronto of the sheik and six advisors. The sheik's host was an unnamed nation-wide trust company who wouldn't say what was on the sheik's shopping list, but the *Financial Post* guessed that it included some income properties, some blue-chip stocks, and a company or two.

It is estimated that foreign companies own over one-third of downtown Vancouver, and this proportion is growing. Each year approximately half of all non-residential real estate sales in Vancouver involve foreign buyers or sellers. Disregarding the hazy emotional arguments surrounding this situation, one point is crystal clear: by allowing foreign companies to buy our land, we are penalizing ourselves, driving up the price which we ourselves must pay.

Allowing foreign ownership of downtown land means there are more buyers with money to spread, who are willing to pay much more than most Canadians can afford. With more potential buyers, the price of real estate automatically escalates, because the supply is limited — you just cannot create more land.

For example, in May 1974, Ark Developments, a Hong Kong-based company, sold a downtown Vancouver block to Grander Development, a British-based company for $9 million. This worked out to $180 per square foot, a record for Vancouver real estate. Ark paid less than $4.5 million for the property which it had assembled in four separate transactions between 1967 and 1972. Ark also had assembled three other development sites in the area, and decided to unload this one. But no Canadian buyer could be found who

was willing to pay the inflated price that Ark was asking. Ark thus sold to a foreign investor, incidentally making an almost untaxed 100% speculative gain. Because the land cost so much, whoever does develop the site will build a much higher, denser development that he would normally, to bring in the higher revenues required to pay the inflated price. If foreign investment in real estate was prohibited, land values would automatically fall to more reasonable levels.

But there are many bankers, politicians, and real estate agents who fallaciously argue that foreign investment in Canadian real estate is not harmful, and may even be necessary for our own good.

One of the most vociferous of these has been Tom Boyle, past president of the Real Estate Board of Greater Vancouver and vice-president of Macaulay, Nicolls, Maitland & Co., one of Vancouver's leading realty firms. In one newspaper interview Boyle argued: 'If local buyers will pay me only $25,000 for my property, whereas I am offered twice as much by a British investor, then by not being allowed to sell to him, I have had half the value of my property expropriated.'

In other words, Boyle was agreeing that the

removal of foreign buyers from the market would lower the cost of real estate.

Boyle failed to complete his line of reasoning, however. In his example, the British investor has driven up the price to $50,000 without having done a single thing to the property to increase its usefulness to society and hence justify the increased price. It is a pure speculative gain for Boyle.

The only thing that the British investor has done is to put the price of the property beyond the reach of most Canadians.

Why does Boyle want real estate to be as expensive as possible? Is it because the real estate agent is paid a percentage of the selling price, and the higher the price, the larger the commission?

Just by coincidence, Boyle's company, Macaulay, Nicolls, Maitland & Co., is itself partly owned by two foreign interests — the British-controlled Hambros Bank, and the Hong Kong and Shanghai Banking Corp. So Boyle is hardly an unbiased observer.

Foreign money loves Canda. A flood of this money has found its way into Vancouver property — money from southeast Asia, from Germany, from the United Kingdom, from the United States, from Switzerland and Italy, and quite probably, from the Arabian states of Kuwait, Oman, and Bahrain.

Each country has its special reasons for investing in Canada but for all of them Canada is attractive because of its excellent reputation. We have been overly accommodating to them all. And we are about the most politically stable country in the world. Consider the investor choosing between Latin America and Canada!

Foreigners also see Canada's long-range growth potential. British Columbia, in particular, they see as a place where the population is going to expand. All they have to do is buy property and just sit back and wait until it increases in value. They can then sell it and take home the almost untaxed profits.

The British were the original investors in B.C.'s land and resources, and they still own a significant proportion of the province. In the past year British-controlled development companies have gone on a rampage of mergers and take-overs, perhaps in anticipation of some action by the federal government, however ineffectual that is likely to be.

One of the largest British ventures in Vancouver has been the Grosvenor-Laing group of companies, a partnership between the estate of the Duke of Westminister which owns large parts of central London, England, and the Laing Construction firm. Among other ventures the partnership developed the Annacis Island Industrial Estate.

The partnership has recently split up, with the Laing half becoming a major shareholder in Project 200 along with the CPR. Project 200 was engaged in blotting out Vancouver citizens' view of the harbour and the northshore mountains with a string of waterfront executive high-rise office buildings. But the most familiar British presence in Vancouver has long been the Guinness beer interests, better known as British Pacific Properties, developers of British Properties and Park Royal Shopping Centre, builders of the Lions Gate Bridge, and owners of most of the Municipality of West Vancouver.

British Pacific Properties has also been active along Vancouver's waterfront, first with the Marine Building in 1929, and more recently with the 23-storey Guinness Tower, another project blocking out the view of the waterfront.

The major reason for the British presence in Vancouver is a very tight, highly-competitive real estate market at home. Consequently, British developers expanded overseas, into the booming and accommodating markets of Canada and Australia.

The Americans had a very different reason for buying up Vancouver property. During the 1950s much of downtown Vancouver was owned by wealthy American families such as the Rockefellers and the Phipps (Dodge Motors).

The main motivation for this flow of funds into Canada — reaching an estimated $100 million per year in the late fifties — was a tax loophole which allowed U.S. residents to save up to 60% in taxes on the amount invested in Canada.

Wealthy families would transfer their holdings that were subject to succession duties to Vancouver real estate. The beneficiaries could then liquidate the estate and take the money back to the U.S.A., paying only a 15% withholding tax to the Canadian government. In effect, it was more profitable for an American to buy property in Vancouver than in Seattle.

The Canadian government aided this process by simplifying regulations for Americans through the Estate Tax Act. However, in 1961 President Kennedy closed the loophole and American money started moving back to the U.S.

This American money had a very harmful effect on Vancouver. There was little development in downtown Vancouver during the 1950s. A state of stagnation had set in. This was not because new facilities were not needed. Vancouver was growing and most of the growth was taking place in the suburbs.

Downtown Vancouver stagnated because the Americans owned most of it, and the Americans were not interested in developing; they just wanted to keep their estates intact. And Vancouver suffered for it.

For historical reasons, Vancouverites react most strongly to property transactions which involve Hong Kong and other southeast Asian money.

Hong Kong, known as the Switzerland of the Orient, is the centre of financial activity for southeast

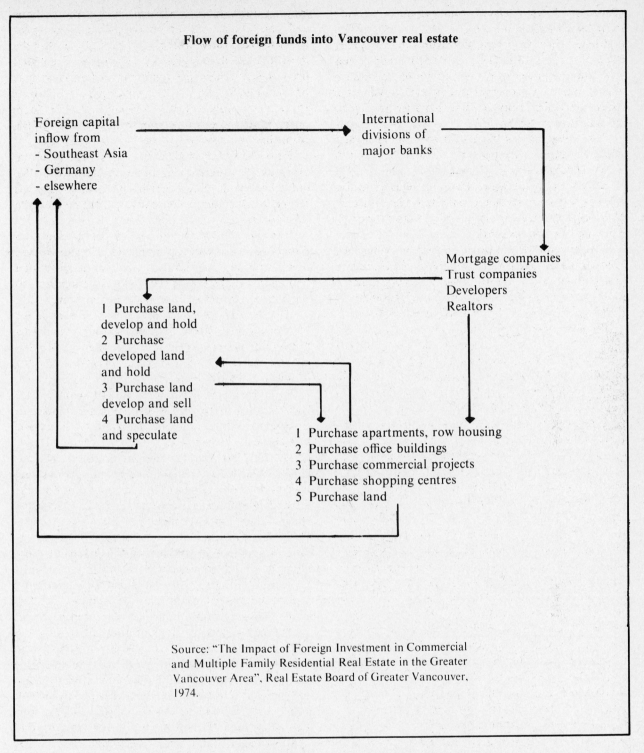

Flow of foreign funds into Vancouver real estate

Foreign capital inflow from
- Southeast Asia
- Germany
- elsewhere

International divisions of major banks

Mortgage companies
Trust companies
Developers
Realtors

1 Purchase land, develop and hold
2 Purchase developed land and hold
3 Purchase land develop and sell
4 Purchase land and speculate

1 Purchase apartments, row housing
2 Purchase office buildings
3 Purchase commercial projects
4 Purchase shopping centres
5 Purchase land

Source: "The Impact of Foreign Investment in Commercial and Multiple Family Residential Real Estate in the Greater Vancouver Area", Real Estate Board of Greater Vancouver, 1974.

Asia. It has been undergoing an economic boom of late, and money has been flowing freely in from the U.S., Japan, and Switzerland — in this latter case, money flows from one unnumbered bank account to another.

However, during the mid-sixties, there was a sudden outflow of capital from the wealthy Chinese community because of financial and political uncertainties — the 1965 banking crisis and the 1967 labour riots. Much of this money found a haven in Canada, particularly in Vancouver real estate.

With a return to stability, this flow of funds was reversed, but money from other parts of southeast Asia — Singapore and Malaysia — has become increasingly important, so that there is still a net inflow of capital.

Hong Kong money has the same result as German, American or British money — it drives up the price of real estate for all Canadians.

Robert H. Lee, president of Vancouver-based Wall & Redekop Realty, and David Lam, head of its international investment department, have been instrumental in channelling much of this money into B.C.

Rumours abound as to just how much property each of the foreign interests owns, but there are just no statistics available. There is no master registration of land sales, and even if there was, buyers are not legally required to register their property.

Lawyers, trust companies, and holding companies can easily hide the true identity of an owner. Foreigners are reluctant to reveal their interests, for if the extent to which B.C. is already foreign-owned was made public, there would be a massive outcry and pressure for restrictive legislation.

This action would be bad for the real estate industry — it would mean lower prices — so they are very careful to mask foreign owners.

12 Bentall Centre: Case study of a downtown development

Next time you are in downtown Vancouver, take a close look at the Bentall Centre — that's the three buildings on Burrard St. between Dunsmuir and Pender streets, in the so-called 'superblock.' Look at how tall the buildings are — 21, 17, and 30 storeys. Then look at how little open space there is at street level. Tower One comes almost to the sidewalk on Burrard St. Tower Two is crammed in beside Tower One. And Tower Three is also too tall for the site it's on — it comes almost to the sidewalk on the Dunsmuir-Melville connector. There seems to be too much building packed onto such a small site.

And it's true. There is indeed too much building packed onto the site. At least, if the developer had gone by Vancouver's zoning by-laws.

Zoning by-laws set the maximum height of buildings; they establish how far buildings must be set back from the street; they set light angles for view and sunlight; and they set the maximum density of development.

The main purpose of zoning is to protect the person who owns property. He wants to be sure that no one will be allowed to build a slaughterhouse next door to his stylish boutique and hence lower his property value. Zoning has a secondary purpose of protecting the public. By specifying a maximum height for a building and a maximum density of development, the zoning by-law effectively limits the number of people who can live or work in the buildings. This maximum is then tied to the level of existing facilities, so that roads, public transportation and area of parkland will not get overloaded.

But somehow, Bentall Towers One and Three are much taller than allowed under the zoning regulations. Tower One should be no more than 247.5 feet in height. It is actually 281 feet high. Tower Three should not be taller than 165 feet. It is actually 385 feet high, *more than twice as tall as it should be.*

Most people must obey every provision of the zoning by-law, and sometimes this is carried to ridiculous extremes. But if you are a big-time developer, you can easily by-pass the zoning requirements. The book on how to circumvent city regulations in Vancouver was written by well-known developer Ben Wosk, but Clark Bentall, president of Dominion Construction Co. and Bentall Properties, builders and owners of Bentall Centre, could do almost as well.

Here's how you do it. When you are making your

By cramming people together in the Bentall Centre like this...   ...Clark Bentall can afford to live spread out like this.

application for a development permit you ask for much more than you are allowed under the zoning by-law — a taller building, and a much denser development. The city planning department must turn down your application because it doesn't meet the requirements. But that's alright. You can just appeal the planning department's decisions to the board of variance (formerly called the zoning board of appeal, which was more descriptive of what it did). This board has the power to relax the provisions of the by-law. It can permit you to build a much taller building than is allowed under the by-law. If the board accepts your appeal, you are home-free and can build yourself a taller building which incidentally is much more profitable for you. The board allowed appeals on both Bentall Towers One and Three. The board also allowed Ben Wosk to make his Plaza 500 much taller than it should have been.

Was it coincidence that Ben Wosk himself was on the board of variance when he made his appeal? He didn't vote on it although another member of the board who did vote, J. Arthur Charpentier, was, as columnist Allan Fotheringham pointed out, shortly afterwards, a director of Wosk's firm.

Even though there was no such blatant conflict of interest in the case of the Bentall Centre, Clark Bentall

did have an enviable record in getting what he wanted. He got two relaxations from the board of variance for Bentall Towers One and Three. And he got city council to rezone land at the corner of Pender and Seymour streets, to allow a five-storey parking garage, even though the city planning department strongly recommended against allowing the development.

Away back in 1956 city council had set a policy not to allow any further parking facilities in the down-town core area because they tended to disturb the continuity of street level activity. However, Dominion Construction Co. bought land on the nothwest corner of Pender and Seymour streets in the spring of 1967 and applied to get the property rezoned so that it could build a parking garage. The city planning department recommended strongly against allowing Dominion to build the garage. The Rathie-led city council ignored its planners' advice and voted to allow Bentall to build his garage.

A few months later Bentall was able to get his hands on the next 52 feet along Pender St. and was back asking to have this property rezoned as well. A compliant city council gave him that too. Bentall then proceeded to build a 400-car garage at a cost of $1.2 million, and another half block of the downtown core was lost to automobiles.

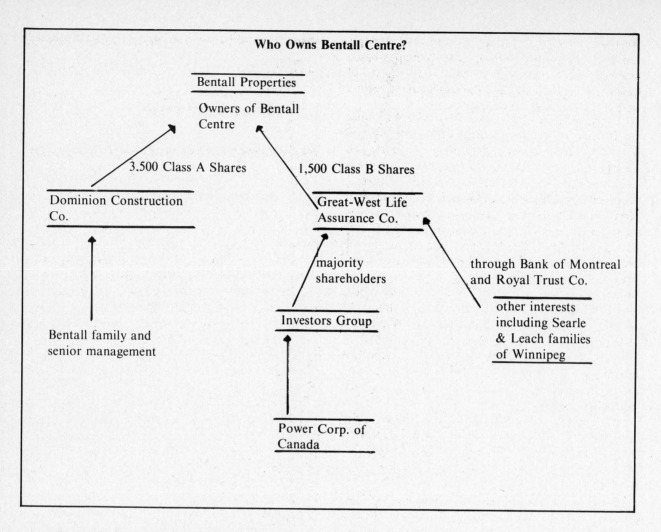

Who Owns Bentall Centre?

Bentall Properties
Owners of Bentall Centre

3,500 Class A Shares → Dominion Construction Co.

1,500 Class B Shares → Great-West Life Assurance Co.

Bentall family and senior management → Dominion Construction Co.

Investors Group → (majority shareholders) → Great-West Life Assurance Co.

other interests including Searle & Leach families of Winnipeg → (through Bank of Montreal and Royal Trust Co.) → Great-West Life Assurance Co.

Power Corp. of Canada → Investors Group

Dominion Construction Co.'s partner in the Bentall Centre venture was Great West Life Assurance Co., the third largest life insurance company in Canada. Great West was an equity partner with Dominion in the subsidiary Bentall Properties, which would actually own the project. Second, Great West provided the mortgage money for the project. Third, Great West became the primary tenant in Bentall Tower One. It was a very neat deal for all concerned. Bentall couldn't get mortgage money without a prime tenant; Great West became the prime tenant and provided the mortgage money. Great West also took an equity position so that it would not only collect the interest payments on the mortgage, but also share in the profits of the development.

This combined role of both equity participant and mortgage lender was a new wrinkle in financing developments. The life insurance companies, major sources of mortgage money lent for long periods of time at fixed interest rates, were becoming concerned about the long-term effects of inflation upon their investments, and demanded direct participation in the ownership of the project in order to capture some of the capital gains from the appreciation of the develop-

ment.

Also, by being the prime tenant in the project which it both financed and owned, Great West Life Assurance Co. was assured of tenant security as well as gaining from the benefits of self-ownership — lower rental costs.

There was more to these cosy financial arrangements. Every project requires short-term financing as well as the mortgage financing. The short-term financing is the money with which the developer actually constructs the building; the lender is then paid back out of the mortgage money which becomes available after the construction is complete. In this case, short-term financing was provided by the Canadian Imperial Bank of Commerce, who also took considerable space in Tower One.

Until the mid-sixties, control of Great West Life Assurance Co. was shared between American and Canadian interests. American control was exercised through the Canadian Imperial Bank of Commerce. In fact, Great West and the Commerce had four directors in common at one point. So it was only natural that the Commerce would pick up the short-term financing for the building. However during the mid-sixties Great

West was subject to a number of take-over attempts and in 1969 Investors Group, the Winnipeg-based financial empire controlled by Power Corp. of Canada, bought 50.1%, and the Commerce directors were removed from the board.

Canadian control of Great West Life Assurance Co. is exercised through the Bank of Montreal/Royal Trust Co. power group representing the Searle and Leach families in Winnipeg who are linked together as owners of Federal Grain Co. (now Federal Industries). At the present time A. Searle Leach is vice-president of Great West, chairman of Federal Industries and a vice-president of the Bank of Montreal. Prominent Winnipeg lawyer J. Blair MacAulay is a director of all three companies. C. Antoine Geoffrion, a Montreal lawyer, is a director of Great West and of Royal Trust. There are thus very intimate relationships between Great West and Bank of Montreal/Royal Trust. It should come as no surprise then that with Great West providing the mortgage money for both Towers Two and Three, Royal Trust was the prime tenant in Tower Two and the Bank of Montreal in Tower Three. Such are some of the practical consequences of interlocking corporate directorships.

And the Bank of Montreal Tower was placed right across the street from the Royal Bank Tower so that the executives of the two banks could glare at each other across the Dunsmuir-Melville connector from their corporate boardrooms.

On August 31, 1968, Bill Fletcher, business columnist for the Vancouver *Sun* wrote an article about the Bentall Centre. The occasion for the article was the topping off of the Bentall Centre. In his article Fletcher bragged about the development of the Bentall Centre, which was going on 'in the heart of the city without any subsidies, debates in city hall or haggling with eastern financiers.' As we have seen, things weren't quite like that.

13 The pattern of downtown development: Boom and bust

The current boom in downtown development in Vancouver is just the latest upward trend in a cycle of boom and bust which characterizes the history of the city. In every boom period, real estate agents flourish, money is easy to find to finance building projects, millions of dollars are made overnight by a few fortunate speculators, and everyone imagines that unparalleled prosperity will continue forever. When the inevitable bust comes, either as a result of a general economic collapse (as in 1930) or because of local over-building, the marginal speculators lose their shirts, and the most solidly entrenched local property interests consolidate their holdings and devote their energies to persuading the city to embark on projects and policies which will get a new boom cycle underway again.

Vancouver and land speculation have always been closely associated. From the moment that the Canadian Pacific Railway announced Vancouver as the terminus for the railway, the crowds descended on the place to make their fortunes in real estate. Hundreds of real estate speculators arrived in town to buy up the land as quickly as possible and then to sell it later as more real estate speculators arrived in town; they would then sell it to the succeeding speculators, and so on.

One of the first speculators to arrive in town was A.W. Ross, MP for Lisgar, Manitoba, and a CPR flak in Ottawa. He was first going to invest in Port Moody but suddenly in 1884 invested all he had in the Granville townsite.

Ross set himself up in the real estate business in 1886 as did his brother-in-law, Malcolm Maclean, Vancouver's first mayor. Vancouver was incorporated in 1886. Jack Boultbee, a prominent lawyer and later magistrate, whose descendants have been important in real estate ever since, was selected to go to Victoria to push the bill incorporating Vancouver through the provincial legislature.

Other Vancouver landowners were very happy when the CPR made Vancouver its terminus over Port Moody. They gladly gave the CPR a third of their land holdings, a donation which the CPR required as part of their deal to move to Vancouver. One of the largest property owners in the new town was a syndicate which owned 1,460 acres of east end land. The group received advance notice of the CPR's intentions, and managed to buy up another 85 acres of Hastings Mill property after they knew the CPR was coming. The

Vancouver's first city council, 1886. Seated left to right: the vacant seat is for Harry Hemlow, in Seattle on business when the photo was taken, and proprietor of the Sunnyside Hotel; C.A. Coldwell, foreman of Hastings Saw Mill, Vancouver's largest employer at the time; E.P. Hamilton, contractor and builder; J. Northcote, grocer; Mayor M.A. Maclean, real estate agent; L.A. Hamilton, assistant land commissioner of the CPR; Peter Cordiner, blacksmith at the Hastings Saw Mill; and on the extreme right city clerk T.F. McGuigan.

Standing left to right: Joseph Griffith, real estate agent; R. Balfeur, proprietor of the Burrard Hotel; Thomas Dunn, hardware dealer; city solicitor J.J. Blake; Joseph Humphries, agent of the Moodyville Saw Mill; city treasurer G.F. Baldwin; city coroner Dr. W.J. McGuigan.

Standing in the background is G.W. Gibson, founder of Gibson's Landing, B.C.

Of the eleven elected city politicians in Vancouver in 1886, seven made their living directly or indirectly from the real estate and land development business.

group included David Oppenheimer, Vancouver's second mayor, and John Robson, member of the provincial Smithe cabinet, and a future premier of British Columbia. The holdings of this group were large enough to rival those of the CPR itself, and the result was a drawn-out struggle between the two groups about the direction which development should take in Vancouver. The CPR wanted everything pushed west onto their land, and the Oppenheimer-Robson syndicate wanted development to go east. This division between east end and west end property interests has persisted, and helps explain why in the 1930s city council decided to locate the new City Hall on Cambie St., a location which favoured east and west end interests equally. On the whole, however, the CPR was the dominant group and succeeded in having most valuable developments go westward.

Even Rudyard Kipling came to Vancouver in 1889 to get in on a piece of the action. Kipling did very well for himself before trundling off to darkest Africa. As

Water Street, 1887, looking west. This was the first development in the city in the Granville townsite (now Gastown) after the fire of 1886. *B.C. Provincial Archives*

he put it: 'You order your agent to hold a town lot until property rises, then sell out and buy more land further out of town ... I do not quite see how this helps the growth of the town ... but it is the essence of speculation.'

Vancouver's history has been nothing but a series of real estate booms and busts:

REAL ESTATE BOOMS	REAL ESTATE BUSTS
1886-1893	1893-1898
1905-1913	1913-1918
1925-1929	1930-1941
1946-1955	1955-1964
1967-1976(?)	1976(?)-?

Each orgy of speculation has been followed by an inevitable collapse in land values. The first era of rapid increases in land values occurred after Vancouver was incorporated in 1886. For example, in 1891, a 50-foot lot on Granville St. was priced at $16,000. An offer of $13,500 was refused by the owner. Two years later, when the bust hit, it was sold for $6,400. Then in the mid-1900s it sold for $90,000. When the Imperial Bank was built on the lot in 1911, the land itself was valued at $175,000.

The earliest commercial centre in downtown was in the area surrounded by Cambie, Hastings, Carrall and Water streets, with the most desirable property being on Cordova St.

The recession of 1893 hit Vancouver hard and a

Malcolm Maclean, Vancouver's first mayor and a real estate agent. Ever since Maclean, selling real estate and running city hall have been almost synonymous in Vancouver. *B.C. Provincial Archives*

J.W. Horne set himself up in the real estate business in this tree stump in 1886. Within a few years he had become Vancouver's richest resident. *B.C. Provincial Archives*

The West End and downtown, looking across False Creek from Fairview in the 1890s. This extensive building took place during Vancouver's first boom from 1886-1893. *B.C. Provincial Archives*

The centre of downtown moved from Cordova to Hastings St. when Woodward built this new department store there in 1904. *B.C. Provincial Archives*

recovery did not begin until 1898 with the discovery of gold in the Klondike. Vancouver became the setting-out point for the gold miners. Prosperity returned and by 1905, Vancouver embarked on its greatest real estate boom, dwarfing even the 1967 boom by comparison. The population of Vancouver more than trebled in the ten-year period from 1901 to 1911. The rate of expansion was particularly strong after 1904. The downtown area expanded enormously. The centre spread first from Cordova St. to Hastings St. —

During the boom of the 1900s, the centre of downtown spread westward from Woodward's store along Hastings to Granville, then up to meet the CPR-dominated corner at Granville and Georgia. Here is a view of the new Hudson's Bay store under construction at the north-east corner of Georgia and Granville. Across the street can be seen the recently-completed Vancouver Block and the Birks Building nearing completion. *B.C. Provincial Archives.*

Woodward's department store moved there in 1904 — then west to Granville St., and up to meet the CPR-dominated node at Georgia and Granville streets. The eight-storey Leigh Spence Building at 553 Granville St. went up in 1911; the 15-storey Vancouver Block in 1912; and the 11-storey Birks Building in 1913. At the height of the boom in 1910, the city gave the first demonstration of a continuing theme in its history when it annexed the Hastings Townsite and other land in the east end to extend its boundary to the present city limit at Boundary Rd.

Land values just sky-rocketed. Some rises in values along Hastings St. were phenomenal. The Province Building site first sold in 1886 for $2,800. Three years later it went for $20,000. In 1895, during the depression it was down to $10,000. Then in the early 1900s it went for $30,000, in 1908 for $70,000 and in 1911 for a cool $200,000.

The old Dominion Trust site between Hamilton

and Richards streets sold for $750 in 1887. In 1911 it went for $100,000. A 52-foot frontage on Hastings St. was sold by Lady Mount Stephen (wife of CPR president Donald Smith) in 1904 for $26,000. Four years later it went for $175,000.

Granville St., just then developing, saw even more spectacular increases. Twenty-five foot lots between Nelson and Pacific streets were put on the market by the CPR in 1886 with an asking price of $1,000. Twenty-five years later they were worth $40,000, an increase of over 3,000%.

Needless to say some men became very wealthy indeed. One notable example was Walter E. Graveley, who set up his real estate business in 1886. He had the distinction of buying the first piece of property put on the market by the CPR from its land grant, the triangle surrounded by Cordova and Carrall streets and the CPR tracks. Graveley — after whom is named Graveley St. in the Grandview area — specialized in east end real estate. Graveley would buy a large piece of property, subdivide it, and sell the lots to builders.

J.W. Horne was another who became fabulously wealthy from Vancouver real estate. He got his start in Brandon, Manitoba, through speculating on land after 1882. He made several visits to British Columbia following the railroad, and moved to Vancouver in 1886 where he invested much of his money in real estate, buying choice properties and erecting business buildings on Cordova and Granville streets. He eventually became the largest property owner in Vancouver. He was, of course, elected to city council in 1888, to the parks board in 1889, and to the provincial legislature in 1890, where he remained for four years. He was president or director of many real estate, insurance, and utility companies, and one of the founders of the B.C. Electric Railway. While an MLA he was offered the posts of minister of public works and minister of lands, the two cabinet posts most intimately tied in with the real estate business, but he refused because he was too busy in his many business affairs.

In the period before World War I foreign capital just poured into Vancouver, buying up everything in sight with the more than accommodating help of succeeding provincial governments. Much of the money coming into Vancouver was British and German. One of the major conduits for British funds was through the Yorkshire Guarantee and Securities Corp. (later the Yorkshire Trust Co. and finally the Yorkshire Financial Corp.) sponsored by a group of Yorkshire businessmen in 1898. It loaned its own funds and those of its clients on mortgages on property in B.C. It also acted as executor and manager of estates, as trustees for debenture holders, and as general agent for Yorkshire Insurance Co. — a large fire insurance business. The company also bought and sold real estate.

Yorkshire's resident manager in Vancouver at first was William Farrell, a Yorkshireman, who was also the company solicitor. Farrell was also a general broker and shipping agent. He acquired a large interest in one of the predecessor companies of B.C. Telephone Co., and when a number of companies were amalgamated in 1904 he became president. Farrell, and his son who succeeded him as B.C. Telephone president in 1928, became one of the major business forces in the province. His four granddaughters were highly desireable marriage material among the up and coming businessmen.

By 1912, Yorkshire's business had expanded to such an extent that it constructed a new nine-storey office building at 525 Seymour St.

One of the major conduits for German money was the colourful Count Alvo von Alvensleben, acting for German investors — some say Kaiser Wilhelm was behind many of the deals. He invested over $7 million in Vancouver real estate and other B.C. resources in a three-year period.

In spite of these foreign sources, capital was in scarce supply for the booming Vancouver real estate market. One local response was the Dominion Trust Co., set up in 1908 by local businessmen because of the remoteness of the other financial institutions in eastern Canada and elsewhere. The company set about lending money using real estate as the principal type of collateral, and built itself a magnificent office tower, Vancouver's first skyscraper, a 13-storey building at the corner of Cambie and Hastings streets. Toward the end of 1913, however, British and German capital (including von Alvensleben) began to pull out because of the impending war, resulting in an immediate deflation in real estate values. In 1914 the company (but not the building) collapsed, leaving over 5,000 customers without any recourse to compensation. The sudden death of the managing director in October 1914 precipitated an enquiry which revealed that some directors had borrowed over $1 million of the depositors' money without authority or security. The enquiry also showed that the provincial government had not investigated the company's financial solvency before incorporation, and that the government had particularly lax laws governing the activity of trust companies. It also was revealed that provincial attorney-general Bowser's law firm were solicitors for the company.

The Dominion Trust Building was Vancouver's tallest for a scant two years. One of its backers was a business rival of Louis D. Taylor, editor of the Vancouver *World* and oftentimes mayor of Vancouver. Not to be outdone, Taylor began work on a 17-storey tower, which became the tallest building in the British Empire.

The Dominion Trust Building. When completed in 1908 it was the tallest building in the British Empire...

...for 2 years until business rivals built a taller building, the World Tower, now the Sun Tower. *B.C. Provincial Archives*

The failure of the Dominion Trust Co. and the pullout of foreign capital led to a collapse in the real estate market. Vancouver had grown faster than her speculative economy warranted and the whole flimsy structure came crashing down around her ears in 1913-14. Hundreds of buildings were vacated, and subdivided lots were worthless. As World War I began, many young men went off to save the Empire. During the bust, Vancouver suffered her only population loss in history, declining from 122,000 in 1912 to 96,000 in 1916.

The establishment of war industries in Vancouver in 1917 meant the beginning of the return to prosperity. The opening of the Panama Canal in 1914 had reinforced Vancouver's position as a pre-eminent seaport and by the mid-twenties Vancouver real estate was again booming. A number of hotels were built — the Georgia in 1927, and the Devonshire in 1925, the Ritz completed in 1924 as apartments and converted to a hotel in 1929. In 1928 work began on the present Hotel Vancouver (Georgia and Burrard streets), but it had not been completed by the time of the great depres-

sion and stood unfinished for almost ten years.

This boom reached its peak in 1929. In that year, the city of Vancouver — spearheaded by the downtown business interests — expanded again by amalgamating with South Vancouver and Point Grey to give the city its present area of 44 square miles and a population of 220,000.

By 1929, according to premier Duff Pattulo, Vancouver had 83 millionaires. In the same year, construction was commenced on the Marine Building and the Royal Bank Building at the corner of Hastings and Granville streets. CPR started construction of a tunnel from Coal Harbour to the False Creek yards to eliminate the Carrall St. crossing, something which had irritated Vancouverites for 40 years.

Then came the greatest bust in Vancouver's history and real estate values again plummeted to their lowest levels ever. By 1935 the city had hit rock bottom. Property was almost worthless — a $1,500 lot in the east end could be had for $50 or less. In 1933, 34,000 people were on relief. Families squatted on the Kitsilano Indian Reserve, under the Georgia St.

The 1930 Vancouver skyline photographed from Stanley Park. In the centre is the Marine Building, then moving to the right is the cluster of buildings at Georgia and Granville including Birks, the Vancouver Block and the CPR hotel, and further right is the cluster along Georgia with the CNR's Hotel Vancouver still under construction. This skyline remained virtually unchanged until the mid-1950s. *B.C. Provincial Archives*

Viaduct, on the False Creek flats. During this period, the newly-formed Co-operative Commonwealth Federation posed the first serious threat offered to the city's established political order, a situation which led directly to the formation of the Non-Partisan Association in 1937 and the beginning of its 35-year domination of city council.

However in 1938 the economy took an upturn. During the preceding year several public buildings had been completed, Malkin Bowl in Stanley Park, the Art Gallery on Georgia St., and the new City Hall on Cambie St. Work resumed on the CNR hotel and it was completed just in time for the visit of the King of England in 1939. Construction began on the Lions Gate Bridge. This had first been projected in 1932, by Guinness beer interests — who had recently completed the Marine Building. The bridge was planned as an integral part of the British Properties development on the North Shore, but it had been opposed by the shipping interests who ran the ferries to the North Shore, and by the CPR who saw the bridge as a threat to their Shaughnessy Heights development. The Conservative government in Ottawa, who were the closest of friends with the CPR magnates, resisted pressure for the construction of the bridge for six years

During the 1920s building boom, the Georgia Hotel (foreground), the Devonshire Hotel and the Medical Dental Building were constructed west along Georgia St. Two other major buildings of the 1920s were under construction when this photo was taken — the Hotel Vancouver, built by the Canadian National Railway on the far left, and the Marine Building on the waterfront whose steel skeleton is visible on the far right. *B.C. Provincial Archives*

but finally gave in.

Little major building construction was undertaken during World War II, so Vancouver emerged after the war with a skyline almost completely unchanged from the late 1920s. The boom which followed the war brought a substantial new demand for downtown office space. At first this was met from the stock of half-empty existing buildings, but a few new buildings were begun, including the seven-storey Alvin Building on

Vancouver's first summer resort, The Hastings Hotel in Hastings townsite (also called New Brighton) in 1886. It was a separate community. In 1910, the City of Vancouver demonstrated another aspect of downtown domination of the region when it annexed the Hastings townsite.

Robson St., a four-storey Dominion Bank Building at Pender and Granville streets, a four-storey addition to the former Begg Motor Building at Georgia and Bute streets, a new Yorkshire Building at Pender and Hornby streets, and a Bentall Building at Burrard and Pender streets, kitty-corner to the present Bentall Centre.

Leading this first post-war downtown building boom was the federal government, which used two of the new buildings for the unemployment insurance commission and the department of national revenue. Interestingly enough, there were scandals surrounding both these projects. Opposition member Howard Green raised in the House of Commons in late 1949 the fact that the federal government had made a rent or purchase deal for the Alvin Building which involved placing a value of $1.1 million on the building, double its assessed market value. An addition built on the former Begg Motors Building cost the federal

government $575,000 more than the original estimate of $850,000. Linked to both exposés was Darrell T. Braidwood, a Vancouver lawyer whose father Thomas Braidwood was president of the Vancouver Burrard Liberal Association for 17 years and former president of the Vancouver Liberal Council.

This post-war boom continued into the 1950s and peaked about 1955 with the construction of Dal Grauer's B.C. Electric Building on Burrard St. and the Burrard Building four blocks down the street. A few smaller buildings went up in the late 1950s but none were the size of these two projects.

The lack of much substantial development during this period gave downtown property owners and their friends in city council much cause for concern. The Metropolitan Vancouver area was growing by leaps and bounds but most of this growth was taking place out in the suburbs. Downtown was not receiving its share of new retail growth. Both Park Royal and Oakridge opened as major regional shopping centres in the 1950s, both fairly close to downtown. The Hudson's Bay Co. and Woodward Stores, two of the major downtown department stores, preferred to go into these new centres rather than expand their downtown facilities. Many stores along Hastings and Granville

streets were vacant — in 1962, 15% of the stores along Hastings St. were empty.

Office space was being dispersed in projects like the Fairmont Medical Building on Broadway. No new hotels had been built in the downtown core in over ten years, while many were being built in the outlying districts. Downtown had poor transportation access and even poorer parking facilities. People who had moved out to the suburbs just were not coming downtown any more. And worse still, from the point of view of the politicians, the downtown tax base relative to the rest of the city was declining.

Another problem faced downtown property interests. During the 1950s a large part of downtown had been bought up by wealthy American families such as the Rockefellers and the American owners of

The B.C. Electric building which, with the Burrard Building, capped the building boom which began after World War II and ended in the mid-1950s. There were no major downtown building projects completed for another 10 years, and then the late 1960s-1970s building boom commenced.

downtown land were not interested in developing. They merely wanted to keep their estates intact. So this had a further damping down effect.

As early as 1957 downtown business interests became concerned about the fate of downtown. Development was slowing down. After the completion of the B.C. Electric Building, the Burrard Building, and an addition to the B.C. Telephone Building no major projects had been undertaken or were on the

Get Going or Lose, Vancouver Advised

Business Captain Lecky Urges Quick Start on Development

By ALF STRAND

Vancouver must sail ahead with downtown redevelopment and transportation links without waiting for a long-range navigational chart, the president of the Downtown Business Association said Thursday night.

John MacD. Lecky warned that waiting for completion of a master plan could becalm the city and cause the loss of millions of dollars in downtown investment capital.

However, Lecky added, work should start at the same time on a master plan for land use and transportation on a long-term basis for the city.

In taking his tack, Lecky politely rapped the knuckles of some academic planners who favor delays in building downtown transportation links until a master plan is completed.

"To say that we should do nothing until we have a complete, long-term plan is to short-change us all in the present," Lecky told the 48th annual dinner meeting of the Automobile Dealers' Association of Greater Vancouver.

'GREAT HARM'

"Worse, it risks doing this city in particular great harm.

"For we have problems to solve now — critical ones which can start us moving up or can pull us down for a generation."

These problems, he said, include getting private investment capital into redevelopment projects and starting approved urban renewal projects.

"There is also the problem of servicing these fruits of investment with modern surface transportation facilities — now," said Lecky.

Lecky, who is also a member of the town planning commission, said he laments the lack of development in Vancouver compared to other metropolitan centres.

horizon. In 1958 the Downtown Business Association (DBA) sponsored Project 58, a pie-in-the-sky $700 million redevelopment plan which immediately perished because of the lack of funds. In 1960 the DBA tried again, forming the Downtown Redevelopment Advisory Board (DRAB) to advise city council about downtown development.

With things reaching a crisis state in the early 1960s the downtown lobby took the offensive. They got firm control over city council with pro-downtown development mayor Bill Rathie. They initiated a propaganda campaign to whip up public concern about the plight of downtown. This campaign was spearheaded by the newspapers who churned out a steady stream of it's-doom-and-gloom-unless-we-do-something-immediately editorials and articles. Alarmists such as the head of the University of British Columbia's school of community and regional planning, Peter Oberlander, actively lobbied for downtown development using the silly analogy of comparing the city to a body.

With the campaign under way, the next step was to find out how to get downtown property values and development on the upswing. City council hired Larry Smith & Co., an American firm of economic consultants to recommend a program of downtown redevelopment. There were three aspects to the proposals put forward by Smith and others:

1 Build a freeway system centring on the downtown. This led to a number of major controversies over the next ten years, as the city tried to implement such a plan with the east-west freeway, the Chinatown freeway, the waterfront freeway, the third crossing — all of which were eventually halted or postponed.

2 Continue to locate people close to downtown, mainly in the West End. This was already happening and Smith recommended that the process be accelerated. The purpose of this was to provide shoppers for the downtown stores and office workers for the downtown office buildings.

3 Assemble land with public money and then turn it over to private enterprise for development. Smith proposed that the best area for redevelopment was midway between Woodward's and the Bay department stores — the area east of Seymour St. between Hastings and Dunsmuir streets. The idea was to integrate all shopping in the downtown area by inducing Eaton's to construct a new department store in that area. It would be close to the Queen Elizabeth Theatre and a proposed convention/coliseum centre across the street, and it would stimulate the construction of more office space and hotel rooms.

Council approved the recommendations made by Smith in his report, endorsed the superblock recommended by Smith, and got the city planners and consultants to prepare plans for the superblock. These were completed in October 1963. However, in one of the city's famous turnarounds; they reversed their decision less than six months later when Eaton's announced it was going to build its new store on its property at Georgia and Granville streets kitty-corner from the Bay. The city planners immediately abandoned their carefully prepared plans saying that they were impractical and recommended a shift to Block 42 which just happened to be adjacent to Eaton's property.

This was a typical city council move — letting the developers and other business interests make their plans, then following behind.

No doubt the favourable climate for downtown development created by the new aggressive political role of downtown property interests and the plans and projects which they developed helped encourage the latest downtown boom which got underway around 1967. As it turned out, Smith's freeways were not built, but alternative transportation projects which use rapid transit to move people from the suburbs to the downtown core promise downtown developers the facilities

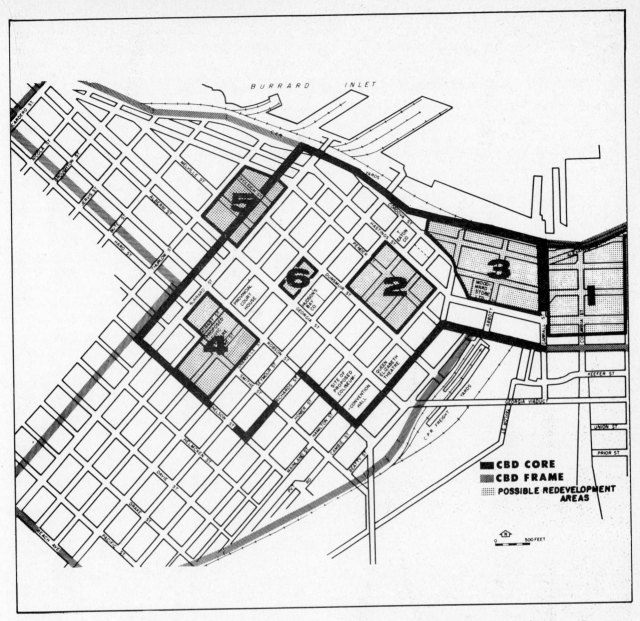

CBD CORE
CBD FRAME
POSSIBLE REDEVELOPMENT
AREAS

0   500 FEET

which they want. Publicly-assisted downtown development has proved time-consuming — after ten years the second phase of the Block 42 project is not yet completed — but the city found other techniques, particularly very generous density provisions in zoning and planning controls, to help the developers along.

The current pattern of downtown development differs in scale from Vancouver's previous boom periods. Just about everything else is the same — immense profits for a few property speculators, both local and foreign-based, behind-the-scenes wheeling and dealing between property interests and political parties, and a city administration controlled by real estate interests actively aiding developers and speculators in their activities.

This map, from the 1963 Larry Smith report on downtown redevelopment, identifies possible redevelopment areas. The report recommended area 2, midway between Woodward's and the Bay, as the best bet. This was endorsed by city council and the city planners. However Eaton's announced that it was going to build its new store in area 6, not area 2. City planners and politicians meekly changed their minds and said that, after all, area 6 was much better.

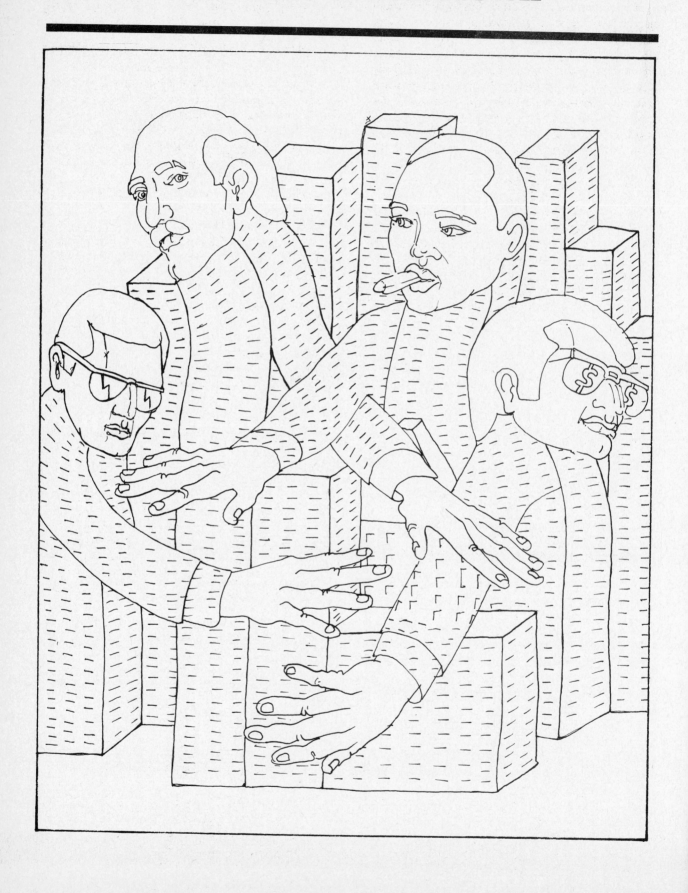

The future of downtown Vancouver looks so rosy for continued rampant development that property owners immediately adjacent to the downtown core are itching to get in on some of the action. The biggest of these adjacent owners is the Canadian Pacific Railway which owns all of the north shore of False Creek, and much of the Burrard Inlet waterfront abutting on the part of downtown that is being most intensively redeveloped at the present time. Several other owners are involved, including the Bayshore Inn which owns the block to the west of the present hotel. Since much of the downtown core is already redeveloped, the next major battles between real estate interests and the citizens of Vancouver will be over these areas. In the long run, the way that they develop will be more important than the downtown itself to Vancouver's well-being, as they are key amenity areas which could provide close contact with the water and water-related activities; or they could be regarded as high-priced real estate, to be developed in the most profitable way possible, which means prestigious office buildings, and high-priced housing accommodation. The way things are going, it doesn't look too good for the citizens of Vancouver.

14 Waterfront politics in Vancouver

Vancouver's Harbour Waterfront is its greatest natural asset. It is important that it be developed in an imaginative way which allows each of us to take advantage of the excitement and variety of opportunities afforded by the inner harbour of this major port city. The Government of Canada and the City of Vancouver have joined together in the Waterfront Planning study to ensure that the Vancouver Waterfront becomes an attraction of lasting benefit to all Vancouver residents.
(Art Phillips, Vancouver mayor, and Ron Basford, federal minister of state for urban affairs from 'Public Information Report No. 2 February, 1974; Waterfront Planning Study'.)

Brave words indeed from our elected federal and municipal politicians, but considering their previous track record on waterfront planning and development, how empty and hollow. The fact is that Vancouver's waterfront is (and always has been) ruled by the National Harbours Board and the Canadian Pacific Railway from their eastern Canadian headquarters. The decisions they make reflect their wider international concerns, and not the needs of the residents of Vancouver.

The reality is that Vancouver's residents have always been denied access to their own waterfront by a solid barrier of railway tracks and private property signs. The tracks are likely to be removed in the near future, not because of any consideration for the general public but because the CPR has realized the tremendous profit potential for high-density high-rise redevelopment. The large multi-national corporations planning to open offices in Vancouver will pay premium rates to be on the Vancouver waterfront, with the spectacular view of the harbour and the North Shore mountains. These proposed developments pose an even greater threat to Vancouver's residents — a solid barrier of high-rise towers and private property signs stretching the full length of the downtown waterfront.

The National Harbours Board, for its part, wants to continue to develop the port of Vancouver to accommodate the increasing outflow of Canadian resources to foreign countries, and the inflow of manufactured goods for Canadian consumption. Vancouver has become one of the major ports on the Pacific coast. In fact, favourable harbour qualities are Vancouver's *raison d'être:* spacious and land-locked,

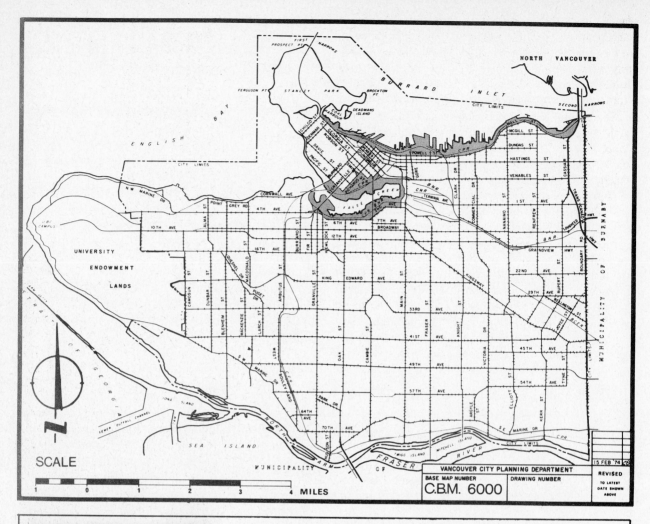

SCALE

1	0	1	2	3	4	MILES

VANCOUVER CITY PLANNING DEPARTMENT

15 FEB '74 28

BASE MAP NUMBER	DRAWING NUMBER	REVISED
C.B.M. 6000		TO LATEST DATE SHOWN ABOVE

Inside City Hall
Alderman H. Rankin

ON THE WATERFRONT

The joint city-federal waterfront planning study group has come up with its third report, this time called Stage 3-Concept Plan, for the development of the area between Stanley Park and Main Street. It calls its plan, "a composite plan based on the 'city by the sea' and 'recreation' concepts favoured at the end of Stage 2''.

It doesn't explain who "favoured" these concepts at the end of Stage 2, but this is obvious from the list of recommendations put forward. These include: —

: a residential-commercial complex providing for a population of 30,000 in 20 years, 10,000 of whom will be permanent residents, the remainder employed in hotels, offices and tourist attractions.

: a 200 foot green strip along the waterfront.

: a fish market, a long time pet plan of Alderman Setty Pendakur and the developers for whom he speaks.

: the re-location of the CPR train and truck ferries.

: the use of Pier B.C. for restaurants, shoppingmalls hotels.

: the creation of two artificial man-made island parks by means of filling in the harbour, one to be known as Burrard Island Park and the other as Gastown Park.

It is a developer's plan brought in by developer-oriented planners. It is no people's plan by any stretch of the imagination.

The tourist attractions, hotels, restaurants and apartments will cater to the wealthy. Their prices will put them beyond the reach of most citizens.

The CPR, the biggest developer on the waterfront, is getting what it wants. It may have to scale down the height of a few of its hotels and towers, but not that much.

In direct contradiction to its previously announced guidelines which provided for substantial public park space, the parks will now be built out in the water, leaving the land area free for the developers.

The proposal of the Longshoremen's Union and the Vancouver and District Labor Council that the section from Pier A to the waterfront be reserved for port facilities, has been completely ignored.

To top it off is the remark about re-zoning. As many of you know, I and the Committee of Progressive Electors (COPE) and the trade union movement have long been saying that when land is re-zoned upwards, say from industrial to comprehensive, by City Council, the increased values brought about by rezoning should go to the city, not to the developer.

The report evades this issue by the following piece of double talk.

"Whatever value is derived through the re-zoning, will, therefore automatically benefit the public. First, we get what we want — second, the developer takes care of maintenance; a cost far outweighing any other consideration."

Summed up, it still means we get nothing and the developer gets it all.

The report is now supposed to be up for public discussion. When this discussion period (less than four weeks) is over, the joint city-provincial waterfront planning study group and/or City Council's Standing Committee on Waterfront will recommend a plan to City Council. What that recommendation will be can be predicted quite accurately right now. It will be whatever the developers want and the people be damned.

However City Council doesn't have to accept the recommendations of this committee. If enough citizens speak up and demand that the waterfront plan center around the declared aim of ensuring that "this Waterfront becomes an attraction of lasting benefit to all Vancouver Residents", perhaps some changes can still be made.

This present plan will bring fabulous profits to developers, create impossible traffic problems for the downtown areas, useful only to a small segment of the population, and intrude still further on the limited waterfront space needed for future port development.

Georgia Straight, July 25, 1974

easily accessible, capable of accommodating the largest ships afloat. The opening of the Panama Canal in 1914 ensured Vancouver's importance as a port, especially for the grain shipping trade to western Europe. British Columbia's timber, mineral, agricultural, and fisheries products are shipped the world over.

The future looks even brighter for Vancouver as a major port. Rapidly increasing trade with Japan and other Pacific Basin countries, and the opening up of the mainland Chinese market mean added port facilities for Vancouver.

Both the National Harbours Board and the CPR are intimately connected to the innermost circles of power in this country. The CPR is Canada's largest corporation with its tentacles in every sphere of economic activity. It is also intimately connected with the largest financial institutions and through them to political power. The National Harbours Board, too, as a government agency, has strong and powerful connections to the political and economic elites.

In brief, the National Harbours Board and the CPR always get what they want. Vancouver's waterfront is already littered with the results of their activities. The foot of Granville St. is marred forever with the beginnings of Project 200, in which CPR is a major partner. And CPR has major plans for westward expansion along the waterfront past Burrard St. Further east, the National Harbours Board has scattered its terminal facilities willy-nilly along the waterfront, where they best suit the board's needs and not those of Vancouver's residents.

And further west, toward Stanley Park, the National Harbours Board has been involved in the most blatant give-aways of public land ever recorded in Canada: the Bayshore Inn and the Four Seasons Hotel sites.

Vancouver, low man on the totem pole, set up a waterfront committee of council in 1973. The members for 1973-74 were alderman Pendakur, chairman (pro-developer), alderman Marianne Linnell (pro-developer), alderman Geoffrey Massey (moderate), alderman Bill Gibson (moderate), and parks board commissioner Bill Du Moulin (pro-developer). So there was not a single pro-citizen voice on the committee. This committee set up a waterfront planning study headed by Dick Mann from the large corporate architectural firm of Thompson, Berwick & Pratt. The study team included only architects and planners. In the whole process, nowhere do the ordinary citizens of Vancouver, the ultimate users of (and taxpayers for) any waterfront development, have any input. The study team carries on secret discussions with the National Harbours Board, CPR, and other government bodies.

Once again, Vancouver is setting itself up to cave in to pressures from the CPR, the National Harbours

Granville Square, at the foot of Granville St., is only the first phase in the CPR's major plans for extending its high-density high-rise development westward along the waterfront over the existing railway tracks.

Board and the pro-development forces for whom they speak. If the Bayshore and Coal Harbour case studies which follow seem like blatant give-aways, they are nothing compared to what is likely to happen along the rest of Vancouver's waterfront.

15 The Bayshore Inn and Coal Harbour: A case study in waterfront corporate giveaways

The Bayshore Inn and surrounding properties.

THE BAYSHORE INN

The average citizen of Vancouver, as he looks about his city, is likely to believe that there must be good reason why the major buildings are where they are. There must be qualified persons around who decide: 'Here is a good location for a park; there a good location for hotel.' One would expect that in making their decisions, these persons would be guided by the principles of good planning and design, ensuring that there is adequate transportation access, that the views are not destroyed, that the site is not over-developed, and that the use of the site is appropriate to its surroundings.

Such is the creation myth of our cities.

Unfortunately the truth is something quite different from the myth, and this is nowhere better illustrated than by the Bayshore Inn. The Bayshore is there, not because it was city policy to build hotels along the waterfront, not because it would fit into the city's planning and transportation guidelines, not even because it was a brilliant stroke of planning genius. The Bayshore is there simply, because someone had friends in Ottawa and on city council.

For many years, the land upon which the Bayshore Inn now stands belonged to the people of Canada. Yet, for some unknown reason, in 1949 the federal government through the *National Harbours Board,* granted to one *Mrs. Isabel Gertrude Spencer,* for 'the sum of one dollar and other due and valuable consideration,' 356,574 square feet of land, approximately 9 acres, north of Georgia St. between the Cardero and Bidwell street ends. The lawyer who handled the transaction was one *Ralph Osborne Campney.*

NOTE: this was the first time in Canadian history that publicly-owned harbour land had been granted to private interests. Every other waterfront user must lease the land from the government. Yet somehow, Isabel Spencer and Ralph Campney were able to bring off the impossible.

Who was Isabel Spencer? She was a daughter of the Winch family one of Vancouver's largest real estate holders, she was also the wife of Col. Victor Spencer, of Spencer's Stores (bought out by Eaton's, in the same year as the property transaction), and one of the guiding lights behind the Non-Partisan Association.

Who was Ralph Osborne Campney? He was a senior partner in law firm of Campney, Owen & Murphy. He was instrumental in organizing the National Harbours Board in 1936, and was its first chairman from 1936 to 1940. Place next to this Campney's unprecedented success in negotiating the land transfer with the same National Harbours Board in 1949. Campney was elected to federal parliament as the Liberal member for Vancouver Centre in the same year, 1949.

Once Isabel Spencer had control of the property, she sold it to the American lumber giant, Crown Zellerbach, who was toying with the idea of building a paper-converting plant on the site (!). Crown Zellerbach finally decided to build in Richmond instead.

The land then passed into the hands of a syndicate of prominent local businessmen, who formed a company called Georgia Centre Estates in 1956. They were:

1 Norman R. Whittall: stockbroker with Richardson Securities of Canada.

2 Ernest L. Boultbee: founder of Boultbee Sweet Real Estate; president of the Non-Partisan Association in 1953.

3 Peter E. Cromie: brother of former Vancouver *Sun* publisher; owner of Dolly Varden Mines; developer on Bowen Island.

4 William G. MacKenzie: partner in Marwell Construction Co.

5 R. Douglas Welch: partner in Marwell Construction Co.

6 Hugh A. Martin: partner in Marwell Construction Co.; president of B.C. Liberal party.

Law firm for this company was Douglas, Symes & Brissenden, another firm with strong Liberal party connections. When MacKenzie died, his place on the board was taken over by George C. Van Roggen, a Douglas, Symes partner, and son-in-law to Norman R.

Whittall. In 1971 Van Roggen was appointed to the Senate by Pierre Elliott Trudeau for his efforts as chief Liberal party organizer in British Columbia.

NOTE: when these men bought the property, only 10% actually was land, the rest being below the high-water mark.

NOTE FURTHER: that the city owned the Bidwell St. end to the west of the property (the extension of Bidwell St. north of Georgia St.) which it had been granted many years before by the federal government to ensure that the public *always* had access to the waterfront.

NOTE FURTHER: that the original grant to Isabel Spencer required that the land be used for 'industrial, general, storage, warehousing, wharfinger or commercial purposes.' Residential uses, including hotels, were not included within the allowable uses.

NOTE FINALLY: that the land was zoned by the city for industrial purposes, as was the rest of the Vancouver waterfront.

In spite of all this, somehow these men were able to:
1 acquire control of the Bidwell St. end;
2 by-pass the conditions of the National Harbours Board grant;
3 fill in the harbour out to the harbour headline;
4 get the land rezoned to allow hotels and a large parking area.

It seemed that these men had inordinately good success in dealing with city council and Ottawa, much better than the ordinary citizen could ever hope to achieve.

Between the time that Georgia Centre Estates acquired the land from Crown Zellerbach and the opening of the Bayshore Inn in the spring of 1961, the company was able to get the northern section of the land rezoned to high-density commercial uses which allowed the hotel: then, even before the rezoning had been granted, they commenced piling and filling the waterlots, and then built the original hotel.

After the hotel opened, the next 100 feet south of the property was rezoned to allow for a parking lot, and the following year, in 1962, the whole site, from the harbour headline to Georgia St. was rezoned to comprehensive development (CD-1), a zoning category which had just been invented by the city hall to let developers do anything they wanted on their property. This CD-1 zoning was to allow the building of a temporary Standard Oil service station which is still there more than ten years later.

In 1963, the original owners of Georgia Centre Estates sold out to the Marwest Hotel Co. at a handsome profit. This company had been formed to develop the Bayshore Inn and operate it. It was 50% owned by Marwell Construction Co. (i.e., Hugh Martin) and 50% by the American-owned Western International Hotels. Marwell had actually built the

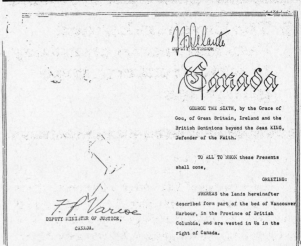

The crown grant by which nine acres of federal government land were transferred in 1949 to Mrs. Isabel Gertrude Spencer.

Bidwell St., sold by the city of Vancouver to the developer of the Bayshore Inn project for $122,960 in spite of the fact that the federal government had given the land for Bidwell St. to Vancouver in 1917 specifically to ensure public access to the water in perpetuity.

hotel, and Western had operated it. Both Hugh Martin and Douglas Welch remained on the board due to their control of Marwell. Western also owned the Hotel Georgia in downtown Vancouver.

Little action occurred over the next three years, while Harbour Park Developments was trying to put together its development for the three blocks between the Bayshore Inn and Stanley Park. Running into financial difficulties when Power Corp. of Canada pulled out of the company, the remaining shareholders decided to cut back on their development plans. The Bayshore Inn on the other hand was a big money earner, and the owners wanted to expand the operation. So Marwest Hotel Co. and Harbour Park Developments made a deal. Harbour Park would sell the block between the Bayshore and Denman St. to Marwest for more than Harbour Park had paid for the whole three blocks two years earlier. Presumably Marwest knew what it was doing, so we must conclude that Harbour Park had gotten a pretty good deal in the first place.

Before the deal went through there were two things that needed doing. One, the block would have to be rezoned, since the CD-1 zoning which city council had passed in 1965 was specifically tied to the Harbour Park development. City council quickly granted the rezoning on December 19, 1966. Less than a week later, on Christmas Day, 1966, the National Harbours Board transferred the long-term waterlot lease from Harbour Park Developments to Marwest Hotel Co. (without that lease the land would have been useless for high-density profitable development). On January

12, 1967, Marwest and Harbour Park closed the deal. And the same month, Hugh Martin and Douglas Welch sold Marwell Construction Co. to the American construction giant, Hawaiian-based Dillingham Corp.

Thus Marwest Hotel Co. became 100% foreign-owned (50% by Dillingham Corp. and 50% by Western International Hotels, both U.S. firms).

There remained one thing to be done. Marwest Hotel Co. now owned the block between Cardero and Bidwell streets and the block from Bidwell St. west to Denham St. But what about Bidwell St. itself ? From Georgia St. north to the high-water mark, that land was owned by the city. And from the high-water mark to the harbour headline, the Bidwell St. end waterlot had been granted to the city by the federal government in 1917 to ensure public access to the water. In the federal grant there was the following reservation: 'to have and to hold the said lands unto the grantee (the city) its successors and assigns forever, for municipal purposes and no other purpose.' This posed a problem for Marwest. But they still seemed to have those right connections; in February, city council approved a report from the board of administration to sell the Bidwell St. end to Marwest for $122,960 (approximately $12.90 per square foot) and to deed the waterlot north of Bidwell St. back to the federal government for $1.00, so that it could then be leased on a long-term basis to Marwest. Thus the public lost further access to its waterfront.

As soon as Marwest Hotel Co. took ownership of the street end, city council rezoned the whole block to allow for higher density hotel and office building development. And within a month Marwest started work on an 18-storey addition (192 rooms). This addition was opened in October 1970, but during construction Western International Hotels (which owned 50% of Marwest) was bought out by United Airlines as part of its plans to tie its air routes to cities in which it owned hotels.

Marwest still owns the block between Bidwell and Denman streets and plans are afoot for massive high-density office building developments in the near future. What were the recommendations of architect Dick Mann's waterfront planning study team for this particular piece of property? The study team proposed high-density high-rise office and hotel buildings. Even though the group presented five alternatives for waterfront developments — recreation, real estate, community, mixed activity, and tourism — there was a surprising consistency to them. Every alternative included high-rise buildings. In the so-called recreation alternative, eight-storey buildings were recommended for the Marwest Hotel Co. property!

COAL HARBOUR

This is the site of the next phase of the planned Marwest Hotel development which will involve more high-rise high-density office and tourist accommodation.

With the success of the Bayshore Inn project assured — the land plucked from the public domain for private gain, the unprecedented zoning granted by city council, the alienation of the public street ends — greedy eyes turned westward and focussed on another ripe plum, the three blocks of land between the Bayshore Inn and Stanley Park. Here were 'run-down' ship repair yards, ramshackle wharfs, and deteriorating storage sheds, ready for redevelopment. There were tremendous profits to be made by redeveloping the three blocks from their industrial uses to high-density residential-commercial-marina uses. The land had all the right qualities: an excellent view, a waterside location, Stanley Park with all its recreational facilities right next door, and the downtown business district close by.

There were only two things standing in the way of successful redevelopment, as there had been with the Bayshore Inn project. One, the land would have to be rezoned from industrial to comprehensive development. This posed no problem because a development-hungry city council was willing to bend over backwards to accommodate the desires of developers. But there was a more formidable stumbling block: the fact was that most of the property lay under water. Only four of the 14 acres of the site were dry land, and could

actually be bought. The remainder, from the high-tide mark to the harbour headline was waterlot under the jurisdiction of the National Harbours Board. This time, the Bayshore gambit — getting an outright gift of the land from the National Harbours Board — didn't seem feasible. And in the normal case the board gave out only 21 year-leases for the use of its waterlots. If the waterlots were to be used for high-rise buildings, they would have to be filled, and the developer, whoever he was, would have to obtain a long-term lease — something the board had never before granted. But without such a long-term lease, intensive redevelopment would not be profitable. Therefore the board would just have to be convinced to take this unprecedented step.

An informal alliance was forged in about 1961 between Hugh Martin, successful Bayshore developer, and William Zeckendorf, just completing his $100 million Place Ville Marie in Montreal. Secretly they began assembling the properties along the waterfront, using a real estate company as a front, so that their intentions would not be known. Finally, with most of the properties tied up under option, Zeckendorf announced his project: a $70 million scheme which

Coal Harbour lands: over 10 years and 4 developers later, the land stands bleak and barren.

---

included 12 luxury apartment blocks 20 to 35 storeys in height set on a two to four-storey parking garage which covered most of the site. The project involved 3.8 million square feet of floor area.

The proposal was flatly rejected by the city planning department: it complained about the exceedingly high density of development, the blocking of the view, the enormous amount of traffic that would be generated, and the loss of public access to the waterfront. The planners recommended a maximum of 1.7 million square feet of floor area, less than half of what the developer wanted. The then-mayor Bill Rathie reacted strongly to the recommendations of his planners: 'I am very disappointed at [their] negative thinking .... Sure we'll ask for their advice and take whatever part of it is good for the city, but we are not going to allow them to destroy the constructive thinking of private developers.' Rathie was able to put enough pressure on the city planning department to get them to agree to a figure of 3.1 million square feet. Because he was not including the city-owned street ends in working out his formula, Rathie was, in fact giving the developers *more* than they had asked for. This recommendation went forward for a public hearing on the rezoning application.

NOTE: The usual procedure is that developers ask for much more than they really want, so that they can appear to be reasonable and compromising when they cut back, but they still end up with what they wanted. However, in this case, even the developers must have been surprised to get more than they had applied for.

In the meantime, Hugh Martin had pulled out of the project for unknown reasons. William Zeckendorf proceeded to set up a subsidiary, Coal Harbour Investments, which would own and develop the

project. He retained the law firm of Campney, Owen & Murphy to do the negotiating with the National Harbours Board.

NOTE: This action demonstrated how well Zeckendorf knew his way around. Ralph Campney, with his background as the man who had set up the National Harbours Board in 1936 and had been its first chairman, was certainly the best person to undertake such unprecedented negotiations with that same board.

Both Ralph Campney and Walter Owen were appointed to the board of directors of Coal Harbour Investments and Owen to the board of the parent company Webb & Knapp (Canada), perhaps replacing A.E. Dal Grauer who had died the year before.

At the public hearing held in late June 1963, Walter Owen appeared for the developer and argued that a number of options were due to expire on June 30, and the company would lose some money if it did not have the rezoning guaranteed by that time.

The argument that the developer might lose some money if it didn't get the rezoning by June 30 seemed to carry the most weight with city council; because instead of waiting for economic consultant Larry Smith's report on downtown development soon to be completed, council held a special meeting three days later to approve the rezoning. This was not surprising considering the make-up of city council at that time: of the ten aldermen who voted *for* the rezoning, two were real estate agents, four were property insurance agents, one a developer, one a construction manager, one a chartered accountant, and the tenth, the ex-fire chief. The sole opponent on city council to the rezoning was a retired druggist.

The rezoning was conditional on Webb & Knapp (Canada) acquiring clear title to all the properties and getting the long-term leases from the National Harbours Board by September 1, 1963, neither of which Webb & Knapp was able to accomplish. It wasn't able to purchase the land outright because of Zeckendorf's severe financial difficulties; and without title to the land even a compliant National Harbours Board couldn't assign long-term leases.

William Zeckendorf began to sell his properties in order to pay off his short-term high-interest loans. Because he failed to make his payments, some of the Coal Harbour property owners filed suits against the company. For almost a year rumours abounded about the state of the Coal Harbour project. Take-over of the company was hinted at, but firmly denied by company officials and mayor Bill Rathie.

Finally, on August 31. 1964, the newspapers announced the take-over of the Coal Harbour project by Power Corp. of Canada and a syndicate of local business men: Peter Paul Saunders and Andrew Saxton, former employees of Power Corp., Harold

Foley, forcibly retired lumber baron, and Graham Dawson, construction heir. With its very substantial resources Harbour Park quickly acquired title to all the properties in the three block area. The Campney, Owen & Murphy law firm disappeared from the scene, but the new developer still seemed to have the right connections in Ottawa: for one thing, there was the famous Liberal party influence exercised by Power Corp.; for another, the lawyer for Harbour Park was Liberal MLA Alan Williams. Harbour Park soon got the precious long-term leases.

Soon afterwards, in March 1965, Harbour Park Developments applied for rezoning of the three blocks. It wanted 15 high-rises as against 12 in the Webb & Knapp (Canada) scheme. There was more square footage of apartment development; the commercial area was doubled. It was a much worse scheme, but this time the city planning department was firmly under the thumb of the politicians and the senior administrators. Many of the planners who had opposed the first scheme had left the planning department in the interim. The planning department approved the Harbour Park proposal. Another public hearing was a mere formality and city council approved the application for rezoning.

Harbour Park Developments never went ahead with its project, as many opponents had predicted. In 1966, the third block adjacent to the Bayshore Inn was sold to the Marwest Hotel Co. for more than Harbour Park had paid for the whole three blocks. Harbour Park then leased the remaining two blocks to Four Seasons Hotels of Toronto, who in May 1969 announced a $40 million hotel-residential-commercial complex. In spite of tremendous public opposition (detailed in chapter 32) city council, now 'led' by mayor Tom Campbell, approved the rezoning. In Ottawa it was a simple matter of transferring the long-term leases from Harbour Park Developments to Four Seasons Hotels. But three years of public opposition to the project finally led to government action. Apparently there was still one waterlot that had not been leased to the developer; and the federal cabinet, after a battle between Jack Davis who wanted the project, and Ron Basford who slowly came to oppose it, finally decided against.

The development proposal was dead. On August 22, 1972, Four Seasons Hotels quietly pulled out of the development after the option to lease with Harbour Park Developments expired, and made plans to build a hotel in the Pacific Centre project. Although pressure was put on city council to acquire the property for open space, the lure of lucrative development was not dead. In May 1973, the owners of Harbour Park sold the company and its assets to Dawson Developments for $6 million. The owners sold the company outright rather than just the land, so the the valuable

The architect's sketch of the Four Seasons' proposed development of Coal Harbour land.

63-year leases would be transferred, rather than Dawson Developments having to renegotiate with the National Harbours Board. Dawson's role in the continuing Coal Harbour story is detailed in Chapter 24.

LESSONS
First: You need to have a pipeline to the city hall bureaucracy.

As it turned out, Hugh Martin, Bayshore Inn developer, was an old friend of Gerald Sutton Brown, head of the board of administration. They had worked together in the Community Planning Association of Canada in the early 1950's; and they collaborated on a proposed high-rise apartment building on Georgia St. between Nicola and Broughton streets (kitty-corner from the future Bayshore site). It was Sutton Brown who advised city council to sell the city-owned Bidwell St. end to Marwest Hotel Co., and to deed the street end waterlot back to the National Harbours Board, so that it could be leased on a long-term basis to Marwest for its proposed development.

Second: You have to have friendly relations with city council

As it turned out, Hugh Martin's father, George, had been one of the founders of the Non-Partisan Association (NPA) in the 1930s and its treasurer for many years. The NPA dominated city council. And NPA aldermen gave the Bayshore Inn developers everything they wanted.

Third: You have to have the right connections to the local business establishment and financial powers

As a further coincidence, Hugh Martin's father-in-law was Gordon Farrell, founder and president of B.C. Telephone Co., and a director of just about every major company in B.C., including Canadian Imperial Bank of Commerce, Canada Trust Co., H.R. MacMillan Export Co., and Cominco. Martin's brothers-in-law included a chairman of Yorkshire

Trust Co. and a vice-president of Inland Natural Gas Co.

FOURTH, AND MOST IMPORTANT: YOU HAVE TO HAVE THE RIGHT POLITICAL CONNECTIONS; THAT MEANS, TO THE LIBERAL PARTY

As it turned out, Hugh Martin had strong ties to the Liberal party. He was a vice-president of the B.C. Liberal Association in 1962 and chairman of the B.C. Liberal campaign committee for Jack Nicholson's campaigns in 1962 and 1963. Martin's Marwell Construction Co. made substantial campaign contributions to both Nicholson's and Jack Davis's campaigns. It was Nicholson who announced that the federal government had granted the unprecedented waterlot leases to Harbour Park Developments in 1965. In 1965 Jack Davis, then parliamentary assistant to the prime minister, candidly stated in a letter that 'the member for Vancouver Centre, the Honorable Jack Nicholson, is very much involved.' Just how much involved he was, we'll never really know.

With the right connections, you too, can be a successful developer.

Once you have got your development under way because of these connections, you can then sell out to an American corporation at a large profit. You can then claim your political rewards.

THE LIBERAL CONNECTION: JACK NICHOLSON

Lawyer Jack Nicholson was one of the men brought to Ottawa by C.D. Howe during World War II, and he helped organize Polymer Corp. which built and operated the huge synthetic rubber plant at Sarnia Ont. Polymer (now Polysar) is presently a wholly-owned subsidiary of the Canada Development Corp. (of which Hugh Martin is a director). Nicholson was general manager and executive vice-president of Polymer until 1951.

Nicholson was then appointed chief executive officer of Brazilian Light and Power Corp. (Brascan), and went to Brazil for five years. (He was succeeded in Brascan by Mitchell Sharp, former deputy-minister of trade and commerce under Howe). Nicholson returned to Vancouver and the law in 1956. The following year he received notoriety as the defence lawyer for Socred minister of lands and forests Robert Sommers who had been accused of accepting a bribe from B.C. Forest Products for the granting of logging licences. Nicholson had come up with an ingenious line of defence. According to the account in the *Toronto Star*, Nicholson had argued that 'no cabinet minister has ever before been convicted under British law for accepting bribes, nor is it a crime under present Canadian legislation.' The judges were not impressed; one was quoted as saying that 'I would not imagine

that a minister could accept $25,000 for granting timber licences without committing an offence of some kind. I would be astonished if that were so.'

Sommers was convicted and sentenced to five years in prison, but Nicholson's career really took off after that. He must have impressed the lumber companies because within two years he was appointed president of the Council of Forest Industries of B.C. Two years after that he ran for MP in Vancouver Centre, was elected in 1962, and re-elected in 1963. He was immediately appointed minister of forestry where he could carry on his work for the lumber companies. He was then moved on to postmaster-general, minister of immigration, and the minister responsible for housing.

Nicholson received his ultimate reward by being appointed lieutenant-governor of B.C. in 1968, and he remained in Victoria until his wife's ill health caused his resignation in 1972. He was succeeded by Walter Owen.

Nicholson retired to private life, but his connections in the forest industry were too valuable to waste and in 1973 he was appointed a director of Crestbrook Forest Industries, owned by Honshu Paper Manufacturing Co. and Mitsubishi Corp., and in 1974 a director of Weyerhaeuser Canada.

THE LIBERAL CONNECTION: CAMPNEY, OWEN, & MURPHY

During the 1940s and 1950s, the Vancouver law firm of Campney, Owen & Murphy was one of the most prominent, with strong connections to the Liberal party in Ottawa, as well as with the local business establishment.

There have been some very illustrious partners in the firm:

John Valentine Clyne, recently retired chairman of MacMillan Bloedel, was a marine law specialist and partner in the firm, leaving in 1950 to become a supreme court judge. Elected chairman to the newly merged partnership between the MacMillan and Bloedel Co. and the Powell River Co. as a neutral arbiter, he took the side of the MacMillan interests and forced out the Foleys, who controlled Powell River. His son is presently a partner in the Campney firm.

Walter Stewart Owen, appointed lieutenant-governor of B.C. in 1973 by Pierre Elliott Trudeau, was also a partner in the firm. Owen was a director of Webb & Knapp (Canada) when they were negotiating their own deal with the National Harbours Board for the Coal Harbour lands. His first wife, Jean Margaret Dowler died in 1970. In March 1972, he married the wealthy widow of Dal Grauer, a fellow ex-director of Webb & Knapp (Canada).

In politics, Owen was an 'ingrained Liberal' and managed election campaigns for Liberal candidates in Vancouver. He succeeded Jack Nicholson as

FOREIGN-CONTROLLED CORPORATE CONNECTIONS OF WALTER S. OWEN, Q.C., LL.D., LIEUTANT-GOVERNOR OF THE PROVINCE OF BRITISH COLUMBIA.

Chairman, Monsanto Canada, 100% owned by Monsanto Corp., *U.S.A.*

Director, East Asiatic Co. (Canada), 87.5% owned by East Asiatic Co., *West European*.

Director, Greyhound Computer of Canada, 82.0% owned by Greyhound Computer Corp., *U.S.A.*

Director, Greyhound Lines of Canada, 61.3% owned by Greyhound Lines Inc., *U.S.A.*

Director, Canastel Broadcasting Corp., 100% owned by Associated Broadcasting Development Co., *U.K.*

Director, Western Forest Industries, 60.0% owned by ITT Rayonier Inc., *U.S.A.*

Director, Phoenix Overseas Operations, 100% owned by Phoenix-Rheinrohr A.G., *West European*.

---

lieutenant-governor of B.C. who was retiring for personal reasons.

Walter Owen pulled out of Campney, Owen & Murphy in 1969 with all of his corporate clients and set up his own firm. And he certainly has an impressive list of directorships under his belt, involving all sectors of the economy: finance, property, communications, shipping, forest products, steel, construction, mining, oil pipelines, etc. The preponderance of foreign-controlled corporations is striking, given that in his most recent job he is supposed to be a symbol of Canadian unity.

However, *Ralph Osborne Campney*, who died in 1967, was the most illustrious partner in the firm. He had been private secretary to Liberal prime minister William Lyon MacKenzie King in 1925-26. He was called back to Ottawa in 1936 by C.D. Howe to reorganize and centralize the administration of Canada's port system — to remove the ports from a local system of political patronage, and to put them under the political patronage of the Liberal party in Ottawa.

After serving as the first chairman of the National Harbours Board from 1936-1940, Campney went back into private practice. In 1948 he moved into the political arena by running for MP in Vancouver Centre, but he was defeated by an unknown CCF candidate. However, he was elected in the general election of 1949 and re-elected in 1953. He was appointed solicitor-general in 1952 and minister of national defence in 1954.

In 1955, the law firm was rocked by a scandal that threatened to see Campney removed from his seat. It was discovered that Campney, a minister of the crown, was a director of a company, along with law partners Owen and Murphy, which owned property in Burnaby being leased to the federal government as a postal station.

The House of Commons Act expressly forbids a member of parliament from transacting any agreement or contract with the federal government for which public money is being paid. Any MP found guilty of violating this act is required to vacate his seat in the Commons. However, legal technicalities saved the day for Campney, who claimed that it had been an 'oversight' on the part of his law firm not to have removed his name as a director of the company when he became a cabinet minister.

Campney lost his seat anyway in 1957, when the Liberal party was swept out of office because of the scandals surrounding Trans Canada Pipe Lines. He went back into private practice, becoming a director of several American-owned companies.

The firm is still in business (although Ralph Campney died in 1967 and Walter Owen pulled out to set up his own practice). Campney's son, Allan, is now the senior partner. Allan has been keeping up all the right connections, having been vice-chairman of the Port of Vancouver's development committee (set up by the National Harbours Board) and was in 1973, president of the Vancouver Board of Trade, and president of the Canada-Japan Society of Vancouver, which promotes friendly trade relations with Japan.

In early August 1974, Allan Campney came out strongly against the provincial government's proposed Public Officials Disclosures Act, which went into effect in September 1974. 'The public will lose tremendous benefits because of the understandable reluctance of successful business men and women to disclose their interests in order to run for public office,' he was quoted as saying. The Bayshore Inn and Coal Harbour stories demonstrate just the opposite, that the public can only gain by a full disclosure of interest on the part of all public officials.

16 False Creek and Marathon Realty: The CPR's next deal

False Creek, immediately adjacent to the downtown core on the south and now used for warehousing and other low-value industrial purposes, is the area next in line for profitable redevelopment. Vancouver owns a substantial chunk of land on the south side of the Creek, and plans are well under way for its development. The bulk of the north side of the creek — 155 acres — is owned by the Canadian Pacific Railway subsidiary Marathon Realty Co. who has a massive redevelopment in mind. In June 1974, Marathon was given the go-ahead for the first phase of that scheme involving the 95 acres between the Granville and Cambie bridges when the city rezoned the area from industrial use to a special comprehensive development zone.

Marathon Realty Co. plans to throw up a high-density high-rise project for 8,000 middle and upper middle-income earners. With 180 people per acre, the scheme challenges the West End for title as the most densely packed area in Canada. Not only that, Marathon plans to cram in 1.5 million square feet of commercial-institutional-recreational development, equivalent to three Royal Centres, or to five Project 200 Buildings on Granville Square.

It is a mammoth development, unprecedented in Vancouver's history and one that will go a long way toward the transformation of Vancouver into Developer City. And, as usual, it is the ordinary citizens of Vancouver who end up paying for it through an incredible string of concessions and handouts granted to the CPR.

City council, again abdicating its responsibility to the electorate, has aided and abetted the CPR at every turn, giving the smooth CPR negotiators everything they asked for, and, on occasion, even more than they wanted. The simple act of rezoning the CPR's 95 acres of land in June 1974 brought enormous windfall profits. Much controversy surrounds the question of just how much the CPR did pick up as a result of this action but there are some indisputable facts.

In March 1971, the provincial government sold 12.3 acres of crown land in the False Creek area to Marathon Realty Co. for $545,788, or exactly $43,560 per acre.

In December 1972, the total CPR holdings of 155 acres on the north side of the creek was assessed at $5,114,271, or $33,000 per acre.

These figures establish that the value of the land

NOTICE
CITY OF VANCOUVER
PUBLIC HEARING

NOTICE IS HEREBY GIVEN THAT, pursuant to the provisions of the Vancouver Charter, a meeting of the Council of the City of Vancouver will be held in the Council Chambers, Third Floor, City Hall, 453 West 12th Avenue, on THURSDAY, JUNE 27th, 1974, commencing at 7:30 p.m. to consider the following:

A. PROPOSED BY-LAW TO AMEND ZONING AND DEVELOPMENT BY-LAW 3575
A portion of the area commonly known as False Creek (Areas 1, 2, 6, 9, and 10) as indicated on the map below be rezoned from a M-1 Industrial District, M-2 Industrial District, and a CD-1 Comprehensive Development District to a False Creek Comprehensive Development District.

B. PROPOSED OFFICIAL DEVELOPMENT PLAN BY-LAW
And Further to consider the adoption of an official development plan by-law relating to the area aforesaid as indicated on the map below.

C. PROPOSED AREA DEVELOPMENT PLANS
And Further to consider the adoption of specific development plans for the areas designated as Area 2 and a portion of Area 6 within the said areas as indicated on the map below.

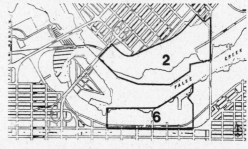

All persons who deem themselves affected by the proposed by-laws and development plans shall be afforded an opportunity to be heard before the Council on the matters contained herein.

A copy of the proposed draft by-laws, development plans may be inspected at the City Clerk's Office, Third Floor, City Hall, or the City Planning Department, Third Floor, East Wing, from 8:30 a.m. to 4:30 p.m. on regular working days.

D. H. Little
City Clerk

On June 27, 1974, Vancouver city council rezoned Marathon's False Creek property (areas 1 and 2 on the map) from industrial to comprehensive development. The increase in value of the land due solely to the rezoning is estimated at $23,460,000.

---

before rezoning was somewhere between $33,000 and $43,560, say $40,000 per acre.

In June 1974, in its negotiations with Marathon after the rezoning had been granted, the city assessed the value of the land on the north side of the creek at *$500,000 per acre.*

Of the 95 acres involved in the rezoning, actually 51.0 will be developed by Marathon. The value of those 51.0 acres for industrial use is 51.0 times $40,000 or *$2,040,000.* The value of those same 51.0 acres after the rezoning is 51.0 times $500,000 or *$25,500,000: a net gain of $23,460,000.* And a totally untaxed gain,

Looking north over False Creek, 1946. Most of the north shore was owned by the CPR or the provincial government. Part of the land was used for railway yards and an engine house, and part was leased to heavy industry that generated railway traffic. *B.C. Provincial Archives*

since the CPR can write it off against oil exploration costs, or railway track relocation expenses, or a hundred other possibilities.

At one time, soon after their election in 1973, The Elector's Action Movement (TEAM) members of city council had talked about the city participating in some of the increased value of land due to rezoning, since it was the city's action in rezoning that caused the increase in value. The TEAM members seemed to think that the city should get 50% of the increased gain. Alderman Pendakur put it in a nutshell: 'If we are serious about it, it would not be difficult to do.' Alderman Fritz Bowers, chairman of the city's finance committee, and one of the aldermen later involved in the negotiations with Marathon Realty Co., felt that

the 50% figure was a fair one and that 'all we need is a mechanism to ensure that it works properly.'

Yet, on March 20, 1973, Committee of Progressive Electors (COPE) alderman Harry Rankin introduced a motion in city council asking the provincial government to change the city charter to ensure that at least 50% of the new value created by rezoning would go to the city. It was turned down by a vote of 6 to 5. Who

Fancy p.r. drawings of the Marathon proposal for False Creek were prepared by the consultant architect. Notice in this one how high-rise towers are carefully hidden by foliage.

voted against the motion? Alderman Bowers for one, along with mayor Phillips, and aldermen Volrich, Hardwick, Linnell, and surprisingly, Marzari. Voting with Rankin were Harcourt, Pendakur, Gibson, and Massey. Council then voted 6 to 5 to study the matter, and there it remained forever.

Thus Marathon Realty Co. was able to pocket the entire increase. True, the city did assess some costs. They deducted 15 acres of land for roads, but this was necessary so that people could get to the Marathon project. And they deducted 25 acres for parks, but this was only to provide some amenity for all those people Marathon would bring into the area in the first place. And they deducted three acres for a school for the children in the development.

There were cash costs assessed as well: $3.5 million for development of the parkland; $4 million for construction of the seawall; $3.5 million for installation of utilities; $0.5 million for construction of a perimeter road; $1.25 million for construction of a community centre; in total $12.75 million. But do not make the mistake of regarding these as a tax on Marathon Realty Co.'s windfall profits; they are costs incurred solely because of Marathon's development, and they will be passed on to the residents of the project in the form of higher rents, a standard practice among developers.

Yet the deal is even worse than this. Alderman Walter Hardwick, who was in charge of dealing with Marathon, himself set minimum standards for parkland in the False Creek area: six acres of parkland for every thousand people. Simple arithmetic shows us that the 8,000 people in the Marathon Realty Co. project will need 48 acres of park. But we see that there will be only 28 acres (including the school). Marathon

is 20 acres short. And how does the city plan to make up this 20 acre deficit? By including them in the city's development on the south side of the Creek, which means another subsidy for Marathon.

Mayor Art Phillips had been pretty proud of the deal he had made with Marathon Realty Co., bragging to the press that the city got about everything they could from the developer. The reality is something quite different.

There were the windfall profits gained from the rezoning that we have already seen. But Marathon Realty Co. stands to make more, much more, from the project itself. Usually high-rise developers have to pay for their sites, and still they make large profits from their high-rise apartment buildings. But CPR will make much more. The CPR already owns most of the False Creek land, which was given to it free and the few remaining acres not owned were purchased at industrial prices, less than one-tenth of what the land is now worth. Also, the CPR created more land, having been busy filling in the creek, creating acres of new land and consequently reducing the size of the water area, until a freeze was finally imposed on further filling. With the land provided virtually for free, the CPR is still developing as if it had had to purchase the land on the open market, as if it had had to pay $500,000 an acre for it.

There is another way that the CPR will be able to

As this drawing shows, the Marathon project with its four proposed 'neighbourhoods' takes up a substantial proportion of Vancouver's downtown peninsula.

In other drawings, the high rises are there in the background, but the focus is on the affluent life-styles of the proposed project residents: the theatre-going, sailing, leisure society.

development statistics

	COOPERS COURT	ROUNDHOUSE SQUARE	YALE LAKE	RICHARDS	TOTALS	
NEIGHBOURHOOD AREA	26.5 ACRES	26.8 ACRES	17.0 ACRES	23.7 ACRES	94.0 ACRES	
DEVELOPMENT AREA	15.0 ACRES	14.0 ACRES	7.5 ACRES	14.5 ACRES	51.0 ACRES	(1)
PUBLIC OPEN SPACE	5.5 ACRES	9.0 ACRES	7.0 ACRES	6.5 ACRES	28.0 ACRES	(2)
ROADS	6.0 ACRES	3.8 ACRES	2.5 ACRES	2.7 ACRES	15.0 ACRES	
NUMBER OF UNITS	1000	1800	300	1400	4500	
NON RESIDENTIAL SPACE (SQ. FT.)	500,000	250,000	100,000	650,000	1,500,000	
NEIGHBOURHOOD DENSITY (GROSS AREA)	38 UNITS/ACRE	67 UNITS/ACRE	18 UNITS/ACRE	59 UNITS/ACRE	48 UNITS/ACRE	
AVERAGE NET DENSITY	100 UNITS/ACRE	140 UNITS/ACRE	40 UNITS/ACRE	100 UNITS/ACRE	100 UNITS/ACRE	
POPULATION	1750	2700	1000	2450	7900	
MAXIMUM BUILDING HEIGHT	20 STOREYS	30 STOREYS	6 STOREYS	30 STOREYS		
NUMBER OF BLDGS. OVER 8 STOREYS	6	9	0	7		
MAXIMUM SITE COVERAGE	60%	65%	70%	65%		

(1) 45 ACRES RESIDENTIAL, 6 ACRES NON-RESIDENTIAL
(2) 25 ACRES PARKS AND PLAZAS, 3 ACRES SCHOOL SITE

increase its profit, perhaps even more than through the land. All developers have to borrow money to construct a building, and the cost of borrowing — a change of say even one per cent in the interest rate —

MARATHON REALTY CO.: INTERCORPORATE CONNECTIONS

TO OTHER CORPORATIONS
   NORTHERN & CENTRAL
   GAS CORP.
   GAZ METROPOLITAIN
   TRANS CANADA
   PIPELINES
   COMINCO
   MACMILLAN BLOEDEL
   JOHN LABATT
   DILLINGHAM CORP.
   MARINE INDUSTRIES
   RIO ALGOM MINES
   LORNEX MINING CORP.
       TO ROTHSCHILD
       INTERESTS

TO CP INVESTMENTS
   & OTHER CPR SUBSIDIARIES

MARATHON
REALTY CO.

TO OTHER DEVELOPERS
   INTERNATIONAL LAND CORP.
   MACAULAY, NICOLLS & MAITLAND
   FRANCANA DEVELOPMENT CORP.
   CANBOROUGH CORP.

TO FINANCIAL INTERESTS
   ROYAL BANK OF CANADA
   BANK OF MONTREAL
   MONTREAL TRUST CO.
   CREDIT FONCIER FRANCO CANADIEN
   SUN LIFE ASSURANCE CO. OF CANADA
   ALLIANCE MUTUAL LIFE INSURANCE CO.
   GRANVILLE SAVINGS & MORTGAGE CORP.
   SELKIRK MORTGAGE CORP.
   SUN-ALLIANCE & LONDON INSURANCE GROUP
   MORTGAGE INSURANCE CORP. OF CANADA
   CHASE MANHATTAN CORP.
       TO ROCKEFELLER INTERESTS

can make or break a project.

However, the CPR has another subsidiary, Canadian Pacific Securities, which acts as the bank from which other Canadian Pacific subsidiaries can raise their money, so that Marathon Realty Co. can raise money much more cheaply than the ordinary developer.

The cost of land and the cost of borrowing money are by far the two greatest expenses in a building project. With so many advantages, Marathon could have subdivided the property into single-family suburban-sized building lots, and they still would have made an enormous profit.

Marathon Realty Co. has found that with the promotion of Vancouver as an executive city, a market does exist for the type of accommodation they propose to provide: high-priced suites at high density, returning maximum profit. Marathon's proposals eminently suit Marathon's needs. The fact that these plans do not serve the needs of ordinary Vancouver residents is no concern to Marathon. And city politicians, rather than protecting the public interest, are following the long-standing tradition of giving the CPR what it wants.

Marathon Realty Co., as the real estate subsidiary of the CPR, is a relatively recent corporate creation, but the CPR has been involved in real estate right from the beginning. It was not until 1955 that the CPR reorganized to reflect its status as Canada's largest corporation, and a massive multi-national corporate conglomerate. The transformation began when Norris R. Crump took over control of the railroad with a new management team. The owners of CPR — whoever

they were — wanted to take a close look at all of CPR's assets and see if they couldn't be put to more profitable use. For example, the first oil discovery at Leduc, Alberta, in 1947 had been on CPR land. The company was receiving revenues from the oil companies, but perhaps the CPR could set up its own oil company and make much more money out of the oil reserves.

The same was true of CPR's extensive timber lands on Vancouver Island. CPR had acquired the land — almost one-quarter of Vancouver Island — in 1905 when it bought the Esquimalt and Nanaimo Railroad from the Dunsmuir family. It had been selling off the land gradually to the big lumber companies — MacMillan Bloedel, Crown Zellerbach. But perhaps it could set up its own lumber company to make more profitable use of the remaining forests under its control.

The CPR's assets were so extensive that it took Crump seven years to find out exactly what the CPR did own. During that time a separate subsidiary company was set up for each activity: CP Oil and Gas for the oil reserves, Pacific Logging for the timber lands, CP Hotels for the chain of hotels, CP Transport for the trucking assets, etc. In 1962, Crump set up CP Investments, wholly owned by CPR, to control all the non-transportation assets. The following year Marathon Realty Co. was established to own and develop all CPR lands not required for transportation activities. Even the historic name was changed. There is no such company as the Canadian Pacific Railway any more. The overall corporate name is Canadian Pacific Limited. CP Rail is merely the subsidiary that

THE BOARD OF DIRECTORS OF MARATHON REALTY CO.

1 Herbert M. Pickard, CHAIRMAN: also executive vice-president and director of CP Investments; director of Cominco, CP Oil and Gas, and many other CPR subsidiaries; chairman of CP Hotels. Calgary.

2 S.E. Eagles, PRESIDENT: also director of Mortgage Insurance Co. of Canada (insures mortgages) and of MICC Investments, Project 200 Investments and Properties (Vancouver waterfront developer), Metro Centre Developments (Toronto waterfront developer), and other development subsidiaries of Marathon. Toronto.

3 M.J. Field, VICE-PRESIDENT: also president, vice-president or director of many Marathon Subsidiaries. Toronto.

4 Robert D. Armstrong, DIRECTOR: also president of Rio Algom Mines, Lornex Mining Corp. and Preston Mines; vice-president and director of Tinto Holdings, the company that owns Rio Algom (controlled by the Rothschilds in England). Toronto.

5 Frederick S. Burbidge, DIRECTOR: also president of CPR; director of the Bank of Montreal, CP Investments, Cominco, and other CP subsidiaries. Montreal.

6 Raymond Lavoie, DIRECTOR: also vice-chairman and president of Credit Foncier Franco Canadien (largest trust company in Quebec); director of Alliance Mutual Life Insurance Co., Associate Acceptance Co., Gaz Metropolitan, General Investment Corp. of Quebec, John Labatt, Miron Co. Marine Industries, Northern and Central Gas Corp., Ogilvie Flour Mills. One of Quebec's most powerful figures. Montreal.

7 J. Douglas Maitland, DIRECTOR: also chairman of Hastings West Investment, Anglo-Canadian Shipping Co., International Land Corp., Macaulay Nicolls & Maitland; director of Dillingham Corp., Granville Savings and Mortgage Corp.; a powerful figure in the Vancouver development scene. Vancouver.

8 Hon. Duff Roblin, DIRECTOR: also director of CP Investments, Cominco, CP Hotels, and many other CP Investments subsidiaries; director of Montreal Trust Co.; was chairman of Marathon until he ran in last federal election; former premier of Manitoba; was merely a figurehead for CP Investments. Montreal.

9 Ian D. Sinclair, DIRECTOR: also chairman of CPR, CP Investments, CP Air Lines; vice-president of Cominco; director of most CPR subsidiaries, Royal Bank of Canada, Sun Life Assurance Co. of Canada, Trans Canada Pipe Lines, Canadian Investment Fund, MacMillan Bloedel; the most powerful figure in the whole CPR empire. Montreal.

runs the railroad.

What was really happening was that the managers realized that the non-railway assets had much greater profit potential than the railway itself. In the United States, many of the larger railroads had, in fact, gone bankrupt. So the CPR managers were setting up a corporate structure through which, when the appropriate time came, they could dump the railway — or at least the unprofitable passenger service part of it — in the government's lap, and keep all the money-making assets.

What was most reprehensible was that the federal government was letting the CPR get away with it. Bear in mind that all of the assets stemmed from the original grant to the CPR to subsidize the building and operation of a railroad. The CPR promoters had picked up 25 million acres of the best land in western Canada, an outright gift of $25 million, and the parts of the railroad that had already been completed, worth at least $37.8 million. It was an unprecedented giveaway, but it was justified by the argument of how costly it was to build and run a railroad.

The non-transportation assets have been highly concentrated in B.C. The CPR is the largest shareholder (12.3%) in MacMillan Bloedel, the province's largest corporation. The CPR owns 56% of Cominco, B.C.'s second largest corporation. Its wholly-owned subsidiary, CP Air Lines, would be B.C.'s tenth largest company if it was a separate company. Its subsidiary, Fording Coal, owns substantial coal deposits in southeastern B.C. The coal is mined, then transported to Roberts Bank superport by CP Rail, where it is then transferred to one of the CP ships for transport to Japan. Another subsidiary, Pacific Logging, already mentioned, owns substantial timber reserves on Vancouver Island. Another subsidiary, CP Transport, is one of the largest trucking companies in the province. The trucks and rail cars are shipped to Vancouver Island by CP Ferries. Once on the island, the truck drivers can stay over at the CP-owned Empress Hotel. Indeed, B.C. is the company province.

But the most potentially profitable of all the CPR holdings in B.C. are the extensive urban land holdings. Marathon Realty Co., which owns all the CPR land not required for transportation, is probably Canada's largest real estate company. Marathon has its own board of directors, who interlock with the other firms in the CPR structure and to outside corporations which are associated with the CPR and its two rival banks, the Bank of Montreal and the Royal Bank of Canada. While Marathon's board of directors includes a galaxy of corporate interests, it affords little cause for optimism for people concerned about Vancouver's expanding downtown and the pivotal role in that expansion of the CPR's lands and the CPR's real estate arm.

Part III Housing

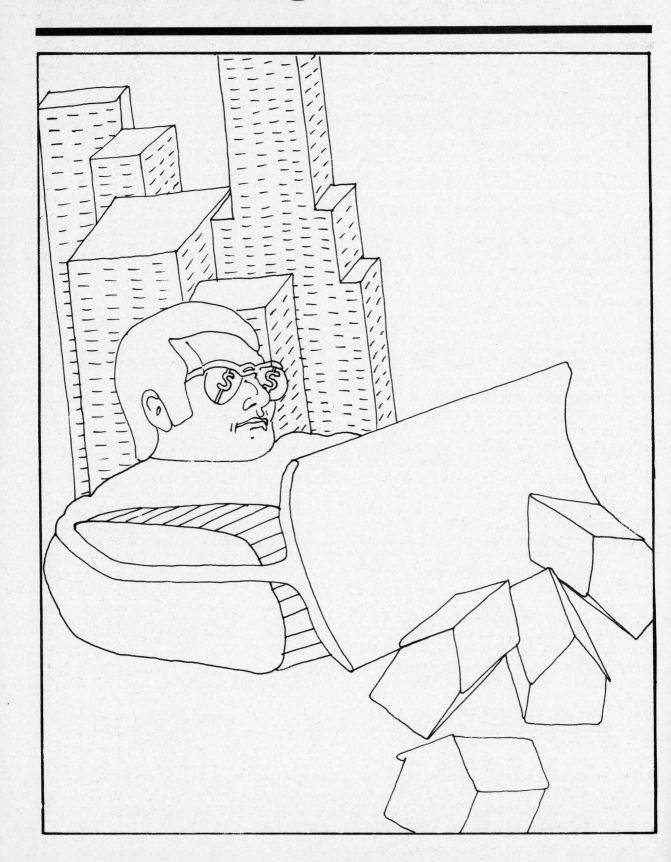

17 Introduction: Housing for whom?

Most Canadian families want to own their own home. For years every survey has come to the same conclusion, and for the same reasons: building up equity; security of tenure; privacy; suitability for child-rearing, control over one's surroundings.

And yet, given the present trends, most Canadian families are destined never to achieve this goal. A Vancouver area survey of house prices completed in December 1974 showed that the average 'less expensive' house — a basic detached brick bungalow, five to eight years old with three bedrooms, one and a half bathrooms, one-car attached garage, and full basement; but no recreation room, fireplace, or appliances — would cost $56,000 in North Vancouver or $52,000 in Richmond. Prices vary in cities in Canada, but they are high in relation to incomes everywhere.

Housing prices are so high and mortgage money so difficult to obtain, that the single-family house has become a luxury item, available only to those who earn at least $18,000 per year. In fact, so few people could afford to buy that in late 1974 there was a *glut* of new homes on the Vancouver market. This surplus had accumulated even though builders had severely cut back on new construction. The municipality of Richmond led the ranks of unsold houses. Incredible to have a glut of unsold houses in the midst of the area's severest housing shortage ever.

Yet, if the market for single-family houses is critical, the rental housing situation is a disaster. With a vacancy rate of approximately 0.2% there are just no apartment suites for rent. Moreover the situation is even worse than the statistics indicate. There are about 100,000 apartment suites in the greater Vancouver area. But this figure is declining. Not only are very few new suites being built but existing ones are being converted to condominiums or to long-term leases since by doing this the developer can expect to double his rate of return over a rental unit.

Obviously those hardest hit by the squeeze are the poor — low-income and single-parent families, senior citizens, and the people on fixed incomes — who are falling way behind in the race with inflation. There has always been a drastic shortage of low-priced accommodation in the Vancouver region, but even the small supply that does exist — much of the remaining older housing stock in the West End and inner residential neighbourhoods — is being rapidly destroyed to make way for more profitable higher-cost condominium

Vancouver's shortage of rental accommodation has been made even worse by the widespread practice of converting existing apartment buildings to condominiums or long-term leases.

'Local real estate tops Toronto'

Vancouver is now the most expensive residential real estate market in Canada, having overtaken Toronto, according to a survey prepared by A. E. LePage Limited.

Frank Hodges, the company's vice president and corporate relations manager, says:

"Residential house prices have stabilized across Canada. For the fourth quarter of 1974 the only noticeable change was Vancouver's move into the highest price category. Most of the 24 reporting cities experienced increases and decreases of less than $1,000 in the last quarter."

The company says the average residential price during 1974 was $52,356 in Vancouver compared with $50,831 in Toronto.

Meanwhile, the Central Mortgage and Housing Corporation reports total housing starts in all areas of Canada in 1974 fell to 222,123, a decline of 17.3 per cent. For British Columbia, the corresponding figure was 31,420, a decline of 16.5 per cent from the record total of 37,627 starts in 1973.

CMHC says total completions in all areas of B.C. reached 34,540 units, a higher figure than in any previous year.

"However the number of units under construction in the province at the end of the year at 22,861 was relatively low. It is interesting to note that the decline in B.C. multiple starts (21.4 per cent) was less severe than the national decline (26.3 per cent). However, B.C. multiple starts were largely made up of subsidized low income rental units and condominiums and very few rental starts."

units.

And yet, in the midst of a 'crisis' situation, those who provide the housing accommodation — the builders and developers — are making more money than ever before. Block Bros., one of Vancouver's largest real estate and development companies, in one of its frequent press releases bemoans the state of the housing industry, accompanied by many statistics to show how badly off the poor house builder really is; yet tucked away in the last paragraph of the article is the interesting fact that Block Bros.' profits have doubled over the past two years.

Block Bros. is typical. Of the five large local developers for whom statistics are available, profits increased from a low of 45% for BACM Industries to a high of 160% for Wall & Redekop Corp. from 1972 to 1973. Where profit figures are available for 1974, the picture is even more staggering.

STATED PROFITS IN 000'S

	1974	% INCREASE	1973	% INCREASE	1972
Block Bros.	4,110	(135%)	1,741	(53%)	1,142
Daon Development Corp.	3,096	(86%)	1,666	(70%)	984
Nu-West Development Corp.			4,654	(125%)	2,064
Wall & Redekop Corp.			679	(160%)	249
BACM Industries			10,311	(45%)	7,035

Just how is this possible? How can the developers be rolling in money in the midst of Canada's most serious housing shortage? To hear the developers tell it, there is one simple reason for the shortage of housing. It is because of the restrictive provincial and municipal laws, by-laws, development policies, and procedures. The developers are being *strangled* by a morass of conflicting laws, confusing policies, constantly changing regulations, and time-consuming procedures.

Developers see the cause for this situation in the negative attitude of city councils and planners who want to see 'controlled growth.' Municipal politicians are elected only by the people who already live in the community and are concerned about the quality of life there. But developers are, of course, preoccupied with those whom the developers would like to attract to the municipality to buy their products.

Everyone blames speculators for the high price of urban land, but no one admits to being a speculator — whenever someone is found buying up vacant land or old houses and holding them while the market rises, he claims to be not a speculator but a contractor-builder doing his little bit to help solve the housing crisis. When the Ontario government slapped a tax on specu-

lative land profits in early 1974, it collected less than $1 million in revenue from the tax in the first year. When speculation is taxed, somehow no one is a speculator anymore.

There is, of course, another explanation why housing costs are so high, and why there is a shortage in one of the richest and largest countries in the world. Simply put, it is because of the unconscionably high profits being made by the developers with the concommitant monopoly control held over the land market, the building industry, and access to financing for housing.

According to a confidential report prepared for the Central Mortgage and Housing Corp. (CMHC), the federal government agency concerned with housing policy in Canada, housing 'is almost a by-product' for an agglomeration of builders, developers, and financial insitutions committed to the routine of making money in the housing business.

There are a number of methods that developers use to increase their profits. One is to keep land values high and constantly rising by controlling the rate at which the land comes on the market. Keeping land costs high keeps up not only the price of new houses on the market but the price of all houses.

Large-scale private land assembly is a long-standing fact in most Canadian cities, but a recent phenomenon in Vancouver. In a relatively short time five or six major companies have built up substantial land banks. One of the largest, over 1,000 acres in size, had been assembled by Western Realty Projects, a Calgary-based company that sold out to British interests in 1973. Other large landholders are Daon Development Corp. with over 700 acres. Marathon Realty Co. and Imperial Ventures.

Two fast-growing western Canadian development corporations have moved into the Vancouver market recently, the Calgary-based Nu-West Development Corp. and the Winnipeg-based BACM Industries (owned by Genstar, a Belgian-controlled conglomerate). Through their own efforts and through interlocking contracts, these companies are rapidly becoming major forces in the Vancouver area. Nu-West owns 400 acres in its own name, and a further 300 acres through its subsidiary, Sur-Del Builders Development. Further Nu-West holds 35% of the shares of another company, Carma Developers, set up by a group of builders and developers to assemble land for their use. Carma owns over 10,000 acres in the Calgary area, but has only recently moved into Vancouver.

Carma Developers holds marketing contracts with 23 builders in the Vancouver area who will be able to acquire land through Carma, thus giving the group potential control over the entire building process. One of the developers holding a Carma contract is Engineered Homes, one of the largest subdivision developers in western Canada, and another subsidiary of the Genstar conglomerate.

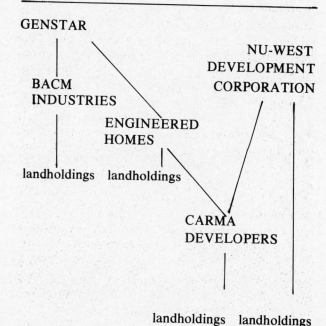

GENSTAR

BACM
INDUSTRIES

NU-WEST
DEVELOPMENT
CORPORATION

ENGINEERED
HOMES

landholdings   landholdings

CARMA
DEVELOPERS

landholdings   landholdings

Another way that developers are able to increase their profits at the expense of the house buyer is through a string of government concessions and handouts which at the same time have pushed the industry in the direction of becoming more centralized and monopolistic in operation. The government helps the developer by letting him deduct from his taxes the cost of holding land for development (including interest payments on money borrowed to buy the land, and municipal taxes), but this priviledge is not extended to the individual landowner. Even though the developer deducts these expenses from his tax load, he may still add them on to the cost of the land when it is sold, or to the final cost of the houses if he develops the land himself.

The system of federal corporate income tax deferrals also gives the developer another way of increasing his profits. The government lets the developer defer payment of all or a part of his income taxes by allowing him to depreciate his property at a faster rate for tax purposes than he actually shows on his books to the shareholders. The result is an interest-free loan amounting, in many cases, to millions of dollars a year. The developer can then use this money to buy more property or to pay off other loans.

One other way that the developer increases his stated profit is through a difference between the book value (what the property was actually bought for) and the market value (what the property is currently appraised at), which during a real estate boom is always increasing. Suppose that the developer buys a piece of land for $10,000, holds it for five years, then builds a house on it. During that five-year period the value of the land may increase to $20,000. In his calculation of what to charge for the house, he figures the land at current market value, i.e., $20,000, and adds this to the price, pocketing the extra $10,000.

In this example the developer actually built a house on the land, but if he had sold it to another developer for $20,000 it would have been a sheer speculative gain. One example shows the extent of such speculation. In 1968, Canada Permanent Trust, acting as executor for an estate, sold 50 acres of land in Richmond to Sawarne Lumber Co. for $230,000. In 1972 Sawarne sold the land to Dunhill Development Corp. for $915,000, roughly a 400% gain in four years. Dunhill then applied for a land-use contract with the municipality to build 411 single-family homes, townhouses, and apartments, finally receiving approval to go ahead with the scheme. Instead of building, Dunhill turned around and sold the property to another developer, Imperial Ventures, in March 1974 for $1,800,000. This represented a gain of $885,000, almost as much as the original purchase price. Yet even if Dunhill had built the project itself, it would have calculated its land cost at the $1,800,000 price, not the $915,000 it actually paid.

Because housing costs are so high, developers have to resort to gimmicks to convince the buyer to pay for their over-priced products. Thus they have developed the concept of the 'life-style'. 'Today you have to sell life-style as opposed to square-footage,' says Bart Wassmansdorf, Ottawa-area manager for Richard Costain (Canada). That means the extras, the central air-conditioning, garbage compactors, indoor barbecues, fancier kitchen cabinets, and eye-catching colours. Outside the house they add on the prestigious recreational facilities, such as golf and country club or a man-made lake. Both of these, in fact, were provided by Keith Construction Co., another subsidiary of Genstar, in an extremely high-priced subdivision outside Calgary.

'Human beings are like sea gulls,' says Fred Witzu, vice-president of sales for Costain Estates, a subsidiary of Richard Costain (Canada). 'They like to pick up things that shine. If they walk in and it takes their breath away, you can consider the sale closed already.' And according to Jack Gillett, vice-president of marketing for Consolidated Building Corp., 'All good salesmen are high-pressure salesmen. It's just the bad

Imperial Group series

The Imperial Group illustrates well the operation of large land development companies. An important aspect of this business is ensuring smooth relationships with governments. President of Imperial Developments is Saul Zitzerman, a law partner of Izzy Asper, until recently head of the Manitoba Liberal party. Herbert Hignett, the former president of the federal government's housing agency, Central Mortgage and Housing Corp., was appointed a director of another Imperial Group

Apple Greene – The reality

company five months after he left his job at CMHC.

Another important aspect of the land development
business is the ability of a developer to sell not just housing but
'life-style'. That is exactly what Imperial offers in its leaflet for
a development called 'Apple Greene.' In its original form, the
leaflet is a bright lime green. In tiny type on the cover of the
leaflet is the qualifying phrase 'All sketches artist's
impression'. Note too the stamped-on afterthought,
'ADULTS ONLY'.

ones who get caught at it.' And *Canadian Building,* the trade journal of the building industry, explained the requirements of today's real estate salesman:

Higher prices limit the market to more affluent sophisticated buyers seeking more sophisticated home features and fixtures. This has spawned a need for more sophisticated salesmen — people who can discuss financing, legal and tax details with the acumen of a banker/lawyer, while probing the buyer's psyche with the insight of a Vienna psychologist.

To talk about a housing market is really stretching the truth. On one side may sit a gigantic vertically-integrated development conglomerate, controlling all aspects of building from land assembly to servicing and subdividing, from construction to selling, with its own legion of lawyers, tax specialists, accountants, financial consultants, engineers, and technicians figuring every conceivable way to squeeze every last penny of profit from their products; on the other side is a young couple, barely able to make a down payment, with little knowledge about houses or construction. It is hard to imagine this one-sided situation producing anything like a fair transaction.

The one thing that developers require in their continuing quest to keep up the high levels of profitability is continued urban growth.

A little growth is enough to protect property values. A lot of growth serves to produce rising property values everywhere in the city.... Booming business conditions help ensure a steady market for all kinds of existing accommodation as well as attracting new city residents who in turn create new housing demands. Slow-growth or no-growth cities do not attract new businesses or people; rather a slow growth rate threatens to depress property values.
(James Lorimer in *A Citizen's Guide to City Politics*)

Governments at all levels seem to share a common goal with the major economic interests — to drive the mass of Canadians into a handful of urban areas. Canada's economy is becoming based more on service industries which have one essential requirement — an endless supply of office workers at all levels. Thus large pools of potential labour need to be concentrated in the few major urban areas.

Direct pressure on urban areas is also caused by the federal government's immigration policy which encourages the immigration of people who are most likely to move to the cities. This policy is in marked contrast to the one which was in effect during the latter part of the 19th and early 20th centuries when the goal was to populate the vast prairie region as quickly as possible (and hence make the CPR's land that much more valuable).

Even by concentrating its own services and facilities in the larger urban areas, the federal government helps increase the pressure on growth.

The provincial government, for its part, could do a great deal to take the pressures off the cities, especially Vancouver. Many plans have been put forward for developing the vast northwest sector of the province, for establishing new towns, for discouraging the flow of industry to the overcrowded areas, but there has been little action so far.

The traditional stance of municipal politicians was to favour as much growth and development as possible. Many of the politicians themselves were involved in real estate or development, and they took the view that what was good for the developer was good for the city as a whole, the city's progress being measured by additions to the tax rolls. The 'new' breed of civic politician takes a somewhat different tack. He is not so blatantly pro-developer, being very conscious of the hostility of the majority of his voters to the pro-growth policies of a few years ago. But he often tries to instill a sense of resignation among them. The growth is inevitable and it cannot be stopped no matter what we can do. Walter Hardwick, former Vancouver alderman for The Elector's Action Movement (TEAM), captured this attitude well: 'Although zero population growth would suit many of us, that goal will not be attained in British Columbia for years to come, if ever, because of the freedom of migration within Canada, to say nothing of natural increase and external immigration.'

Thus the Vancouver situation can only get worse. The population of the Greater Vancouver Regional District is growing by an estimated 35,000 per year, equivalent to the West End in numbers. In 1971 the population passed the 1,000,000 mark. At the rate it is growing, it will double by the year 2000, in 25 years from now. What will the increase in population do to the city as we know it?

Up to now, the housing crisis has affected Vancouver in a number of different ways. The West End, for example, was substantially redeveloped during the 1960s when developers were making large profits from high-rise rental accommodation. Such redevelopment, whose primary purpose was to provide shoppers for the downtown department stores and workers for the downtown office buildings, also had the effect of driving out many of the lower-income families and people on fixed incomes who lived in the older houses. When construction dried up in 1972, rents began to escalate quickly, thus making the area more and more a preserve of the wealthy.

The inner residential neighbourhoods — Kitsilano, Fairview, Mount Pleasant, Grandview, and parts of North Vancouver City and Burnaby — are affected by

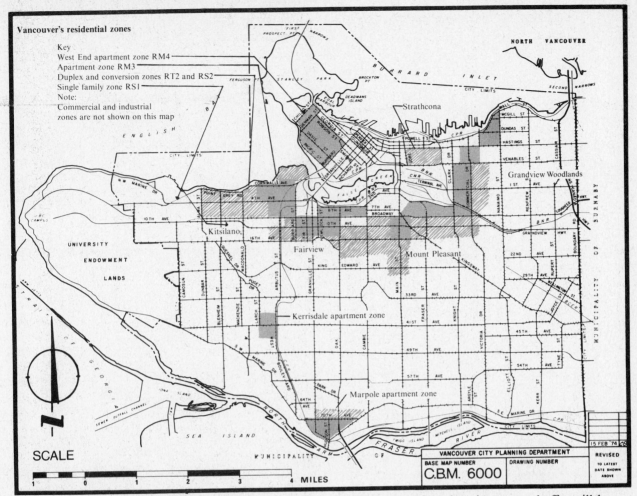

Vancouver's residential zones

Key
West End apartment zone RM4
Apartment zone RM3
Duplex and conversion zones RT2 and RS2
Single family zone RS1
Note:
Commercial and industrial
zones are not shown on this map

SCALE

VANCOUVER CITY PLANNING DEPARTMENT
BASE MAP NUMBER   DRAWING NUMBER   REVISED
C.B.M. 6000

the housing crisis in a rather different way. They are in the midst of redevelopment; the older homes providing cheaper accommodation are being destroyed and replaced with much more costly accommodation. The city, through its zoning policies, aids the developers in their quest for more profitable ventures. Kitsilano, as other inner areas, has three different housing zones, each under a slightly different kind of pressure. The inner zone, closest to downtown, has been zoned for multiple dwellings for years, but only in the recent past has a trend to this type of occupancy become widespread. The remaining houses and conversion units providing the cheapest accommodation in the city, are rapidly being demolished for condominium suites.

In the mid-zone, the area of conversions and duplexes, RT-2 and RS-2, the houses are bought up by speculators and blockbusters in the expectation they will be rezoned eventually for apartment buildings. Families are being driven out, breaking the existing community spirit so that there will be few to resist when the area is rezoned. This mid-zone area acts as a buffer between the apartment zone and the outer zone, the RS-1 or single-family area. It is city council policy to destroy this mid-zone area; once the conversion dis-

trict is rezoned to high-rise, a new buffer will be required. Then the single-family area will be rezoned to conversion dwellings.

A third type of area affected by the housing crisis is found in the suburban municipality, where development follows a process from the conversion of rural land to urban use, to the subdivision and servicing for single-family houses. An area such as Richmond underwent its greatest expansion during the early sixties after the construction of the Oak St. Bridge in 1957. Subdivisions leapfrogged across the municipality. The pace of development has slowed down recently accompanied by a shift to multiple-family housing and condominiums, although some single-family housing continues to be built. The major problem here is the exorbitant price of new houses and condominiums.

18 The West End: Developers' paradise

In 1955, the eight-storey Sylvia Hotel, on the English Bay waterfront, was the tallest building in the West End. Today, 20 years later, it is hidden beneath a forest of high-rise apartment buildings; the fine old mansions that once surrounded it are gone; the inexpensive rooming-houses destroyed; the human scale of the area obliterated; and all in the name of progress and profit.

In 1973, with a population of over 40,000 in a one-square-mile area, the West End was one of the most densely populated places in the world; it was by far the densest in Canada. And of course, with so many people being packed together into mainly one-bedroom apartments, a whole host of problems have appeared: children, families, the poor, those on fixed incomes being forced out of the area; noise, air and traffic pollution; alienation and loneliness in the midst of thousands of people; high crime and suicide rates; and a lack of community spirit.

How did such a drastic situation arise? Quite simply, because the downtown business interests needed a high-density residential development close to downtown. By the mid-fifties, the post-war building boom had petered out in the downtown core. The downtown business interests were looking for ways to boost business. A number of suggestions were entertained. One was to make sure there were many people living close to downtown. This would do two things:

1 It would ensure large numbers of shoppers for the downtown stores — the Bay, Eaton's, etc. NOTE: a survey in 1966 showed that one-third of all shoppers in the downtown area did live within one mile of downtown.
2 It would ensure an endless supply of clerical workers for the downtown office buildings — the key raw material for a concentration of such buildings. NOTE: a survey of the MacMillan-Bloedel building showed that a majority of the workers did live in the West End.

Thus the West End and the downtown could feed off each other. More office buildings meant the need for more office workers, and hence, more high-rise apartment buildings in the West End. And more office workers meant that more developers would move into the downtown area and build more office buildings.

Other developers were only too happy to step in and provide block after block of highly-profitable high-rise apartment buildings in the West End. They were helped at every stage by a development-crazed

Until 1910 the Vancouver elite build their homes in the West End overlooking Burrard Inlet and English Bay. In 1910 the CPR opened its exclusive Shaughnessy Heights development, and these large homes were soon converted into rooming houses. *B.C. Provincial Archives*

The central portion of the West End was filled with row upon row of working men's houses. *B.C. Provincial Archives*

city council who rezoned the area to one of the highest potential densities in the world. Although the city planning department continually recommended that the West End should not have such a high density because the amenities of the area would be destroyed, the planners were slapped down by city council every time. The West End property owner, perhaps with a deteriorating rooming-house, looked forward to the day when he could sell out to a developer at a big profit, and retire. The owners began to look upon this as their God-given right; any interference by the city planning department would not be tolerated. For 20 years, city council agreed.

This transformation of the West End in a 20-year period is only the most recent in a number of dramatic changes. Until 1886, the West End was covered with dense stands of prime timber. Beginning that year, the area was cleared, graded, and subdivided by the CPR. By 1910, it had been completely built up with two

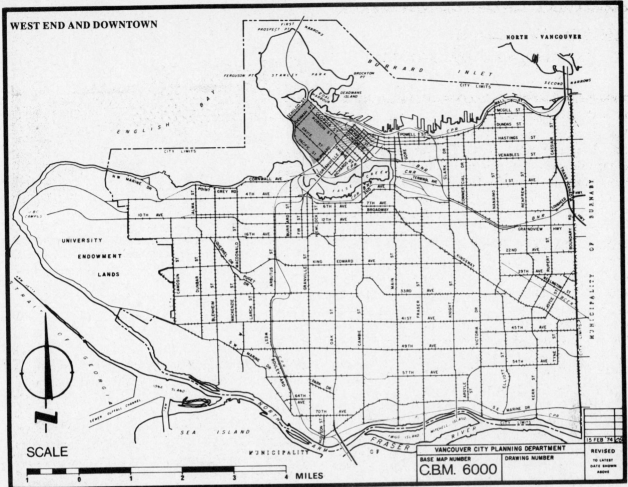

SCALE

1　0　1　2　3　4　MILES

VANCOUVER CITY PLANNING DEPARTMENT		REVISED
BASE MAP NUMBER	DRAWING NUMBER	TO LATEST DATE SHOWN ABOVE
C.B.M. 6000		

distinct types of development. At first, CPR officials and others of the Vancouver elite built their grand mansions along the bluffs of Burrard Inlet. (Later, the scene shifted to Davie St. overlooking English Bay). Until the opening of the Shaughnessy Heights area by the CPR in 1910, the West End was Vancouver's finest residential area. The central portion of the West End, during the same period, was developed with row upon row of small frame working-men's houses on 33-foot lots.

Since there were no zoning by-laws and few regulations governing building until the late 1920s, a number of other developments began to appear after 1910. Corner grocery stores were built helter-skelter throughout the West End. Many of the larger houses were converted into suites and rooming-houses after their former owners had moved into Shaughnessy Heights. And a number of masonry apartment buildings were constructed — almost 400 suites in 1910, for example.

Another mini-boom in apartment building occurred after 1925; and in 1931, when the city enacted its first zoning by-law, West End property owners were successful in pressuring city council to zone most of the West End area for multiple dwellings. There was a

height limit imposed of six storeys, but the open space requirements were so minimal that a building could occupy most of the site, so that, in effect, it was high-density zoning. Very few apartments were actually built. The vast majority of the houses in the West End were converted into suites and rooming-houses, providing inexpensive accommodation for many lower-income families: in 1941, there were many more children and fewer elderly people in a total West End population of 25,700.

In 1950 the West End began to experience another building boom. This time three-storey frame walkup apartments were the dominant type. Property owners and downtown business interests were putting more pressure on city council to upzone. In 1956, the city enacted its new Zoning and Development By-law, which established a new zoning category of RM-4 for the West End. This zoning allowed a maximum Floor Space Ratio of 3:00 or 3:35 on corner sites.

The RM-4 regulations didn't set a height limit, but all buildings over 80 feet were subject to the approval of the technical planning board. Later, regulations regarding sunlight angles and views were added.

With this rezoning, the West End's biggest boom was on. The number of suites built doubled between

Vancouver's West End. With a population of more than 40,000 people living in a one-square-mile area, the West End is by far the densest area of its size in Canada.

During the building boom of the 1900s a number of six-storey masonry apartments were scattered throughout the West End. These buildings covered almost the entire building site, leaving virtually no space.

1955 and 1956, and went over 1,000 for the first time in 1958. There was a severe cutback around 1960 because of a nation-wide economic recession, but in the years after 1962, at least 1,000 suites were added each year in the West End until 1971.

In 1972 the West End population reached 40,000.

But even within two years of the adoption of the RM-4 zoning, the city planning department was having second thoughts about the wisdom of such potentially high-density development. A report entitled 'Apartment Zoning,' published in 1958, recommended that the West End should be down-zoned to a FSR of 2:0. The report noted that under the current zoning of a FSR of 3:0, the potential West End population was something of the order of 63,000. The downzoning would reduce that to about 45,000.

However, city council rejected the planning department's recommendations.

The issue surfaced again in 1963, when the planners again recommended a reduction in the allowable FSR to 2:00. They argued that experts the world over had recommended maximum densities of 200 to 300 people per acre, and this over relatively small extents. In Vancouver, the RM-4 zoning allowed up to 380 people per acre over the *whole* of the West End. There was also a system of bonuses in effect where the developer, by building on a larger site, with more of the site as open space and more of the parking underground, could achieve densities as high as 500 people per acre!

The city planners argued that even if the FSR was reduced to 2:00 it would still be high compared to standards in every other city. But city council not only rejected the planners' arguments again, they were prepared even to *increase* the existing FSR above 3:00. The pressure was really on from the downtown business interests.

In June 1963, the Downtown Business Association (DBA), in a brief to city council, made these points:

- *the DBA contains the major taxpayers in the Central Business District;*
- *if the Central Business District is to be retained, the West End must be intensively developed; even a recommended maximum of 65,000 in the West End is too few;*
- *a greater density will increase tax revenues and land values in the Central Business District;*
- *density ... is one of the most important factors to create value and to make the best economic use of the land;*
- *we recognize that aesthetic and economic viewpoints may conflict at times in development, but we feel that the former must not be so restrictive as to discourage enterprise.*

As part of its program to support the downtown business lobby, city council had hired Larry Smith & Co., an American firm of economic consultants, to

Downtown and the West End, 1959. The West End building boom was just underway. The first two high-rise apartments were built on the English Bay waterfront near Stanley Park (on the far left). The rest of the West End was still covered with old rooming houses and six-storey apartments. *George Allen Aerial Photos*

The West End, 1974. Just 15 years later, the area had undergone one of the most amazing transformations in the city's history. The main effect of this change was to provide a large pool of workers for the downtown office towers and shoppers for the downtown stores. *George Allen Aerial Photos*

recommend a program of downtown redevelopment. Smith devoted a substantial portion of his report to an analysis of West End zoning and apartment 'demand', and their effect on downtown redevelopment. Smith flatly rejected the planning department's proposal to downzone (i.e., lower the density of development) the West End to an FSR of 2:00. 'This indicates a possible loss of approximately 20,000 people at the time of ultimate development' (i.e.; when the West End was totally built up with high-rises). Smith calculated that 20,000 fewer people in the West End would mean $5 million less spent in downtown stores in 1981. Even though this figure represented only 1.2% of all downtown sales forecast for 1981 (in other words, it was negligible), Smith concluded that the city should retain the current West End zoning. City council was very favourably impressed with Smith's report.

The final group to be strongly, almost violently, opposed to the planners' ideas to downzone the West End were the owners who, according to a 1963 brief,

'have been hanging on to old rooming-houses for generations in hopes of selling to apartment builders.' City council rejected the downzoning requests, and another ten years of apartment building went on before another look was taken at the zoning by-laws.

The building boom reached a frenzied pitch during 1968 and 1969, when 37 buildings were started. At the same time there was considerable speculation and land assembly, and land values were driven up from about $4 to $5 per square foot in 1960 to $10 to $11 in 1970. Higher land costs meant inevitably higher rents and taller buildings. A slump hit the West End in 1970 and new construction dried up: in 1971 there was only one high-rise building started, and in 1972 there were none. Petty speculators who had been assembling sites over the past few years got caught in a tight money crunch. Some of them took severe financial losses when they couldn't find the money to buy up the options they had taken out. The situation eased somewhat in 1973 and a few more buildings were constructed. These however, were mainly of the condominium variety.

Downtown Vancouver, 1974, is a vastly different place from downtown 1964. In 1964 there hadn't been a new building for years. The downtown business interests desperately needed high-density West End development in a hurry. In 1974 the situation was completely reversed. Downtown construction was booming. Developers couldn't find enough tenants to fill up all their office space. Therefore, they were not too concerned with the West End any more. They knew that a rapid transit system would be built in the near future, and this would bring in thousands of office workers. Thus the pressure was off the West End to provide that manpower and those sales dollars. Further, other proposed developments around False Creek and along the waterfront would take up the slack in providing that still essential ingredient for continued downtown growth — an inexhaustible supply of clerical workers.

As a result, the city in the mid-seventies became more willing to consider some downzoning for the West End.

19 Kitsilano: Neighbourhood in transition

In 1971 the population of Kitsilano was 34,000. This was a meagre 6% increase over the population 20 years earlier. (In contrast, the population of Vancouver as a whole had increased 25% over the same period, and the metropolitan area a whopping 93%). And yet Kitsilano had been undergoing an incredible amount of redevelopment. Many older homes were being torn down and replaced first with three-storey walkup apartments, then with high-rise apartments and finally, during the early seventies, with three-storey condominiums. What was happening, of course, was not population growth, but population change.

As downtown Vancouver continued to grow, to expand its retailing activities and office functions, greater pressure was being put on inner areas such as Kitsilano as well as the West End for accommodation to suit downtown-oriented people. The existing residents of the area, the working-class and lower middle-class families, the many people who had grown up in the area, were being displaced by another group, the more affluent singles and childless couples who would live in smaller bachelor and one-bedroom units and who could afford to pay much more for that accommodation. Thus developers saw many opportunities for profitable redevelopment. Many long-standing families desiring to remain in the area were no match for the alliance of city hall with its control over zoning and planning and the real estate agents and developers who swarmed over the area. Large parts of Kitsilano were, by 1974, already lost to the developers' bulldozers, even though the majority of houses were only 50 to 60 years old

The demographic facts tell the story. From 1951 to 1971 the number of children under 14 dropped by 20%. The number of people between 35 and 54 dropped by almost 25%, as did the senior citizen population. The big increase was in the 20-to-34-year-old group which skyrocketed by 55% to the point where one out of every three persons in Kitsilano is in that age category; whereas in the greater Vancouver region that age group makes up less than one in four of the total population. The results are everywhere evident. Schools are half-empty, the church congregations are dwindling, and the streets are becoming clogged with automobiles.

In fact, Kitsilano is not homogenous. There are at least three distinct districts corresponding to the three types of residential zoning. Roughly 30% of the residential area is zoned for single-family, 45% is

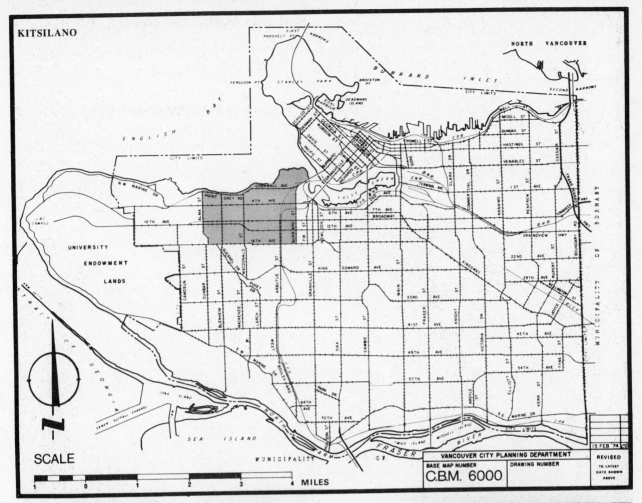

duplex (two-family) or conversion (suites), and the remaining 25% is zoned for apartments. All three areas are threatened in different ways by the pressure for redevelopment to higher density and more profitable uses.

Kitsilano's history as a residential area really began

Broadway (9th Ave.) in what was to become the Kitsilano area, in 1889. The land was being cleared and subdivided by CPR work crews. *B.C. Provincial Archives*

5th Ave. and Arbutus St., Kitsilano in 1904, looking north along Arbutus to the Kitsilano Indian Reserve on the English Bay waterfront, with Stanley Park just visible on the other side. The area had poor accessibility until 1905 when a streetcar line was built from downtown along the waterfront. *B.C. Provincial Archives*

after the construction in 1905 of a streetcar line over the Kitsilano Trestle Bridge, and along the water to the foot of Balsam St. A further streetcar line was built in 1909 along Fourth Ave. to Alma Rd. By 1913, at the height of the boom, both areas had been substantially built up with single-family homes.

The easternmost and westernmost parts of Kitsilano, were the first to be built up, with the centre being filled in later.

Until 1928, 16th Ave. and Alma Rd. were the boundaries of the city, as Point Grey had split off from the municipality of South Vancouver in 1908 to form a separate municipality (extending to Cambie St. on the east). This move seemed to have been inspired by the CPR, which had plans to develop the exclusive Shaughnessy Heights area and did not wish it to come under the control of the municipality of South Vancouver which was more a working man's area. However, the boom of the 1920s witnessed the continuing expansion of the downtown core with its insatiable yen for land, and in 1928 Point Grey and South Vancouver were annexed by the City of Vancouver.

This little affected Kitsilano, which was totally within the city limits. Another important event which occurred the next year also had little effect on Kitsilano for a number of years. That was the adoption of the city's first zoning by-law. This zoning by-law provided for three distinct types of residential areas: single-family, two-family, and multiple-family — these latter being restricted predominantly to the inner areas of the city. Because zoning was imposed after Kitsilano had been substantially developed, many single-family houses were found in all three areas. There were many older three-storey brick or frame apartment buildings scattered throughout Kitsilano.

The major explicit goal of the zoning by-law was to protect the single-family areas in the belief that the single-family home owner was the backbone of society. The two-family dwelling areas were to be used as buffers between areas of denser development — the apartment zone — and the single-family areas.

Little redevelopment occurred between the time of the adoption of the zoning by-law in 1928 and the end of World War II. There was a spurt of redevelopment after the war and parts of eastern Kitsilano were rebuilt with three-storey frame walkup apartments. At the same time a number of secondary suites in single-family houses were being built, these being illegal although quite widespread.

In 1951 the city threatened to crack down on the illegal suites in two large areas of Kitsilano: Fourth-Alma-Waterloo-Bayswater, and Fourth-Bayswater-Broadway-Trafalgar. A group calling itself the Kitsilano Improvement Association quickly formed to

pressure for rezoning to two-family, which would thus legalize the suites in the area. It was soon discovered that most of the suites didn't meet the city's standards, so that the city both postponed the crackdown on the suites and refused the rezoning.

In 1956 city council passed a new zoning by-law which retained the inner apartment zoning in parts of Kitsilano along with the outer single-family zoning, and in between rezoned 445 acres of single-family from RS-1 to RS-2, which would permit conversions (making the illegal suites legal in those areas) and would allow low-density multiple dwellings (garden apartments and townhouses) as conditional uses.

Subsequent amendments in 1961 encouraged construction of apartments in the inner apartment areas. The height limit was raised from 40 feet to 120 feet, and bonuses which allowed denser development were given to developers who used larger sites, left more open space, or put their parking underground. Between 1962 and 1968 about ten high-rises were built on the lower slopes of Kitsilano under this amendment.

Roughly speaking, the three zones form concentric rings centring on the downtown core: the inner apartment ring (RM-3), the middle duplex and conversion ring (RT-2 and RS-2) acting as a buffer, and the outer single-family ring (RS-1).

Gradually the inner RM-3 area is being re-

Construction of the Burrard bridge (centre) in 1931 opened up access to the lower slopes of Kitsilano. The scrub area on both sides of the bridge is the remains of the Kitsilano Indian Reserve. The bridge was a recommendation of Harland Bartholomew, an American planner hired by Vancouver city council to prepare a master plan for the city. Another of Bartholomew's recommendations was to connect the bridge with Arbutus St., a proposal which Kitsilano residents have been fighting for the last 45 years. *B.C. Provincial Archives*

developed from the older homes that exist now into three-storey or high-rise structures. It is estimated that this process will be complete by 1980, in only five years from now. At the same time that the RM-3 zone is being redeveloped, speculators and developers have been buying up the remaining single-family homes in the RT-2 and RS-2 areas, breaking them up into suites and renting them out to a more transient type population with less of a stake in the community. Then, when the RM-3 zones are filled in by 1980, it will be an easy matter for the planning department to rezone the conversion districts to apartments: there will be few left to oppose the rezoning. Many owners in the conversion zone consider it to be transitional; the present zoning is not considered to be permanent, and increasing pressure is being exerted for upward zoning in west Kitsilano and Kitsilano Point. Consequently much speculation is taking place in these areas. After this area has been rezoned it too will then need buffering, so that the city will have to rezone another ring of single-family homes to conversion units. This ring will probably include the remaining single-family area of Kitsilano, and then the pressure will be on West Point Grey and Dunbar, the way it is on Kitsilano today.

1 THE APARTMENT ZONE — RM-3

In 1960, 25% of the apartment-zoned land in Kitsilano was occupied by apartment buildings. By 1968 this had increased to 42%, 293 buildings. Twenty-two per cent was still single-family and 23% multiple occupancy, either as duplexes or conversions. Many of these were demolished over the next six years, so that by the end of 1974, about 1,000 suites were left accommodating 2,000 to 3,000 people. Due to pressure from the community, city council agreed to downzone the apartment area of Kitsilano for a one-year period, during which time a local area planning program was supposed to come up with a new plan for Kitsilano. It wasn't really downzoning. It merely restricted the height of buildings to 40 feet rather than 120 feet which had been on the books since 1961.

However, during 1974 there was a rapid escalation in the rate of redevelopment, as many small-time developers cashed in on the housing squeeze by churning out a series of shoddy three-storey condominium apartments. Fifteen to 20 of these were approved during 1974, causing the demolition of approximately 75 to 150 houses, which in turn had provided low-cost accommodation for 400 to 600 people. This low-priced accommodation was not being replaced anywhere — the city wasn't building any, the province didn't have any plans for building any, and the federal government wasn't providing money for building any. So when the low-priced housing went, the people being displaced — senior citizens, families with children, people on low and moderate incomes — were out of luck.

The story of Mrs. Helen Chester is a poignant illustration of the plight of people living in these older homes. Mrs. Chester, a 57-year-old widow, had lived in the West End since 1954. She moved to a small two-storey house on W. Eighth Ave. where she rented the whole house for six years. Two rooms were rented out to senior citizens whom she looked after and she also had an in-home daycare license looking after two children. On July 27, 1974, she received notice to vacate the premises by August 31, as the owner was planning to demolish the house and construct a three-storey condominium building. The tenants in seven houses on the block received the same notice. The developer promised Mrs. Chester that he would find suitable replacement housing that would allow her to continue providing daycare and accommodation for her senior citizens. But at the same time the deve-

In 1974, community pressure in Kitsilano brought about a temporary freeze on high-rise apartments. One building was able to slip through the freeze, however, and another block of homes fell to the bulldozer.

loper's management firm sent a letter to Mrs. Chester threatening that the firm would not be responsible for damage done to any of her belongings. The developer did not produce any alternative accommodation for Mrs. Chester, and she stayed put. Instead, he went to the office of the rentalsman, which went into operation on October 1, to have Mrs. Chester thrown out. The rentalsman, former Liberal MLA and radio hotliner Barry Clark, told Mrs. Chester that she had to vacate by October 15. If she didn't, the owner could apply for an immediate order for possession of the house from Clark.

In the meantime, the developer had applied for, and received, a demolition permit from city hall for all seven houses, the issuance of such permits being a mere formality. By this time, the tenants in the other six houses had moved out. On the morning of October 15 the bulldozer arrived on the site and began ripping down the houses, starting at the end away from the house where Mrs. Chester was living. The rentalsman had instructed the developer not to interfere with Mrs. Chester until a court order had been issued or a reasonable solution found. At 10:00 a.m. that morning he requested a meeting with Mrs. Chester for 9:00 a.m. the following morning to discuss whether a court order giving possession to the developer should be issued.

At about 11:45 a.m. that same morning, the

developer directed the bulldozer operator to smash through Mrs. Chester's backyard — destroying daycare equipment and knocking down trees, one of which crashed against the house, smashing the back porch and causing a large crack in the kitchen wall only a few feet from where one of the daycare children, Mrs. Chester and two other adults were having tea inside. The developer had not bothered to turn off the electricity, gas, or water. As it turned out, he 'inadvertantly' knocked the top off the gas meter, causing live gas to freely escape for hours. A city gas inspector quickly called to the scene ordered the operation to stop.

In a state of panic, Mrs. Chester called a mover and cleared out, storing her possessions in a warehouse, and moved to a cousin's house on the other side of Vancouver. The two senior citizens disappeared without a trace.

The rentalsman immediately took the position that since the tenant had left voluntarily, there was no longer any need for the services of his office. Accordingly the developer called his bulldozer in the next morning to demolish the remaining two houses. In the meantime, Mrs. Chester had been in contact with members of the West Broadway Citizens Committee, and when the bulldozer arrived on the site a group of citizens were standing in front of the house protecting it, with Mrs. Chester's permission and blessing. It seemed that since the rentalsman had still not issued an order for possession to the developer Mrs. Chester, having regained her composure, was still the legal tenant, and she wished to get back in the house until alternate accommodation was found for her. This meant that the developer would have to repair the damages he had caused the day before.

West Broadway Citizens Committee members and other residents stood in front of the house all day October 16 and some slept over that night to prevent a surprise midnight foray by the bulldozer driver. During the day the driver had several times tried to attack the house and several of the defenders were shaken up — being scooped up in the bulldozer, then dropped. The conflict was a standoff for four days, until the morning of the 19th when a truce had been called so that a meeting could be held in the rentalsman's office. However, as soon as the defenders left the site, the bulldozer operator, who had been waiting in the wings, moved in and quickly finished off the job.

Mrs. Chester, unable to find alternate accommodation in Kitsilano, was forced to move in with relatives on the other side of town. Of 26 tenants who were displaced from the six houses and later contacted, nine relocated in Kitsilano, 16 moved out of the area, and three were without accommodation two weeks after the eviction. There were at least nine other tenants who could not be found.

The seven houses containing altogether about 35 people were to be replaced by 39 condominium suites to accommodate roughly 80 people, so that the population in this particular stretch of Kitsilano would be roughly doubled. The suites were put on the market at $37,000 to $41,000 for a one-bedroom unit, hardly a price that anyone who had lived there before could afford.

2 THE CONVERSION ZONE — RT-2

The duplex and conversion zones comprise roughly 45% of the residential area of Kitsilano. However, well over half of all the houses in the area are still single-family in spite of the multi-family zoning, and a substantial proportion of these are owner-occupied rather than tenant-occupied, many by families who have lived in the area for years. The process of redevelopment in this area differs from that occurring in the apartment zone. There have been a few demolitions when older houses were destroyed to make way for very expensive luxury townhouses. But basically redevelopment in this area involves forcing out families, breaking up houses into suites and renting them out to a more transient population, driving up rents through various means, and in many other ways preparing the area for upward zoning when the apartment area is totally redeveloped.

The story of real estate salesmen Stanley Silverman and Edward Walmsley illustrates well how this process works.

On February 14, 1974, the results of an investigation by the attorney-general's department into possible breaches of the B.C. Real Estate Act were revealed in the Vancouver press. Subjects of the investigation were Stanley Silverman and Edward Walmsley, salesmen for real estate company Fullbrook, Bertram and Brown. The company, in turn, was seeking a supreme court injunction to stop the investigation and damages against the provincial investigators.

The company had good reason to want the investigation halted, because it was revealing how two salesmen, using a maze of interrelated holding companies, were speculating in revenue properties, leading to astronomical rent increases and to subsequent evictions of hundreds of people who could not afford the new rents. In the process, Silverman and Walmsley had become very rich men.

The story would never have come to light if it had not been for the work of staff members of the Kitsilano Information Centre and the West Broadway Citizens Committee. The Information Centre operated a housing referral service, and the staff began to notice that an unusually large number of people looking for housing in Kitsilano had recently been evicted from the places in which they had been living. The also noticed

that many of these houses were managed by a firm called Silverlane Management. They noted the addresses of these houses, and noted also in the Saturday papers lists of suites for rent by Silverlane. They then began checking out the ownership of these properties through the assessment records and the land registry office, and tracing out the shareholders and directors of the holding companies.

They discovered that the two salesmen, Stanley Silverman and Edward Walmsley, operated a network of companies involving associates, friends, and relatives, which over the past year had set a pace of buying and selling real estate, inter-company trading, mortgaging, and remortgaging that Vancouver *Sun* reporter Hal Lieren described as 'dizzying'.

Through contacts with previous and new tenants in Walmsley-Silverman controlled houses, the West Broadway Citizens Committee and Kitsilano Information Centre completed the other half of the picture — the astronomical rent increases, the massive evictions. What was most reprehensible was that Silverman, Walmsley, and associates preyed on the conversion and duplex districts. These districts provided much of the lower-cost housing in Vancouver. The supply of this type was being reduced in apartment and industrial areas because of redevelopment. But the city planning department had concluded in a 1968 study that 'efforts should be made to preserve and enhance these districts as they will continue to provide the majority of the city's low cost housing units.' What little lower-cost housing remained in Vancouver was single-handedly being destroyed by Silverman-Walmsley et al.

Here's how they did it.

First they would buy a property on the open market. Because they were real estate salesmen they had access to a great deal of information that the ordinary home owner didn't have. They would keep their eyes open for sellers who were not asking as much as the market might pay. They would buy this house for themselves and, if a revenue property, would raise the rents in the house. In this manner they increased the appraised value of the house. The rough rule of thumb to determine appraised value is to multiply the yearly income of a property by a factor of between 8.5 and 10. Thus if a rooming-house had an income of $5,000 when they bought it, it might be appraised for up to $50,000. If they raised the rents by 50%, the income would then increase to $7,500 and the appraised value up to $75,000. They could then remortgage the house, receiving a mortgage for, say, 75% of the value, or $56,250. The $6,250 was sheer profit.

In practice they did this by mortgaging and remortgaging a property by way of repeated sales through the various companies until the rents and mortgages had been driven as high as they would go. Then they might sell the house to a developer who was assembling property for an apartment building. Each time the house was resold, Silverman or Walmsley would collect the real estate commission, 5 to 7% of the selling price. And Silverlane Management, owned jointly by Silverman and Walmsley, would charge a fee for collecting the rents for the Silverman-Walmsley holding company that owned the house. This, presumably, had tax write-off advantages.

Government records show 560 property transactions carried out through Fullbrook, Bertram and Brown (FBB) in 1973, 80 involving company employees as principals. Walmsley and Silverman were at the top of the pyramid of companies that did the buying and selling. They controlled two companies themselves, Silverlane Holdings and S&W Investments. Immediately below were a number of companies involving Silverman and Walmsley along with other associates. These were:

Blacklane Investments	Edward Walmsley, Stanley Silverman, and Peter Black, meat market owner
Greater Vancouver Holdings	Walmsley and his wife Lynn
Magoo Investments	Silverman, Walmsley, Michael McCleery, and Barry Dunn
Lincoln Holdings	Walmsley and Ian McFarlane, manager of Zephyr-Mercury Sales
Westfield Holdings	Walmsley and John Laxton, lawyer and former provincial president of the NDP
Marian Holdings	Silverman and Ian G. and Maryanne Belcher
Kawi Holdings	Silverman, Walmsley and Brian Heard
Mandy Holdings	Silverman and Patricia and Andrew Krieger
Napoleon Enterprises	Silverman, Walmsley, and Michael and Lois Gurvin
Serin Holdings	Silverman and his wife Mary Jane
Mishigana Investments	Gerald and Karen Lecovin (she is Silverman's sister; he is Silverman's lawyer)
Rosmore Investments	Karen Lecovin and Rose Silverman (Silverman's mother)
Excelsior Investments	Ron Boulter, FBB salesman
Magnexx Holdings	Fred James Walker, FBB salesman
James B. Spieran	J.B. Spieran (owns property jointly with John Fullbrook, FBB owner)

How the system worked is best illustrated by looking at a typical property.

On January 19, 1973, T.A. Streiling of Hollywood, California, sold a Point Grey Rd. property to William Brian Harrison of 5460 Gilpin, Burnaby, for $37,750. On April 9, Harrison sold it to Silverman for $45,000. Sometime in September, Silverman sold the property to Silverlane Holdings for an apparent sum of $45,000. The land registry office data were reported to be fuzzy on this point. Sometime in September or October, Silverlane sold the property to Westfield Holdings for $55,000. On November 2, Westfield sold it to Napoleon Enterprises for $63,000.

NDP lawyer John Laxton (a partner with Edward Walmsley in Westfield Holdings), who should have known better, said he was unaware that Walmsley had sold the property to another company in which Walmsley was also involved. Laxton was told by Walmsley that the house had been sold at a profit of $8,000 which, after Walmsley's $3,000 commission, left a net of $5,000, or $2,500 each.

From January 19, 1973 to November 2, 1973, it was sold and resold at least five times. At least four of the transactions were between Silverman-Walmsley companies. The property rose from an initial price of $37,750 to $63,000. Silverman had bought it at $45,000. By February 1974, there were mortgages on it of $59,500. Thus the minimum profit taken out of the place in eight months was $14,500, plus a fee for collecting the rents and the commissions for selling and reselling. And Silverman and Walmsley still owned the house.

Because of the publicity surrounding the revelations of the operations, Walmsley left Fullbrook, Bertram and Brown, going over to Malcolm Boot Realty, where he continued to wheel and deal. In June 1974, he listed the Point Grey Rd. property for sale at *$89,500.*

As Walmsley puts it, 'I'm not a charitable institution.' This is certainly true judging from Walmsley's opulent waterfront home in West Vancouver (5240 Marine Dr.) estimated to be worth $500,000.

This house, on Point Grey Rd. in Kitsilano, was bought and sold five times in ten months. Four of the transactions involved companies related to real estate agents Stanley Silverman and Edward Walmsley. The price was driven up from $37,750 to $63,000. In June 1974 Walmsley had the property up for sale again at a price of $89,500.

And what about the increased rentals necessary to support such inflated prices? In most of the Walmsley-Silverman houses, rents at least doubled over an 18-month period. Many tenants of course had to leave the area, or people had to double up and cram two or three into space suitable for one. The files of the West Broadway Citizens Committee are packed with pathetic stories of people being exploited during the housing crunch. The institution of rent controls and a Landlord Tenant Act which finally gave tenants an even break against their landlords by the NDP government was a direct outcome of the exposure of the Walmsley-Silverman saga. With more stringent controls the whole venture lost its attraction for the Walmsley-Silverman duo, which explains why they later listed their properties on the open market.

3. THE SINGLE-FAMILY ZONE — RS-1

The third type of accommodation in Kitsilano is the single-family housing zone, comprising roughly one-third of the whole residential area of Kitsilano. There are, of course, many single-family homes in the conversion district, and even a few remaining in the apartment district, although most of these are tenant-occupied.

A substantial proportion of single-family homes in the RS-1 zone are owner-occupied. Thus there are many people in the area with a strong commitment to maintaining it, and preserving the area's desirable qualities. These people are a potent opposition to any would-be developers or blockbusters.

Yet the area is vulnerable. Legally, there should be one family to a house. However, for years a substantial number of houses have had a secondary suite — 'illegal' according to the by-laws but known about and tolerated by the city, even given semi-official sanction

over the years. But the city always intended to do something about the problem.

Many of these suites were built during and after the war when accommodation was at a premium and no housing was being built. In 1959, the city undertook a ten-year plan to phase them out. Anything built before 1956 was exempt from the phase-out. Three categories were set up for phasing the others out in 1963, 1968, and 1970. The vast majority were to be phased out in 1970. However, when 1970 rolled around, they received a two-year reprieve to 1972, and after that another two-year extension.

Legalizing the suites meant in fact rezoning to a two-family area. This would result in a crackdown on the suites, requiring that they be brought up to city standards. City council's community development committee held a public meeting on the matter in February 1974. Two distinct points of view were expressed. On the one hand there were those who were opposed to making the suites legal, for example the affluent members of the West Point Grey Civic Association. Making the suites legal, i.e., rezoning, they argued, would be a reversal of city council's established policy of keeping the area as a single-family dwelling neighbourhood. The laws could be relaxed to permit some illegal suites in single-family homes in hardship cases, but as their spokesman argued, 'When the number of these suites rented out by absentee landlords is allowed to increase without restriction, the neighbourhood rapidly deteriorates into a commercial area.'

Opposing this view was the Frog Hollow Information Centre representing the lower-income east side area, which argued that extra suites should be encouraged to help fight the near-zero vacancy rate for rental units. All such suites would be required to meet standards set by the city and enforced by inspectors.

This put the city in a quandary. The way out was to let each area decide for itself in a 'test' plebiscite. Yet the four of the areas in which the test plebiscites were to be held — Kitsilano, Riley Park, Kensington-Cedar Cottage, and Grandview-Woodlands — are areas immediately adjacent to the apartment zones, and presumably the next to go once the existing apartment zones had been totally redeveloped.

Legalizing the illegal suites by rezoning would serve to prepare the area for further upward zoning in the not-too-distant future. Although the regulations might require that only resident owners be allowed to build an extra suite, nothing would prevent the resident owner from selling to an absentee owner. Once the single-family area has been rezoned, property values will rise (because the houses can then bring in more revenue legally). In this fashion, another area is set up for slow but steady redevelopment by real estate interests.

20 Richmond:
Bedroom suburb

Vancouver's vast increase in population over the past 20 years has taken place in the suburbs. While the City of Vancouver proper gained a mere 25% over that 20-year period to reach a population of 425,000, suburban municipalities such as Surrey, Richmond, and North Vancouver district increased by over 300%. The Vancouver metropolitan area as a whole increased by 93%. Although some suburbs developed commercial and industrial activities, the primary function of a community like Richmond was as a bedroom suburb of Vancouver. The growth of Richmond and the other bedroom suburbs has been a direct result of the growth of downtown commercial activity.

Richmond was one of the first suburbs to be opened up after World War II. Its growth reached a frenzied pitch following the construction of the four-lane Oak St. Bridge in 1957 across the north arm of the Fraser River, giving the municipality direct access to downtown Vancouver. Speculation and subdivision construction was rampant in those early days. Subdivision developers would leapfrog over farmers and speculators holding out for higher prices than the developers needed to pay. Thus the typical pattern emerged of tightly-packed subdivisions next to operating farms.

Richmond, mainly comprising Lulu Island, retains its strong agricultural base; to the east and south can be found the larger mixed farms of dairy, potatoes, raspberries, and strawberries; to the north are the remaining truck-garden farms and greenhouses.

The folly of having a solely residential base led the municipal leaders to promote industry in the municipality, and manufacturing is on the increase. B.C. Packers operates a major fish cannery, and Crown Zellerbach Canada, a paper converting plant. Richmond's largest single employer is Vancouver International Airport, with over 5,000 persons on its payroll.

Richmond is focussed on Richmond Square, which contains the main commercial, municipal, and institutional functions. Richmond Square has an interesting history. The area had its beginning in 1864 as part of the 700-acre estate of Samuel Brighouse, one of the 'three greenhorns' who originally settled in the West End of Vancouver.

In 1907, gentleman farmer Brighouse built Minoru Racetrack (named after one of Queen Victoria's racing thoroughbreds). He selected the worst agricultural land on his estate for the racetrack, where the hard clay on a deep peat base was particularly well-suited for a track surface. These soil conditions made it one of the best tracks in Canada.

At about the same time, Brighouse's friends, who owned the B.C. Electric Railway Co., built a line from Vancouver to Steveston on the south side of Lulu Island, running along the edge of Brighouse's property. One of the railway stops was located at the southeast corner of Brighouse's land.

In 1914, the municipal council built its town hall adjacent to the racetrack clubhouse, thus securing the Brighouse site's future; this lessened the importance of both Steveston, a fishing community, and Bridgeport, an old settlement at the south end of the original bridge to Marpole on the mainland.

The Minoru racetrack facilities remained in operation until the late 1950s when the building of the Oak St. Bridge made it desirable for more profitable uses. The land was purchased by real estate tycoon William Zeckendorf and Simpson-Sears for a Richmond shopping centre. The municipality purchased the remaining portion of the Brighouse estate at the same time, and in 1958 the planning department produced a plan designating the Richmond Square area as the only place for regional commercial facilities in the municipality.

The development of Richmond Square paralleled the municipality's greatest spurt of growth. Between 1956 and 1961 the population grew by 65%, from 26,000 to 43,300. After a relative slowdown during the mid-sixties, the population growth took off again towards the end of the decade. It was growing so fast that in the spring of 1971 — with 2,000 dwelling units and 7,000 people predicted for 1971 alone — the Richmond council took the unprecedented step of declaring a 12-month moratorium on comprehensive developments (i.e., developments containing a mixture of housing types, the kind favoured by developers in those days).

The Richmond council did try to institute stringent zoning by-laws — many of the politicians were well-intentioned in that regard because they saw clearly that too much growth would drag down their municipality — but Richmond was just too desirable to the developers. For one thing it was close to downtown. And it was totally flat, without any large trees or rocks, making construction relatively inexpensive. Until the recent past, land values had been low and the land was already in large parcels making assembly easy.

The pressures on Richmond are continuing to increase. In 1974 and 1975, two more bridges from Richmond to Vancouver were under construction, and these put great pressure on the municipality for further development. By 1973, Richmond's population was expanding at an alarming rate, and the planners expected it to double to 120,000 by 1986, in less than 15 years.

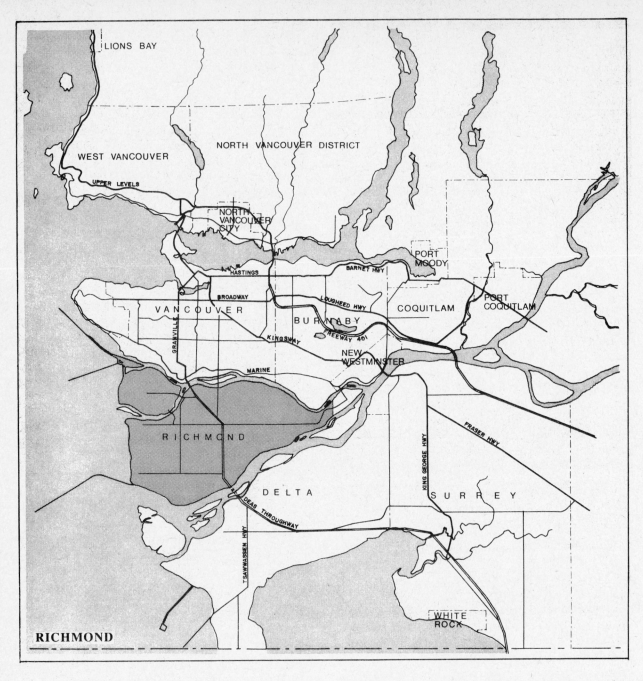

RICHMOND

The fact that Richmond lies in the Fraser River delta and is subject to flooding, especially during the spring run-off, meant that the whole of Lulu Island had to be surrounded by a system of dykes which need continual monitoring and upgrading. Rainwater run-off and sewerage and drainage are also critical problems. These were factors that should have produced a more cautious approach to development. One event did, however, disrupt the pattern of steady development. That was the passage, in 1973, of the NDP government's Land Commission Act, which put a freeze on the conversion of agricultural land to urban uses. The freeze was to stay in effect until each regional district, in this case the Greater Vancouver Regional

District, had prepared and approved a plan designating agricultural reserve land. This was important in Richmond because of the large amount of agricultural land — over one-quarter of the total area — in the municipality.

The land act generated enormous opposition — charges of communism were bandied about — much of it coming from the Richmond area. Harold Steves, the NDP MLA, showed that the source of much of it was local real estate companies and developers rather than farmers.

Although much of Richmond's agricultural land was saved, it was almost too late. The best agricultural land is on the west side of the island, and that had

Industrial development next to an old farm in Richmond.

Two new bridges linking Richmond to Vancouver — the Knight St. bridge (top) and the Hudson St. bridge (bottom) — guarantee that Richmond will continue to experience rapid population growth and continued rampant development.

A typical upper-income residential subdivision in Richmond.

already been zoned for residential and industrial uses.

A development-hungry council can always find ways of circumventing the requirements of the land act. In mid-1974, Nu-West Development Corp.,one of the biggest developers in western Canada, got its hands on 160 acres of agricultural land on the south side of the island. The land had been used as a vegetable farm. Nu-West applied for, and got, from the Richmond council, rezoning of the land to industrial uses. A petition signed by 9,000 persons protesting the planned rezoning was presented to the provincial government. The province requested council to reconsider its decision, but this request was rejected. As a result, the chairman of the council's advisory planning committee, which had also recommended rejection of the rezoning, resigned from his position. Clearly, as in this case, the best of plans and intentions — to save agricultural land — is not enough to offset an alliance of developers and politicians.

Similar special consideration was usually given to the residential developers who did the bulk of the developing and building in Richmond. At first, only single-family homes were allowed, following a standard subdivision layout: arterial roads around the perimeter, interior crescents, a school in the middle. This large-scale layout reflected the relatively simple process of land assembly where the developer acquired up to a quarter-section from the farmer or speculator.

Richmond officials soon came to recognize the costs inherent in such wide-open leapfrogging development — the building of roads and sewers through sparsely-settled areas being the major ones. In the early 1960s multiple-family dwellings made their appearance in the municipality. At first only three-storey apartments and townhouses were allowed. Soon pressure for higher density development led to the appearance of high-rises in Richmond. The first project was built by Block Bros. in 1968, four 15-storey towers containing 60 units each. Because Richmond is delta land, the soil was inappropriate for heavyweight construction. Even though lightweight thin-wall construction techniques were developed, the municipality eventually restricted building heights to seven storeys.

Yet, with the appearance of multiple-family

dwellings in the municipality, one of the major reasons for moving to Richmond in the first place — the desire to acquire a single-family house in a semi-rural setting — began to disappear. Ironically, in the midst of open farmland, were crowded, cramped conditions as bad as anything to be found in the heart of the city. Sharon Gardens, 70 townhouses and 66 suites in a three-storey apartment crammed onto a 5.6 acre site, resulting in a density of 24 units per acre, was a typical example. Each townhouse was allocated a postage stamp-sized yard surrounded by high fences, and the whole complex was ringed with parking. For this project, builder Erick Ramage received an award from the Canadian Housing Design Council.

At the present, roughly three times as many multiple-family dwellings are being built in Richmond as single-family houses. Yet time and time again high- and medium-density developments have evoked a hostile reaction from many Richmond residents. After all, they had moved out to Richmond to escape the crowded city conditions and now they were being faced with them out in the suburbs. Some development issues have been hot indeed.

But Richmond residents have had little success in combatting the interests of the real estate industry anxious to develop the municipality as quickly as possible, and as densely as possible in order to maximize their profits on their land. It was real estate developers who built up Richmond in co-operation with local politicians in the first place, and against this powerful combination the people who now live in Richmond have had little success in slowing down the rapid growth of their bedroom suburb.

21 Who is responsible for the housing crisis? CMHC

As housing prices and rents have risen out of control, as vacancy rates come close to zero and new construction slows down, and as the housing crisis becomes a constant fact of life in Canada, the question of who is responsible has been answered many different ways by different people. Federal politicians blame the desire of Canadians to move to big cities, and to have a real house with a garden and not a tiny high-rise apartment when they get there. Developers blame politicians and bureaucrats for their 'red tape' and their 'regulations' that prevent developers from building more houses and reducing their prices. Municipal politicians who are friends of the development industry often blame citizen groups for objecting to growth and trying to hold up needed new construction.

The truth of the matter is that the high prices, the low quality, and the short supply of urban housing are the collective responsibility of all the financial and business interests and the government agencies who together control the housing business in Canada. Each of them, from the federal government and its housing agency, Central Mortgage and Housing Corp. (CMHC) to the massive development and construction companies like Daon Development Corp. and Genstar, plays its part in creating the constant housing crisis which Vancouver residents and most Canadians constantly face. They all co-operate with each other in creating this crisis because it is immensely profitable to all the businesses involved, and because the politicians and government officials are directly tied into the housing industry.

So the answer to the question 'Who is responsible for the housing crisis?' is 'Everyone who is now involved in the housing business.' In the remaining chapters of this part, we identify the responsible parties one by one, starting in this chapter with CMHC, the federal government agency responsible for administering federal housing policy.

By any standard, CMHC is a housing and financial giant. It has been involved, directly or indirectly, with 35% of all new house funding in Canada since 1960. By 1973 its assets had swollen to $6.6 billion, making it almost as large as the chartered banks. Its budget for 1973 was $1 billion and for 1974 was over $1.5 billion.

What does CMHC do with all this money?

CMHC has had two major policies. Since the economic slowdown of the late fifties, the government has used housing as a means of stabilizing the economy by regulating the number of housing units built each year.

When the economy was sluggish CMHC would lower the interest rate on mortgage loans. This would stimulate developers to build more houses. When the economy heated up, it would raise interest rates and hence slow down the rate of new house construction. Neither of these actions had anything to do with the need for housing.

Furthermore, CMHC was not concerned with the price of the housing being produced, nor did it care about the level of profits achieved by the developers who used its money.

CMHC's second major policy was to step in directly wherever private industry was not doing the job. This was mainly in the low-income housing area, and private industry was not building low-income housing quite simply because there wasn't enough profit in it. What CMHC would do was to make it profitable enough for the developers by pouring in subsidies and incentives, at all costs to keep housing production tightly in the grasp of the private sector.

CMHC has always had smooth and easy relations with the developers. Key personnel from CMHC move out into the industry; developer and bureaucrat understand what the other wants and act accordingly. For example:

David Mansur, ex-president of CMHC, is now president of Kinross Mortgage Corp. a subsidiary of the Canadian Imperial Bank of Commerce and a rival source of mortgage funds. CMHC transacts much of its business locally with Kinross.

Campeau Corp., one of Canada's largest real estate companies, began to move only after Jean Paradis left his job at CMHC where he was administering federal funds being lent to developers, and moved over to Campeau, where he worked at getting those same funds for Campeau projects. After eight years with CMHC, Paradis knew all the ins and outs of the system. Campeau might have prospered enormously anyway, but with Paradis getting the money, everything was much easier.

There are other connections between CMHC and Campeau Corp. through Louis deG. Giguere, a Liberal senator in Ottawa, a vice-president of Campeau, and for many years a director of CMHC.

In August 1973, CMHC got a new president — William Teron, head of a $200 million real estate and financial empire, previously affiliated with Campeau Corp. and with very close ties to the Liberal party. Teron performed a valuable service for the Liberal government in 1972 by getting his hands on a piece of Toronto waterfront property which was then grandiosely donated to the city for a park. The Liberal government with its once-solid Toronto base threatened was able to use this as an election goodie.

Herb Hignett, president of CMHC before Teron, left it to become director of Beacon Hill Lodges of Canada which builds and operates nursing homes for senior citizens using CMHC money. Beacon Hill Lodges of Canada is a subsidiary of Imperial Ventures, one of the largest Vancouver developers, responsible for a blockbusting high-rise in Kitsilano.

It should therefore come as no surprise to anyone that CMHC has maintained abnormally friendly relations with developers and builders over the years. Senior CMHC officials consult regularly with HUDAC (Housing and Urban Development Association of Canada) and the Urban Development Institute (UDI), the two chief lobbies of builders and developers in Canada.

For many years, the main activity of CMHC was to insure loans made by banks and life insurance companies on new and existing houses, to make this type of investment more secure and attractive for the lenders. If the person who bought the house defaulted on his payments, CMHC would guarantee the rest of the loan. In this way the government took the risk. and the bank made the profits — a cosy relationship.

A second major activity for CMHC was to make direct loans to home buyers where private lenders wouldn't, because it was not worth their while. The major lenders concentrated their activities in the large urban centres because it was more profitable. The result was that someone who lived in a small town, in a rural area, or in the north, would not be able to get financing for a house. CMHC stepped in here. This function increased over the years as the financial institutions concentrated on the high-growth high profit areas, leaving the hinterland to the government.

Yet in 1973, both of CMHC's major programs declined drastically, the first by over 20%, the second to less than one-sixth of its 1972 level, simply because so few Canadians could afford to buy houses on the open market.

Until 1970 over 80% of all government funds used in its housing programs went to middle- and upper-income groups, those who needed it least. Less than 20% went into low-income housing. And even this tiny amount was spent in ways which ensured that low-income housing was a profitable activity for private developers. In the past four years CMHC has become involved in bankrolling low-income housing for the simple reason that with soaring housing costs, fewer and fewer Canadians could qualify for a CMHC mortgage.

CMHC has also had an 'urban renewal' program which demolished useful buildings, destroyed neighbourhoods, and created blockbusting monoliths. CMHC's interest here was to add as many new housing units per year to the record, not to provide needed housing. Single-family, often resident-owned houses were torn down by the thousands and replaced with more profitable bachelor and one- and two- bedroom rental units.

Eventually the recipients of the government's handouts caught on to what was being done to their neighbourhoods, and due partly to the efforts of groups such as Vancouver' Strathcona Property Owners and Tenants Association (SPOTA) and partly to the skyrocketing costs of the program, the whole thing was scrapped in 1969.

In between the low-income groups and the decreasing number of people who could afford CMHC's mortgage rates, has been a group of programs aimed at people making between $5,000 and $8,000. These were called 'limited dividend' (i.e., limited profit). The profit which the developer was to receive was supposed to be limited, but there were many loopholes in the programs.

One of the most favoured dodges involved a 90% low-interest loan provided by CMHC for the cost of construction. (The developer was supposed to put up the other 10%). However, the developer would purposely over-estimate the cost of the building when applying for the loan, so that he was able to build the whole project using the 90% loan, and not have to put up any of his own money. In the business, this well-known practice is termed 'mortgaging out'. The developer would pay back the loan out of the rents from his tenants and in 15 years he would end up owning the building, never having put a cent of his own money into it.

There were several other ruses used by the developer. If he had a piece of property he couldn't develop profitably, say, because it was next door to a

William Teron:

William Teron, the current president of Central Mortgage and Housing Corp., had made his first million dollars in real estate by the time he was 25. By the time of his CMHC appointment in July 1973, Teron had moved on from real estate to more diversified financial and political activities.

Teron was born in Winnipeg in 1932. He was trained as a draftsman, and arrived in Ottawa in 1949 to take a $100-a-week job with the federal government. After six weeks, he joined a construction firm specializing in expensive custom houses.

In 1955 he started a company with $412 of his own money. Though he had originally intended only to design houses, he soon found builders getting $40,000 for houses he knew he could build for $25,000. So he went into the construction business, and by the fifth year he was grossing $5-million annually.

In 1959, 30 Ottawa speculators pooled $25,000 each to buy a five square mile tract of land just outside Ottawa's built-up area. Teron was one of the 30, and later he bought out all the other partners. He went on to build a suburb he named Kanata.

In 1967 Teron sold his company and Kanata to Canadian Interurban Properties Ltd., a subsidiary of Power Corp. In 1971 Teron joined up with Liberal Senator Paul Martin and Paul Nathanson to buy control of St. Maurice Gas Co., whose name they changed to St. Maurice Capital Corp. The newly organized company then bought control of General Mortgage Corp. of Canada. By 1972 majority shareholders in St. Maurice Capital included Teron, a family trust of Paul Martin (whose son is now a Power Corp. vice-president) and Maurice F. Strong, a former president of Power Corp. and currently an international civil servant.

St. Maurice's activities were in the real estate and financial services field. It owns 63.9% of Farmers & Merchants Trust Co., headquartered in Calgary, 86.9% of General Mortgage Corporation of Canada, and it has a wholly-owned subsidiary St. Maurice Properties Ltd. which in 1972 was working on eight shopping centres in Western Canada, including a 141-acre project in Winnipeg.

In 1972, St. Maurice president J.B. Whiteley was saying that though ownership

meat-packing plant, he could build limited-dividend housing on it. Or if his normal business was slack, he could cover his overhead by building some limited-dividend projects.

CMHC didn't concern itself with the way the developer managed the building or how he selected his tenants. He could evict welfare recipients, or large families, or Indians, or whomever he liked. He would then go to CMHC and complain about having a high vacancy rate and not being able to meet the mortgage payments. CMHC would then let him increase the rents. He would then go out and fill all the vacancies at the higher rents. Several years ago a study was done of CMHC's housing practices and programs. The report

An example of what CMHC considers to be urban renewal — Maclean Park, in Vancouver's east end.

was so damning that CMHC suppressed it. The authors, Michael Dennis and Susan Fish, had to publish the report on their own under the title *Programs in Search of a Policy.*

Faced with a worsening situation, in 1970 CMHC instituted a $200 million 'innovative low-income housing program.' The purpose of the program was to *entice* builders and developers to experiment with low-income housing forms in the hope of arriving at some magical formulas. This program turned out to be even a bigger rip-off. As one observer put it, 'the only thing innovative about innovative housing is the profit.' A study done of this program was also suppressed by CMHC.

That report, undertaken by architect Melvin Charney of the University of Montreal, examined 22 low-income developments, 11 of which came under the 'innovative housing program'. Charney found dilapidated developments: cheap materials, poor finishing, falling plaster, cramped space, lack of landscaping, no recreation areas. Furthermore the units were expensive — not at all low-income housing.

One of the projects Melvin Charney studied was in Vancouver — Champlain Heights, in the southeast section of the city, developed by Dawson Developments (now Daon Development Corp.). The scheme put forward by Dawson was exactly similar to one it was developing in Burnaby. That is, it was hardly innovative and should not have qualified for the low-interest loan. Charney estimated that one would need an income of at least $9,000 per year to afford to live there. It was hardly low-income.

Because of the scandal surrounding the program — only 14,000 units were produced and eight large firms received most of the money — the program was scrapped in 1971.

In 1972 CMHC was back with a new set of programs. With a great deal of publicity and fanfare, then newly-appointed minister of urban affairs Ron Basford introduced a set of amendments to the National Housing Act. This time Ottawa was really going to lick the low-income housing problem. Basford mentioned that a sum of $457 million would be available. However, it took until June 1973 before these amendments were passed by the government. And a closer look at exactly how much was involved shows that the amendments weren't all that Basford made them out to be.

The largest portion of the amount went into an Assisted Home Ownership Program which, in fact, had already existed for two years, so it was not new. The program provided mortgage loans at an interest rate somewhat below the current sky-high levels. The program was intended to help lower-income families to purchase a home. Gross family income had to be between $6,000 and $11,000. But there were severe restrictions on the maximum price allowed. For a family earning $7,500 per year with two children, the maximum house price allowed was $24,500 (The average house in Vancouver cost $40,000 in 1974). By the end of 1973, CMHC had pumped $130 million into the program, helping to purchase a mere 6,900 houses, when total housing production for the year was 268,000 units.

The next major portion of the money went into public non-profit, and private lower-income rental housing schemes: $200 million in low-interest loans provided 14,114 public housing units; and an additional $51 million went into federal-provincial cost-sharing projects to provide an additional 3,300 units. CMHC also provided $68.5 million in subsidies to cover operating deficits. CMHC loaned $70 million to private developers to build low-rental housing, and $95 million to non-profit groups for the same purpose. However, the housing provided under these last two categories was well beyond the means of senior citizens receiving the provincial government mincome (minimum income benefits) — those who need the housing most desperately.

In total, CMHC's low-income programs helped produce roughly 30,000 units out of a total production of 268,000 in 1973, or 12% of total housing units produced — a figure which could hardly make a dent in the backlog of housing needs.

Two other CMHC programs received a great deal of publicity — the Neighbourhood Improvement Program, and the Residential Rehabilitation Assistance Program (NIP and RRAP) — but a close examination shows them to be more promotion than substance.

These programs were developed to replace the urban renewal programs — the bulldozer approach — which had been scrapped in 1969. They had two aims: 1) to upgrade existing housing in older, 'run-down' neighbourhoods; and 2) to delegate decision-making to the residents of such areas.

In Vancouver the second aim was subverted even before the program got underway. Perhaps the most crucial factor was in deciding which areas of Vancouver should be eligible for rehabilitation and improvement. This was done by city planners and bureaucrats, in many cases going against the wishes of citizen groups and non-city planners. Fairview, for example, was an area in very poor condition, and area residents were extremely anxious to have the area designated for rehabilitation. But this would have gotten in the way of the city's plans that Fairview be redeveloped. Grandview-Woodlands and Hastings

East were also by-passed.

Eventually, the city designated two areas, Kitsilano and Cedar Cottage, as NIP areas and allocated a total of $3 million to the two areas, an amount so small that it could have no serious effect. Assuming, for example, that all the money was used to buy land in the two areas, $3 million could purchase 50 to 60 lots out of a total of over 10,000 separate residential buildings.

Moreover, there were serious inadequacies in the methods used by the city planners in determining 'run-down' areas. For one thing, they relied heavily on the so-called 'windshield survey', where the planners drive around in their cars and take a quick look at the buildings as they drive by. The danger with this method is that a planner might have a preconceived idea about which areas he'd like to see rehabilitated and this could affect his judgment. As it turned out, the areas selected also had to be tied in with the city's local area planning programs. Kitsilano happened to have one these programs in action, even though it may not have been the area most in need of consideration.

Once Kitsilano had been selected, area residents did have some input in determining how the money should be spent, but the final decision remained with city council, even though it was putting up little of the money.

The second program, RRAP, provided a measly $28 million in 1973. Under its terms, low-interest loans and grants up to $5,000 are made to resident home owners and landlords to improve their houses. At $5,000 per unit, $28 million would provide funds to fix up a mere 5,600 units across Canada — hardly making a dent in the problem. Moreover, there is little control over landlords who might raise their rents after making the renovations, or over resident owners who might sell at a profit.

It is clear that both programs are window dressing, and their real purpose is to defuse public hostility to the lack of real government action in preserving and maintaining the existing residential neighbourhoods, which after all make up the bulk of our cities.

The evidence is overwhelming that CMHC has failed in every way possible to provide adequate low-cost shelter to the large number of Canadians who desperately need it.

CMHC is in fact a monolithic bureaucracy, centralized in Ottawa under the thumb of the minister responsible and CMHC's president.

A bunch of old boys run the show. Except for William Teron, every senior CMHC executive has risen through the ranks. Many of them joined CMHC when it was first formed in 1946 and they have just floated to the surface.

The minister approves each low-income project individually on a political basis. Instead of paying attention to local regional differences, one uniform set of housing standards applies all across Canada. This means that a senior citizens' housing project in rural Prince Edward Island must meet the same standards of planning and construction as one in the West End of Vancouver It is an absurd situation.

The local CMHC architects and planners, the ones who might know something about local conditions, do not have final say in approving designs. That is all done in Ottawa.

And the users of CMHC's projects are totally excluded from any say in the design. In 1974, Walter Rudnicki, a senior CMHC executive, was fired by Teron. He had been told to work closely with Indian groups in developing satisfactory housing programs. He did his job too well, and tried to involve the Indians directly in the decision-making process. He was quickly sacked.

Faced with a structure that was becoming unresponsive even to the demands of developers and house-builders, the directors of CMHC in 1973 undertook to reorganize the corporation. According to the 1973 annual report:

The basic objectives of the reorganization are: to decentralize more authority and resources to the field offices so that they may better meet housing and community development needs and to provide, through Head Office, co-ordination of activities and distribution on a national basis; to strengthen the planning function; to anticipate and adapt to changing needs; to organize for the delivery of programs on the basis of program objectives.

However, given the past record of CMHC — its monolithic bureaucratic make-up; its cosy relationships with private developers, its view of low-income housing as so many new 'starts' for the year, with the money it provides for these low-income programs somehow ending up in the developer's pocket, it is hard to believe that these changes are anything more than another attempt at window dressing.

What is required is not a token restructuring, but a total decentralization of all housing functions to local levels — provincial or municipal if necessary, but preferably to the community level. The federal government should pass the money it takes in from taxes directly back to the communities who are qualified to determine their priorities and to allocate the funds to the various housing needs.

22 Who is responsible for the housing crisis? The province

Under the provisions of the British North America Act, the provinces have jurisdiction over property rights and municipal matters. Thus the provincial government is intimately involved in the urban housing crisis. For years the rurally-dominated Social Credit government of British Columbia took little interest in the problems of the cities — especially Vancouver — or in the housing problems of the poor and lower-income groups, preferring to leave it all up to Central Mortgage and Housing Corp.

In 1967, the British Columbia Housing Management Commission (BCMHC) was established to manage the public housing projects in B.C. In effect, this meant Vancouver since it was the only place where there was any public housing. Up to this time, public housing had been managed by the Vancouver Housing Association, a local, politically-appointed body whose members didn't necessarily know anything about housing.

The idea of the BCMHC was to replace the political appointees with knowledgeable bureaucrats. It was composed of two representatives from the provincial government, two from CMHC, and one from the local municipality involved, i.e., Vancouver. The main purpose of the commission was to use the existing CMHC programs as effectively as possible — to get as much federal money as they could.

In reality the BCMHC did very little. For one thing it relied on the local municipality to initiate projects. Normally a municipality tied in its public housing projects with its urban renewal schemes, to house the people displaced by the redevelopment. Decisions about public housing had little to do with the need for low-cost housing accommodation. To the end of 1970, 3,500 units had been built in B.C., most of them connected to urban renewal schemes where the residents' homes had been demolished to make way for redevelopment. The City of Vancouver had never undertaken a long-range study of public housing needs.

BCMHC also relied on a distant CMHC head office in Ottawa for public housing approvals. This inevitably led to a string of poor projects and lengthy delays. A senior citizen high-rise project under construction in 1975 in Vancouver's West End took over six years from the time it was first initiated until the beginning of construction. In the process the design concept was watered down so badly that the accommodation ultimately provided will barely meet minimal standards.

In 1971, the responsibility for public housing was delegated to the Greater Vancouver Regional District.

The only other provincial government involvement during the Socred years were a Homeowner's Grant — designed to remove a portion of the municipal tax load from property — and a system of low-interest second mortgages to make home acquisition easier.

When the New Democratic Party came to power in 1972 there had to be some change — the vacuum couldn't continue. Adequate housing for all members of society was one of the key NDP policies. One of the first acts of the new government was to put a freeze on further development of agricultural land throughout the province and the establishment of the B.C. land commission to oversee the process of designating permanent agricultural reserves. Each regional district in the province — there are 28 — had to produce a plan which set aside agricultural land, greenbelt land around urban areas, land banks, and park lands. By the end of 1974, many of these had been approved by the land commission and the provincial government, leading to permanent agricultural zoning.

The NDP's housing initiatives were not as quick in coming. In mid-1973, MLA Lorne Nicolson was appointed acting minister responsible for housing. In November, a full department of housing was set up with Nicolson as minister, a kitty of $10 million, and the power to establish corporations to develop housing programs.

Nicolson took his first step in early 1974 when the provincial government bought out a private developer — Dunhill Development Corp. — active in building luxury condominiums in North Vancouver and other locations in the lower mainland. The company had assets of roughly $12 million, including a small land bank. Part of the deal was that the existing management team would continue on under contract for two years. In theory the idea was a good one — the only other alternative was to build up management from scratch, a process that could take years. But in practice it did present problems.

The Dunhill managers were typical developers, more than typical if anything, out to make as large a profit as possible on their operations. The company had been known as United Provincial Investments until 1971 when it was taken over by the present managers led by Werner K. Paulus. There had been considerable controversy surrounding the take-over — the question being whether the minority shareholders received a fair deal. When Paulus and his associates sold out to the provincial government, they made a substantial profit on the transaction.

Dunhill continued its development activities as a crown corporation. Nicolson, minister of lands and forests Bob Williams, and Vancouver city council housing committee chairman Mike Harcourt were appointed directors of the corporation, but they did allow Dunhill to continue with some deals already underway. One of these, in which Dunhill reaped substantial speculative profits, did not make the NDP look very good. The transaction involved 50 acres of land in Richmond which Dunhill had bought in October 1972 for $915,000, got rezoned for medium-density residential development, then sold to another developer in March 1974 for $1.8 million — a 100% profit in 18 months without undertaking any development whatsoever.

While negotiations to take over Dunhill Development Corp. were underway, Nicolson was building up his department of housing. George Chatterton, former Progressive Conservative MP for Esquimalt-Saanich, and former chairman of the ineffectual BCMHC (1971-72), was appointed deputy minister of the department in February. John Northey, a Port Moody alderman and also a planner for the Vancouver city planning department, was hired as housing 'expediter' to speed up the delivery of housing in the lower mainland.

Along with an expanded staff, the department of housing got a budget of $75.6 million for 1974. An additional $25 million was to be pumped into mortgages, providing for about 1,000 mortgages in the first year for homes built on leased crown land — none of this would go into the lower mainland where the need was the greatest. Another $15 million was to be available as low-interest loans to allow people to convert their single-family homes into duplexes. With a maximum loan of $5,000, this would provide for roughly 3,000 conversions. However, by the end of the year, only 15 conversions had been approved. The problem was that the conversions normally required municipal rezoning, and the municipalities were moving slowly on this potentially explosive issue.

The bulk of the budget — $50 million — was to go for the assembly and servicing of land for a grab-bag of programs: 2,500 family rental units, 1,000 senior citizen rental units, 1,500 building lots for co-operatives, 2,000 building lots for family housing, as well as additional money for land assembly, neighbourhood improvement programs, and grants.

Under the plan, Dunhill Development Corp. would plan and develop, acquire land, and buy projects under construction by other developers. For example, in mid-June the provincial government bought a 127-unit condominium project in Surrey from Nu-West Development Corp. for $4,725,000 ($37,200 per unit). Nicolson's idea was that the actual building would be done by private developers. As an extension of this, in May 1974 he announced a

This project in Surrey was purchased by the B.C. provincial government from Nu-West Development Corp. and then rented by the B.C. Housing Management Commission.

'proposal call' program, in which developers would make proposals for projects on their own land. The government, selecting the ones it wanted, would then buy them on completion and rent them to a range of income groups.

Another step in the evolving strategy was to re-activate BCMHC. A new chairman, David Davies, from the Ontario Housing Commission, was appointed. This was tied to the plan to move into rental housing in a much larger way. BCMHC would own and manage all the rental units bought by the provincial government for a wide range of income groups — none of the government housing projects would be identifiable as 'public housing'.

The provincial government's most explosive action was the imposition in 1974 of controls on allowable rent increases in rental units. At first the ceiling was established at 8% in any 12 month period; this was later increased to 10.6%. Landlords, of course, felt this was far too low, tenants felt this was too high. There were a number of loopholes which exempted rental accommodation from the controls. All new units were exempt for a five-year period, as were duplexes, or conversion houses containing three suites or less.

As well as the exemptions provided for them by the government, landlords discovered a whole series of tactics to avoid the controls by converting existing buildings to apartment hotels where rent is paid on a weekly basis, to condominium ownership where the tenant must buy his suite, or to 99-year leases, where the tenant in effect buys his tenancy. A wholesale conversion of apartment buildings has been under way in Vancouver since the rent controls came into effect.

Rent controls were part of a new landlord and tenant act that went into effect in October 1974. The main thrust of that legislation was to remove rental disputes from the jurisdiction of the provincial small claims court, and put them in the hands of a rentals-man. The rentalsman would try to mediate disputes arising from the legislation and arrive at a mutually

When the B.C. provincial government enacted a revamped landlord and tenant act former Liberal MLA and radio hot-line host Barry Clarke was appointed to the new office of rentalsman to arbitrate landlord-tenant disputes.

satisfactory solution. Failing that, he had the power to make a binding decision which then could be appealed to the county court, a lengthy and costly procedure for tenants.

The major reform of the legislation was to require the landlord to give 'just cause' for eviction; these are spelled out in the act. For example, the landlord must give four months notice and pay the tenant $300 if he wishes to demolish his building. However, there is no provision for the policing of the act. No one is there to ascertain whether the landlord did, in fact, demolish the building, or if he just rented it out to someone else at a much higher rent.

A landlord can evict a tenant if the landlord requires the suite for use by his family. Some ludicrous situations have arisen in which landlords, living in their large Shaughnessy mansions say they must evict tenants from their run-down house in Kitsilano so that

Landlords threaten strike action

the landlord's family can move in. But it's perfectly legal under the landlord and tenant act, and no one ever checks up to verify if the landlord's family did move in.

In summary, the provincial government seemed to have many good ideas and intentions about the housing crisis. But in 1974, at least, its programs were minimal. As pointed out, the duplexing scheme has not worked because of the need for rezoning and control. The $40 million for mortgages was no more than a drop in the bucket — perhaps 5% of the total mortgage funding in 1974. The $50 million for land assembly was also more of a token than any substantial action. Nor was any of this money to be spent in inner urban areas where land costs were higher, but the need was greatest. One of the major problems with public housing is that provincial housing corporations such as the Ontario Housing Commission often become more bureaucratic and less responsive to the needs of the tenants than private owners. BCMHC seemed in danger of becoming such an organization. And use of private developer Dunhill has exposed the government to charges of exhibiting all the worst excesses of such practices — the speculation, environmental destruction, and lack of concern for surrounding residents.

While the change in provincial government did bring about a change in attitude toward housing, there was still no dramatic effective action to break through the housing industry's control of the housing business to bring down prices and provide a much-needed supply of low-cost accommodation.

Landlord spokesman accused of violations

Chief B.C. landlord spokesman Richard Dolman has violated the law four times in dealings with tenants at a house he owns, the B.C. Tenants' Organization charged Wednesday.

The charge was made by BCTO, president Bruce Yorke who produced documents and an affidavit from the current tenants of the house at 2710 Waterloo, which he said supported the allegations.

In a prepared statement and an interview Dolman, executive director of the B.C. Rental Housing Council, did not deny the charges but said he is contemplating legal action against Yorke.

At a press conference and in a later interview, Yorke charged:

That Dolman raised the rent on the four-bedroom house from $360 to $400 a month in April 1974, contrary to the eight-per-cent rent ceiling then in effect;

That he failed to give the tenants the required three months' notice at that time and that in any case the increase was invalid since the tenants had not lived there for a full year;

That Dolman illegally increased the rent to $450 in October when the current tenants moved in, and gave notice of a further illegal $30 increase to take effect in six months;

That Dolman charged the current tenants an illegal $225 security deposit.

Throughout his period as rental housing spokesman, Yorke said Dolman has claimed landlords do not want to violate the law.

He said he will meet Attorney-General Alex Macdonald in Victoria today and ask him to have Dolman prosecuted for violation of the landlord-tenant laws.

23 Who is responsible for the housing crisis? The Greater Vancouver Regional District

Despite attempts to publicize itself, the Greater Vancouver Regional District remains a shadowy little-known body. Yet the GVRD is assuming an increasing importance in affairs that affect everyone in the lower mainland: hospitals, regional parks, sewers, water supply, and most important for us in this book, planning and public housing.

Yet, for its first six years the GVRD was not directly accountable to the voters of the region. The aldermen and mayors appointed each other. The members of the GVRD are the municipalities of the Vancouver region, every 20,000 people in the lower mainland being represented on the GVRD board by one vote. Currently there are 22 directors who divide up 61 votes among them. Mayor Art Phillips of the City of Vancouver, for example, has five votes. In other words he represents 100,000 people who had no say in electing him to this job.

In 1974, for the first time, representatives to the GVRD were elected by the voters during the municipal elections. But only those who were elected to municipal council as well could serve on the GVRD. Thus the directors of the GVRD are the same people as the municipal aldermen and mayors, with their same friendly relations with private developers.

There was thus some minimal compromise towards the principle of direct representation but GVRD politicians still have no constituency to whom they are accountable. Thus there is little pressure from citizens on the politicians to take any specific actions. For the members of the GVRD, municipal priorities come first because that is where their constituency lies.

The formation of the GVRD represented the victory of municipal and provincial interests over regional concerns. Until 1968 regional planning was under the control of the Lower Mainland Regional Planning Board (LMRPB) which, as its name suggests, was responsible for the planning of the whole Fraser valley area. It did a good job, preparing an overall plan that attempted to deal with severe problems of growth and development.

The LMRPB's chief planner had opposed the provincial government over the establishment of the Roberts Bank superport since it went against everything in the plan. For one thing it meant the loss of 10,000 acres of high quality farmland. Socred Premier Wacky Bennett simply abolished the LMRPB. He was strongly supported by the municipalities. NDP MLA Bob Williams, a former Vancouver city alderman, charged that city commissioner Gerald Sutton-Brown had helped to axe the LMRPB.

In its place, the province set up four regional districts completely under the thumb of the local politicians. The GVRD is one of these. The first chairman of the GVRD (1967-69) was Vancouver Non-Partisan Association (NPA) alderman Earle Adams, one of the strongest pro-development members of Vancouver city council. He was succeeded in 1970 by North Vancouver district mayor Ron Andrews, another old-style pro-developer politician. In fact, in 1971 when Andrews was re-elected, he had been nominated by the Bowen Island representative on the GVRD, Graham Budge, also the island's largest realtor.

Provincial minister of municipal affairs Dan Campbell, the Socred cabinet minister responsible for setting up the regional districts, was careful to point out that the GVRD would not become a fourth level of government. This would have led to a diminution of local politicians' power, something they are always against. To guard against this happening the GVRD was not given any direct taxing power. It must get its money from the member municipalities, or it can issue bonds to raise funds for capital expenditures.

The members of the GVRD themselves determine what functions to take over by a two-thirds vote and provincial government approval. To date, the GVRD has assumed responsibility for regional parks, public housing, hospital planning, regional planning, sewage disposal, water supply and distribution, air pollution control, and municipal labour relations. As well, the GVRD participates in regional transportation planning.

One of the first functions that the GVRD assumed was regional planning which it took over from the dismantled Lower Mainland Regional Planning Board. At the time of the takeover, an Official Regional Plan was in effect which designated all land in the region — some 360,000 acres or 560 square miles — as urban, rural, industrial, park, and reserve. The plan is still in effect. For example, amendments to rezone waterfront land from industrial to urban uses must be approved by the GVRD board. Applications for amendment can only come from the municipal councils who have already approved the proposed change, not from developers. Once approved, control goes back to the municipality. The planning department could plan, but it had no power to enforce.

One of the GVRD planning department's most highly touted efforts was the 'Livable Region Program' established in 1971 'to manage growth and change so as to maintain or enhance the livability of the region.' It was to be a showpiece of citizens' input into the planning process — establishing goals for the region, undertaking technical studies with the help of staff, formulating policies and, finally, producing a plan for the region.

Things began to go wrong even before the program got underway. The terms of reference for the program were set by the politicians. Here is how the citizens were to consider the critical question of growth: 'The Lower Mainland region contains 54% of British Columbia's population. In the last five years the population of Greater Vancouver increased by 13.5%. *'How can we use growth to achieve quality?'* On the basis of these already-biased terms of reference, the planners asked for public response, and by late 1972, the GVRD politicians had endorsed a series of policy statements which were then allocated among nine policy committees of 'concerned citizens', such as transportation and transmission, residential living, and environmental management and pollution control. But the citizens on the committees had to be *nominated* by federal, provincial, and municipal politicians and bureaucrats or by recognised public groups. Room was allowed on the committees for any stragglers that may have happened along, but a large proportion of each committee was composed of professionals and others with a vested interest in the field. The residential living policy committee, for example, was made up of architects and planners, and the chairman of the committee was a real estate agent. Also the terms of reference for each committee were set in advance by the politicians to ensure that the committee's discussions would not get too far off the desired track.

The reports of all committees were completed within eight months and went to the GVRD board. Because it was a rush job, because of the make-up of the committees, the recommendations put forward were hardly revolutionary.

The residential living policy committee recommended that 'action to come to grips with the housing crisis must commence immediately;' that 'land cost should not be the deciding factor in selecting a site for a senior citizens housing project;' and that people should be subsidized directly by rental supplements, assisted home ownership programs, or a guaranteed annual income.'

The reports, however fatuous, seem to have been conveniently forgotten at this point. The next step in the 'public participation' program was a one-day seminar held in February 1974. Of the 100 people in attendance, the overwhelming majority were politicians and bureaucrats plus a few members of the policy committees.

The process of watering down continued. This seminar produced four 'key principles'. The one on overall growth was: 'The GVRD is concerned about

GREATER VANCOUVER
REGIONAL DISTRICT
NEWSLETTER

return requested to:
2294 W. 10th Ave.,
Vancouver 9, B.C.

Canada Postes
Post Canada
Postage paid Port payé
Third Troisième
class classe
2150
vancouver 3

2294 WEST 10TH AVE., VANCOUVER 9, B.C. □ 731-1155   FEBRUARY, 1973

.... what are our goals for the Region?

Wanted: Concerned Citizens To Help Plan Region's Future

The GVRD has accelerated the Livable Region Program, the most ambitious and important undertaking launched by its planning department. But to make it work it needs people — people from all segments of society, from all parts of the Greater Vancouver area. It needs people with a variety of interest, a variety of opinions on how they would like to see this region develop.

As part of the Program, nine policy committees are being set up. While they might include some government or technical representatives all committees will be composed primarily of citizens, people interested in this region as it is today and in establishing goals for its future. All names submitted for committee participation will be considered. We're looking for people who really want to contribute. Over the next eight or nine months the committees will meet regularly before arriving at their recommended policies.

If you have a special interest in any of the nine committees — or know of anyone who does and is willing to contribute — we'd like to hear from you. Send your name, address, phone number, place of employment and the names of organizations (if any) with which you are now associated and the committee you'd like to work with to the GVRD Planning Department, 2294 W. 10th, Vancouver 9. Here is a list of the nine policy committees:

1. transportation and transmission
2. residential living
3. recreational
4. educational and research
5. social services
6. health and public protection
7. production and distribution (economics)
8. environmental management
9. government and society

the problems of accommodating growth at the rate now being experienced in the region and would support provincial and federal initiatives and policies to help control the rate of growth.' The other key principles had to do with sharing growth among all the members of the region, equalizing the financial burden of growth, and getting a piece of the action as far as transportation planning for the region was concerned.

At about this time a split between the livable region program promoters and the politicians came to the surface. The GVRD consultant responsible for the program was sacked and the program dismantled. As the event was announced in the GVRD newsletter for April 1974:

A proposal to hold about 50 more public meetings this spring and summer to obtain further public input on the "Livable Region Program" has been called off for several reasons: public turnout, and the results, at three such preliminary meetings (in Richmond, White

Rock and North Vancouver) was less than anticipated; it was felt the District has received the general views of the public and it should now come up with alternative proposals for handling problems. These proposals will be submitted to the public for reaction.

With the public conveniently out of the way, another seminar was held in May 1974, again overwhelmingly populated by the politicians and bureaucrats. This time they made their desires more specific: they approved a system of regional town centres and some diversion of growth from the City of Vancouver; they designated open space reserves; they called for development of compact residential communities (i.e., residential development at densities higher than current single-family but less than apartment building density); and they proposed speeding up the infilling of areas by-passed over the years by leapfrogging development.

And the original policy committee reports? As one person put it: 'While the GVRD is taking action on a number of policy committee recommendations there is a substantial number on which it is not.'

The GVRD housing department has not been nearly as successful as the planning department. It was in May 1970 that the GVRD board voted to adopt public housing as a function. For many years the City of Vancouver had been pushing for greater distribution of public housing throughout the region. In fact, all public housing, with the exception of public housing for senior citizens, was in the City of Vancouver. It seemed that all the other municipalities wanted to have poor people living in Vancouver and not in their own communities.

The first chairman of the housing committee was Hugh Bird, another of the Non-Partisan Association pro-development Vancouver aldermen. He was replaced the next year by New Westminister mayor Muni Evers, a pharmacist, who has retained the post ever since. The 1974 members of the housing committee were:

Mayor Muni Evers (New Westminister)
Mayor Tom Reid (North Vancouver City)
Ald. Mike Harcourt (Vancouver)
Ald. Doreen Lawson (Burnaby)
Mayor Tom Goode (Delta)
Mayor Tom Hall (Port Moody)
Ald. Marianne Linnell (Vancouver)

Of the seven, only two, mayor Tom Goode of Delta and alderman Marianne Linnell of Vancouver, actually earned their livings from real estate. But developers had friends among the others, so that the committee was unlikely to do anything to antagonize the development industry.

The GVRD will be able to locate public housing anywhere in the region but it must have the approval of the municipality. Costs would be pro-rated across the entire region. The GVRD would need specific authority from the province to locate housing without municipal approval but the provincial government would not likely grant this given the vigorous municipal opposition which would occur.

In late 1971 a director of housing was appointed. Bill Casson, the director, saw his role was 'not to construct housing projects but to *stimulate and encourage* private industry to provide accommodation for the lower-income group.' Was this just the old chummy relationship between public money and private profits? The first scheme undertaken by Casson's department was to buy small groups of houses already built or about to be built by private developers, using federal and provincial funds, then sell them to low-income families with no down payment and monthly payments adjusted to income. This would allow developers to unload their poorly-selling models on the public and make a nice profit of it at the same time.

The scheme was less than successful. By the end of 1973, only 83 out of a planned 300 houses had been sold. At the commencement of the program, the *number* of houses under the program was strongly emphasized by the housing department. But because the program was working so poorly the housing department said that it was quality, not quantity, that really counted.

The housing department had more success with housing for senior citizens, since no municipality is against senior citizens. By the end of 1973 over 700 units had been planned or were under construction, mainly in Vancouver, but also in Burnaby and Surrey. The department also flirted with a few minor schemes involving private developers, and other levels of government.

One of the problems faced by the GVRD housing department is that it cannot do its own developing. It is entirely reliant on the provincial government for funding, and it must have the approval of the participating member municipalities. These are obviously severe handicaps to any effective action.

In an attempt to deal with the problem, early in 1974 the housing committee — the politicians — asked the GVRD board for authority to set up a non-profit housing corporation to produce family rental accommodation. As a separate corporation, it would have direct access to CMHC funding, making it slightly more independent of provincial control.

The housing corporation turned out to be a bad joke — an attempt to give the appearance of dealing with a problem without really touching it at all. The housing corporation's annual target would be set at *250* units. Bill Casson, director of the housing department, admitted that this was a modest target but said the really big problem was to provide quality, not quantity. Nor were the units going to be particularly cheap — rents were to start at $300 per month for a three-bedroom unit.

Casson's view of the housing corporation was that it would intermesh its activities with those of private developers. Said Casson: 'It has no intention of going into the construction business. That will be a job for private industry. I don't think any building should be done by anyone but those in industry.' As a demonstration that Casson meant what he said, five new members were appointed to the housing committee of the GVRD to join the seven politicians already on it. These members, who enjoyed full voting rights, were:

Al Koehli, private developer and chairman of the B.C. council of the Housing and Urban Development Association of Canada, the house-builders' biggest lobby, and provincial government adviser.

Ian Beveridge, land development consultant, president of ICO Real Estate Management & Holdings, who in a report he had recently prepared for the Real Estate Board of Greater Vancouver stated that there was a shortage of land to build on because of the restrictive provincial and municipal laws, by-laws,

development policies, and procedures.

Wally Ross, real estate agent, chairman of the GVRD's residential living policy committee, who in his report to the GVRD said: 'The large developers [are not] responsible for the shortage of serviced land.' He put responsibility for the housing crisis on the three levels of government and 'on all of us for the speculative impulse shared in equality of guilt by the largest and smallest of landholders.'

Joe Wai, an architect with the large corporate firm of Thompson, Berwick and Pratt, although Wai himself had been very active with citizens' groups in the Strathcona area of Vancouver.

Cy Lee, mortgage consultant.

So when it comes to solving the Vancouver area's housing problems, the GVRD is doing little of any significance. Housing industry representatives and politicians friendly to them are firmly in control of this body, and have demonstrated no inclination to tackle a problem which the housing industry and its associates in government created in the first place.

24 Who is responsible for the housing crisis? Daon Development Corp.

One of the main reasons why housing costs are so high is that developers are making incredibly large profits at the expense of the unwitting tenant or house-buyer. A few development corporations are beginning to monopolize the housing market and to charge what the market will bear. These corporations are aided in many ways by government taxation and corporation policies. Accelerated depreciation and other tax loopholes favour the large well-established firms which have increased in size to the point where they now monopolize the housing market.

Daon Development Corp. is one of the larger western-based development companies which has risen to prominence in a scant ten years. It is typical of developers but was selected for a closer examination because (1) its management has been unusually frank in their press statements (a series of articles in the *Financial Post*); (2) it is a public company — its shares are traded on the Vancouver and Toronto stock exchanges so that it must publish annual reports and issue financial statements — both of these mean that more information is available than is usual for a highly secretive industry; (3) it is an extremely aggressive company so that trends show up in greater relief than with other companies. But it is typical.

Dawson Developments (the name of the company until 1973) was formed in 1964 by John W. (Jack) Poole of Moose Jaw and Graham R. Dawson of Vancouver, the son of a long-standing construction family. The first activity the company entered was building detached houses in resource towns throughout British Columbia and the north. They built, for example, housing in Sparwood, B.C., for Kaiser Resources, and in Faro, Yukon, for Anvil Mining. Since 1968, the company has moved increasingly into the more lucrative urban real estate business, first building condominiums and single-family homes for sale, then into building and owning apartment units, then into the assembly of land for development, and finally into commercial properties.

Dawson Developments went public in 1969 when shares were issued on the Vancouver Stock Exchange, and has become one of the largest public real estate companies in western Canada. Today its business is almost totally concentrated on the profitable Edmonton, Calgary, and Vancouver markets.

Dawson's business has grown rapidly: in the five years since it has gone public, its assets have increased

Vancouver Sun 25 September 1971

from $6 million to $86 million, a 14-fold increase, and its stated profits have increased by 500%. While housing accommodation gets poorer and poorer, Dawson seems to be getting richer and richer. Let us take a look at how Dawson got that way.

As mentioned, the Dawson firm started out building housing in resource communities. However, this activity is not too profitable because large corporations such as Kaiser Resources are able to assess the value of the product they are getting. Better to deal directly with the individual consumer (house-buyer).

Consequently Dawson moved into urban real estate in 1968, building condominium units under the previously enacted Strata Titles Act, which was designed to allow outright ownership of apartment units. Dawson's first condominium project was Hi-View Estates in Port Moody, B.C. Shortly after, Dawson began a landbanking program, to cash in on the rapidly escalating land prices around the three western cities of Vancouver, Calgary, and Edmonton.

In 1969, Dawson went public to increase its base of capitalization, and also began to build apartment units

Daon's 'innovative' housing project in the Champlain Heights district of Vancouver. Daon bought the land from the city at a specially-reduced price. Later it sold two acres of the site to the Bay for expansion of the Champlain Mall.

such as Villa Montecito in Burnaby. Finally in 1971, Dawson got into commercial development, building a 12-storey office building on West Pender St., a 500-car parking garage adjacent to it, and the recently completed B.C. Forest Products Building, a 21-storey office tower in the same block.

Dawson is now engaged in every aspect of the development industry. They buy and assemble raw land; they plan, zone, subdivide, and service this land either for sale or for company use; they construct houses, condominiums and apartments; they build commercial buildings (offices, warehouses, shopping centres); they sell their houses and condominiums; they buy and sell rental properties; they own and operate rental properties both residential and commercial. At the present time they are the biggest condominium developer in the lower mainland.

Dawson's condominium activities first achieved notoriety in 1973 through the practice of buying apartment buildings and converting them into condominiums. Expecting a tight money situation in 1974, Jack Poole's corporate strategy was to get the company very liquid, (i.e., to have cash available in

1974) for picking up good real estate buys if less liquid competitors started unloading properties. The way Dawson did this was by buying apartment buildings, improving them, and selling them at a profit within six months. This brought in immediate cash rather than tying it up in long-term rental housing.

This strategy was good for Dawson's liquidity, but unfortunately there just happened to be people living in those buildings that were being bought up and converted to condominiums. One of the buildings was the Crescent View Apartments on Argyle Ave., in West Vancouver. Another was Hycroft Towers on south Granville St., owned by the Capozzi brothers. The tenants had to buy the suites or get out. They were all elderly. Allan Fotheringham, Vancouver *Sun* columnist, reported on a meeting of the residents on June 26th, 1973, to see if there was anything they could do about Dawson's ultimatum:

> ... 'I'm the youngest guy in the whole building,' a man in his early 60s says. 'A year from now a lot of these tenants may not be alive. And they're being told to buy their suites.' One elderly woman had a stroke after hearing about Dawson's plans ....
>
> The tactics of Dawson and the Capozzis are the same. The residents of both Hycroft and the Crescent are relatively well-off. 20 of the 45 tenants in the Crescent are widows. Many of them can be bullied into buying an apartment rather than change the habits of a dozen years and move. Of what use to an 84-year old lady is ownership of an apartment? The Capozzi excuse is that mortgages can be arranged. As one of the mortgage men was quoted yesterday, 'At their age, I wouldn't sell them a long-playing record....'
>
> A full 1½ months went by between the time Dawson bought the Crescent from Manufacturers Life and quietly switched it to condominium status and the time it informed tenants a new landlord had appeared.
>
> What is particularly contemptible is how the high-class quick-profit artists sprinted to evade the authorities moving in. April 18 was the date on which new legislation, requiring municipal approval of any further conversions to condominiums, was to be proclaimed. Somebody knew the need for the hurry. The Hycroft changeover under the Strata Titles Act was registered with provincial officials five days before April 18. Dawson Developments registered the Crescent conversion on April 17, less than 24 hours before the deadline ....

Dawson's second claim to notoriety occurred in relation to some so-called low-income housing which Dawson developed in Champlain Heights in the southeast sector of Vancouver. The project came under CMHC's innovative housing program, a $200 million stop-gap measure instituted by the government in 1970 when it became apparent that not nearly enough housing was going to be produced that year. (See description in Chapter 21).

The city was involved as well. Champlain Heights was all city-owned land, created by the covering of the city garbage dump.

The city initiated a competition among developer groups to present proposals for the seven acres of city land. Three groups were involved. One of the groups, headed by Yorkshire Trust Co., came forward with a scheme of row houses to cost $13,500 to $15,000 per unit. In the proposal made by Dawson, the units would cost $16,200 each. Despite this clear difference in cost, Dawson won the competition!

Dawson would build 132 units, all three-bedroom condominiums, and qualifying purchasers had to have a minimum annual income of $5,500.

CMHC provided a low-interest mortgage (7⅞%) of $1,939,806 under its innovative housing program. There was nothing innovative about the scheme. It was exactly the same as another project that Dawson was building in Burnaby under the same program — Simon Fraser Village.

Dawson paid the city $384,000 for the seven acres of land. This worked out to $55,000 per acre, considerably below market value. The Hudson's Bay Co. paid $125,000 per acre for land adjacent to the site in 1971, for the construction of a shopping centre. The city sold the land to Dawson cheaply because, after all, it was for low-income housing.

However, Dawson only used five acres of the land for the project and the year after it was completed sold the other two acres to the Bay for shopping centre expansion at a healthy profit — perhaps enough to cover the total money that Dawson put in in the first place. City council noted that Dawson was undertaking this entirely out-of-order transaction but did nothing to stop it.

Dawson seems to be able to make profits out of ventures that most developers would hesitate to enter. Take the Four Seasons Hotels site, for example. It was the site of continuing battles between citizens and profit-hungry developers for over ten years, and each time the citizens were able to drive off the wolves. You would think that a developer would take a long hard look before he put his foot into it again. Well, apparently, Dawson Developments did take that look, and seemed willing to take the gamble, because in May, 1973, Dawson bought for $6 million all the outstanding shares of Harbour Park Developments, the owners of the property and of the extraordinary 63-year leases on the adjacent waterlots. Dawson bought the company outright rather than just the property, because it would have had to renegotiate the waterlot leases, and there was no way the federal government would do such a suspect deal again.

As in every single transaction involving the

The Woodcroft Estates project and the bridge across the Capilano River which allows traffic from the project to get to it from North Vancouver, in whose jurisdiction the land falls.

property, it was far from being an 'arm's length' deal — where the buyer and seller were entirely separate. Graham Dawson, the chairman and namesake of Dawson Developments, the buyer, was also the chief shareholder of Harbour Park Developments through his majority interest in Dawson Construction Co. In effect he took the money out of one pocket and put it into the other. It was more complicated than that though. Dawson Developments paid $6 million, but only put up $2 million cash. The other $4 million was financed by Harbour Park, now entirely owned by Dawson Developments, which was to pay interest only over a ten-year period at which time the principal amount would be due. In the meantime Dawson sold the land to the city, collecting the cash which it could then use in other ventures.

Within a month of buying Harbour Park, Dawson announced its plans for the property: four high-rise apartment buildings up to 34 storeys in height, a high-rise office tower, and a 480-room hotel — a proposal as bad as anything that had ever been proposed for the site over the years. Again, there was an immediate public outcry. People could hardly believe that after all this time there was a developer so out of tune with public sympathies to propose such a clearly unacceptable scheme.

Of course it could have been argued that Dawson was only using one of the developer's standard tactics — to propose something that was twice as dense as it really wanted, then to back off, make a seeming compromise, and end up looking good. In fact, Dawson did back off immediately and returned within a month with a second proposal. Although scaled down in height, it still contained over one million square feet of floor area. This too was totally unacceptable to the TEAM politicians and the public. TEAM, it seems, was committed to the city acquiring

BANK OF MONTREAL DIRECTOR

G. R. DAWSON

The election of Graham R. Dawson, of Vancouver, as a Director of the Bank of Montreal, is announced by G. Arnold Hart, Chairman of the Board, following the annual meeting of shareholders.

Mr. Dawson is President of Dawson Construction Limited. He is also a director of a number of companies, among them Kaiser Resources Limited and Zeller's Limited, and is a past president of the Vancouver Board of Trade.

Also elected to the B of M Board of Directors were Raymond Crepault, Q.C., of Montreal, partner in the legal firm of Crepault, Fortin, Raymond & Trahan; J. Peter Gordon, of Toronto, President of The Steel Company of Canada, Limited; and J. Blair MacAulay, of Winnipeg, partner in the legal firm of Aikens, MacAulay & Thorvaldson.　●●●

at least the first block of the two-block site for parkland.

After some behind-the-scenes negotiations, and a public meeting at which the vast majority of briefs argued for acquiring both blocks for parkland, TEAM decided to hold a referendum on the issue. The voters were given two alternatives — buy one block for $2 million, or buy both blocks for $6.4 million. Due to the obscure wording of the referendum and the confusion surrounding the issue, the public voted to buy only the first block for parkland and to allow a substantial development on the second block.

Another case where Dawson had less than congenial relations with the public was the Woodcroft Estates project in North Vancouver. The site is a chunk of North Vancouver which projects across the Capilano River into West Vancouver. It is surrounded by upper-middle-class single-family homes and parkland. In 1966 it was rezoned for seven high-rise apartment buildings by a development-hungry North Vancouver district council — over strenuous objections of area residents and the West Vancouver council. In an attempt to quell the opposition, North Vancouver made approval conditional on the developer's constructing a bridge across the Capilano River so that traffic from the project would use North Vancouver's road system rather than the suburban streets of West Vancouver.

For several years the project lay dormant because of financial difficulties. Then in 1971 Dawson bought out the other partners and hired the prestigious Vancouver architectural firm of Erickson-Massey to prepare a new plan for the site.

The new proposal, while much more elegant-looking than the original, in fact was potentially much more profitable. It was composed of two crescent-shaped structures, one of them rising in a stepladder fashion to a height of 30 storeys. The original scheme had 943 suites, the new one 1,322, an increase of almost 50%. The previous scheme had included some family-oriented accommodation, appropriate to its semi-rural setting. In the new proposal this was all eliminated for more profitable bachelor and one-bedroom units, which would also mean adding more parking space to the project; the height of the original scheme was 170 feet; the scheme proposed by Erickson-Massey increased the height to 300 feet, which would have made it the tallest residential structure in B.C.

A public hearing had to be held because of the major changes in the design. Perhaps Dawson was not prepared for the public reaction, a reaction so strong that none of Dawson's connections could keep the project on the rails. All of the original charges which had been levelled at the previous proposal were reiterated, but there were some new ones for this scheme. Due to the intense public pressure, North Vancouver had to reject the new design, and Dawson, perhaps figuring that it wasn't worth the effort to push further, went back to the original seven-building high-rise scheme, which commenced construction in 1973.

At about the same time, because of the confusion caused by having so many companies with the Dawson name, a new name was selected for the company, Daon Development Corp., but the same old activities continued.

Daon usually restricted its activities to more suburban locations such as North Vancouver, Surrey, etc. On occasion they did move into inner city neighbourhoods. 'Let's face it,' Daon president Jack Poole told an interviewer, 'people like high density.' The result was the inevitable neighbourhood block-busting and redevelopment to higher density three-storey condominiums that threaten to obliterate the inner city. In one Kitsilano case, the company owned three houses in a row. These were allowed to deteriorate — the houses ran down, junk and garbage accumulated on the property, until the adjacent owners agreed to sell. In its haste to get development under way, the demolition contractor gave some of the tenants only half an hour to clear out with all their possessions before he demolished their houses.

For some reason, Daon Development Corp. seems to have a high degree of success in dealing with governments and in expanding its business at a rapid rate. Perhaps this might be explained by looking at the personalities and forces behind the corporate facade.

Who are the directors, and why are they on the board? Nobody becomes a director of a major corporation by accident. There are very specific reasons each person is appointed. Take Daon, for example. There are eight directors: Graham Dawson, chairman of the board, and Jack Poole, president and chief executive officer, are the major shareholders and originators of the company; Norman Cressey and William Laurie are executive officers of the company, and act as a link between the operations of the company and the deliberations of the board; Roderick Hungerford and George McKeen represent the Vancouver business establishment on the board; Robert Thompson represents eastern Canadian financial and real estate interests, and one of Dawson's early sources of financing; finally, H. Richard Whittall, who was Daon's stockbroker and investment dealer. He left the board in 1974 to be replaced by William J. Corcoran, another stockbroker, executive vice-president of McLeod, Young, Weir & Co., Toronto.

Graham Dawson, chairman of the board of Daon Development Corp., is the son of Fred Dawson, founder of Dawson Construction Co., one of the largest heavy construction companies in B.C. Dawson inherited the construction company from his father, and is now chairman and president. Graham Dawson has made it big in local business circles. In 1969, he was president of the Vancouver Board of Trade. He has been a member of the Employers Council of B.C., an organization of the largest B.C. businesses. He is vice-chairman of Kaiser Resources, that American-owned company which sells B.C. coal to Japan. He is a director of a number of smaller companies: Andres Wines, Zellers, the Hamilton Group, Hayes Trucks. In 1971, Dawson reached the pinnacle of his career when he was appointed a director of the Bank of Montreal. Here he joined the other Vancouver directors of the Bank of Montreal. Dawson is also a member of the Vancouver advisory board of National Trust Co. For a number of years he was a member of the Vancouver police commission, where he met regularly with Vancouver mayors Tom Campbell and Art Phillips.

Poole is Daon's president and chief executive officer; that is, the man actually in charge of the company's operations. Poole came from Moose Jaw, Saskatchewan to Vancouver in 1964 as vice-president of Genstar subsidiary Engineered Homes to explore the Vancouver market. He saw a better opportunity in the instant towns market and got the financial backing of Graham Dawson. He severed all other corporate connections to devote his time to the activities of Daon. Poole is a very personable man and likes to be interviewed. Hardly a month goes by without an appearance by him in the pages of the *Financial Post* or *Business in B.C.* or the Vancouver *Sun*.

Poole and Dawson are the major shareholders of Daon Development Corp., between them controlling some 17% of the shares of the company, worth roughly $5 to $6 million on the Vancouver Stock Exchange.

Norman Cressey, an engineer, is vice-president in charge of operations, and along with Poole functions as a link between the company's operations and the board's ruminations.

William Laurie, a chartered accountant, came over to Daon from Dawson Construction Co. as vice-president in charge of finance. This job has been taken over by William Levine for the company, and Laurie now acts solely as a director for the company as well as remaining executive vice-president of Dawson Construction Co.

Both Roderick Hungerford and George McKeen have very strong and intimate connections with Vancouver's oldest and wealthiest families. Hungerford is a vice-president and director of Inland Natural Gas Co. He is a director of Cornat Industries and a number of its subsidiaries — Burrard Dry Dock, Johnston Terminals, and B.C. Ice and Cold Storage — all of which compose that mini-conglomerate controlled by Peter-Paul Saunders, another of Graham Dawson's colleagues on Harbour Park Developments.

Hungerford has also been a Vancouver police commissioner in the past. He is married to one of the Farrell daughters, which may go a long way toward explaining his success in business. Gordon Farrell, who was at one time Vancouver's leading businessman, was the founder of B.C. Telephone Co. Farrell had four daughters, and Hungerford's brothers-in-law include Harry Boyce, chairman of Yorkshire Financial Corp. Hungerford is also a director of National Trust Co., where he sits with Victor MacLean, president of Kelly Douglas and a director of B.C. Telephone and Crown Zellerbach.

George McKeen's father was Senator Stanley Stewart McKeen, who along with Farrell was one of Vancouver's powers to be reckoned with. Senator McKeen formed Straits Towing Co., and was intimately connected with Union Steamship Lines and Burrard Dry Dock and B.C. Ice and Cold Storage (now owned by Peter-Paul Saunders). Stanley was Liberal MLA for Vancouver Point Grey, 1933-37, a founder of the Non-Partisan Association (NPA) and was appointed to the Senate of Canada in 1947 by a grateful Liberal government.

McKeen inherited all his father's connections, being chairman of Rivtow Straits and Burrard Dry Dock, president of B.C. Ice and Cold Storage, as well as being a director of Cornat Industries, Johnston Terminals, and Dawson Construction Co. McKeen is past-president of the Vancouver Board of Trade and of the NPA and a director of B.C. Turf, that NPA stronghold.

McKeen's sister married Richard Wallace, of the ship-building Wallaces, who recently sold their company, Burrard Dry Dock, to the ubiquitous Cornat Industries. Wallace's father, Clarence Wallace,

- Daon director George McKeen's house

- Graham Dawson's house

- Daon director Roderick Hungerford's house

- Graham Dawson's house

was at one time lieutenant-governor of B.C.

McKeen and Hungerford and Dawson thus represent all the right connections in order to do well in B.C.: the Board of Trade, the NPA, the Liberal party of B.C., and the powerful old families.

H. Richard Whittall, a partner of Richardsons Securities, was Daon's stockbroker and investment dealer. It is de rigeur at one time or another to have a stockbroker on your board as Block Bros. had John Chaston, president of Pemberton Securities, and Western Realty Projects had Ross Hanbury, a vice-president of Wood Gundy.

H. Richard Whittall succeeded to his father's position in Richardsons Securities and to many of his corporate connections. He is now a director of many of B.C.'s largest companies (rank in top 50 B.C. companies given in brackets): Weldwood of Canada (7); B.C. Sugar Refining Co. (15); Placer Development (17); Brenda Mines (27); Daon Development Corp. (28); Inland Natural Gas Co. (36). He is also deputy chairman of Canada Cement Lafarge, Canada's largest cement company, chairman of Grosvenor International Holdings, and a director of B.C. Television Co. and Dynasty Explorations.

Daon's directors do not live in the projects they develop, but rather in the exclusive Shaughnessy, South West Marine Drive and British Properties districts. Graham Dawson's house, which is difficult to photograph because it is so huge and well-hidden, is the former residence of an ex-lieutenant governor of B.C.

Finally, we have Robert Thomson of Montreal, who represents eastern Canadian financial and real estate interests. It is a good thing to have one of these on your board: Thomson was executive director of British-owned Standard Life Assurance Co., one of Daon's early sources of financing, and was connected to the giant Taylor Woodrow development interests. Thomson retired from these connections and became involved with large-scale development projects in Hamilton, Ontario.

Thus we complete our list of ingredients for a successful board of directors. Follow these instructions and you too can have your own multi-million dollar corporation.

HOW MUCH MONEY DOES DAON REALLY MAKE?

I have argued that one of the reasons why

housing costs are so high — both the price of condominiums and single-family houses or rents — is because of the incredibly large profits being made by developers such as Daon Development Corp. An examination of Daon's published financial statements gives an astonishing look at just how much money Daon is really making. 1973's figures are being used, although that was by no means the best year that Daon has had.

With inflation hitting 10% per year, an investor would have to make that much on his investment just to stay even. Therefore, a profit of 15 to 20 % on invested capital would seem to be a reasonable return and certainly not out of line. Daon's stated profit for the year ended October 31, 1973, was $1,667,000, up from 1972's $983,000 by a healthy 70%, but giving a return on shareholders' equity of roughly 20%. Not bad, but it doesn't seem to be out of line.

However, in arriving at its profit Daon listed certain expenses that it never really paid out. One of these was $166,000 for the depreciation of the buildings it owns. Now the buildings never really depreciated in the sense that an automobile would, i.e., wear out and hence lose some of its value. In fact, the opposite is the case — the buildings, apart from the land they stood on, actually increased in value. Therefore eliminating this expense increases the net profit to roughly $1,833,000.

Another expense listed by Daon is the money it pays for income tax, yet Daon pays no income tax. As David Lewis pointed out in his book, *Louder Voices: The Corporate Welfare Bums,* large corporations are able to avoid paying a great part of their taxes because of a tax dodge that is perfectly legal. The government allows the company to count depreciation of buildings and equipment as a business expense, and to depreciate the buildings at a faster rate for tax purposes than the company does on its own books.

Daon Development Corp. claimed $1,740,000 as an expense for income tax it did not pay in 1973. Adding this amount to the profit figure almost doubles it to $3,580,000.

In passing, it should be noted that up to 1973 Daon has never paid one cent in income tax because of this loophole even though its net profit from 1969 to 1973 totalled just under $4 million. Its deferred income taxes during that same period amounted to over $5 million.

A further profit, neglected in its published figures by Daon, is the appreciation in the value of the land it owns. All together, Daon owns over 4,100 acres of land around Calgary, Edmonton, and Vancouver. Land held for development was valued on its books at $16 million. But this was the price that Daon paid for it. Assuming that it increased in value by 10% over the past year (actually a very conservative estimate given

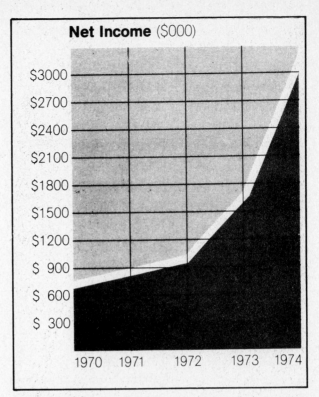

The graph shows Daon's declared after-tax profits for 1970-74.

the astronomical increase in property values) adds another $1,600,000, making a total real profit of $5,180,000 for 1973, not $1,666,000 as stated.

Total shareholders' equity in Daon was $8,480,000. Using this as the basis for calculating return on investment, we get a somewhat different figure from the published one — 61%! Not bad. But it is even better than that. The actual cash investment by shareholders in the company was considerably less than shareholders' equity — $3,130,000. The rest was retained earnings — profits from previous years ploughed back into the company and not taken out as dividends.

Daon's real rate of return on invested money turns out to be 165% for the year 1973. That was not even its best year. In 1971 return on invested capital was *205%.*

No wonder Daon has been able to grow so quickly to become one of the largest developers in western Canada. Daon's plans for the future involve two related targets: to restrict themselves to western Canada, and to grow in assets and profits at a rate of 15% per year. As part of the first strategy, in 1973 Daon bought out Paragon Properties of Calgary, a $20-million development company. However, Daon seemed to have trouble in sticking to the 15% growth rate target. For the year ending October 31, 1974, Daon's stated profit was $3.1 million, up 86% over 1973. Daon's real profit was somewhat more — $11.3 million or a return on shareholders' equity of 233%.

25 Who is responsible for the housing crisis? Genstar

Another reason why housing costs are so high is because a few building material suppliers — such as the cement and wood products industries — have a near monopolistic control over their markets, and can and do charge whatever the market will bear. These costs are automatically passed along by the builders to the consumers in the form of much higher housing costs.

Vancouver residents had a glimmering of such monopolistic practices in February and March 1974, when four firms that together control the cement and ready-mix concrete business in British Columbia — two of them, Ocean Cement and Canada Cement Lafarge, controlling 80% of the market — were found guilty of 'conspiracy to curb competition by fixing prices and allocating jobs.' The four firms were fined a total of $432,000. During the trial the crown introduced into the record a list of projects which had received cement through the illegal system of market allocation used by the combine. Nine of these involved public funds, including the Georgia Viaduct, the Hudson St. and Knight St. bridges, and a project at the Vancouver General Hospital; privately financed projects included the Royal Centre, the Bentall Centre's Tower Three, and a 60-unit condomium at 49th Ave. and Elliott St. How many similar price-fixing agreements are never discovered?

The situation is much worse than mere price-fixing. Not only do a few companies enjoy monopolistic control of an industry — such as Ocean Cement and Canada Cement Lafarge in the cement industry — but often the same companies are vertically integrated, and own their sources of supply and their markets. In the development industry a vertically-integrated company is one that buys and assembles land, does the subdividing, supplies the building materials, does the construction, and markets the products. Under such a system, the company's subsidiaries make a profit at each stage of the project, as they sell their output to the next subsidiary, and so on. Increased profits at each stage mean superprofits for the company as a whole. And all of the costs are inevitably passed on to the home buyer.

Canada has an outstanding example of the vertically-integrated development company in Genstar, a $500 million corporation whose subsidiaries — BACM Industries, Inland Cement Industries and Ocean Cement, Con-Force Products, Engineered Homes and many others — are engaged in every aspect of land development in western Canada. Subsidiary Ocean Cement was one of the firms found guilty of price-fixing; subsidiary BACM Industries was the subject of a recently-released report which showed that it had a near-monopoly position in the Calgary housing market; and subsidiary Engineered Homes is one of the two or three largest house-builders in Canada.

Genstar is a foreign-owned corporation. It attained its position of pre-eminence solely through buying up existing Canadian companies, making their previous owners millionaires in the process, with the use of Canadian money made available to it because of particularly close ties to the Royal Bank of Canada and the Liberal party.

Although its branches have been nourished by the savings of the Canadian people, its roots lie buried in darkest colonial Africa, in the Belgian Congo. Genstar's previous name was Sogemines, named after the parent company, Société Générale de Belgique.

Société Générale de Belgique is one of the two or three largest investment concerns in Europe. It is said to control one-fifth of the Belgian economy. The company is intimately connected to the 'august Société Générale de Banque, the most powerful bank in Belgium where attendants in black ties glide across marble floors, and the electric lights are set in gilded brackets.' Shareholders are rumoured to include members of both the Belgian and Dutch royal families.

Société Générale's most important venture outside Belgium was in the Belgian Congo, where, along with Rockfeller and British interests, it was the major shareholder in the Union Minière du Haut-Katanga, the copper- and cobalt-producing giant. The Union Minière achieved its pre-eminence in its field during the 1920s and 1930s by charging up to $70,000 per gram for radium, until competition in the 1950s from the Canadian company Eldorado Nuclear forced the price down to about $20,000 per gram, at which price both companies were still able to make a good profit. For years the company extracted huge profits from the colony, whose government and economy were dominated by company officials. In 1960 the Toronto *Globe & Mail* estimated Union Minière's profits to be about $60 million per year.

In 1959 the Congolese government was overthrown in a bloody revolution, which saw the company hiring a mercenary army to protect its interests. Seeing the writing on the wall, the company withdrew as much of its money as it could from the Congo. Much of this money was invested in Canada.

Sogemines was just one of a number of vehicles for investing in Canada. Other Société Générale-controlled companies include Canadian Petrofina, currently in the $400 million range, and the Miron Co., a $50 million Montreal-based cement and construc-

DEVELOPMENT AND CONSTRUCTION ACTIVITIES OF GENSTAR LTD.

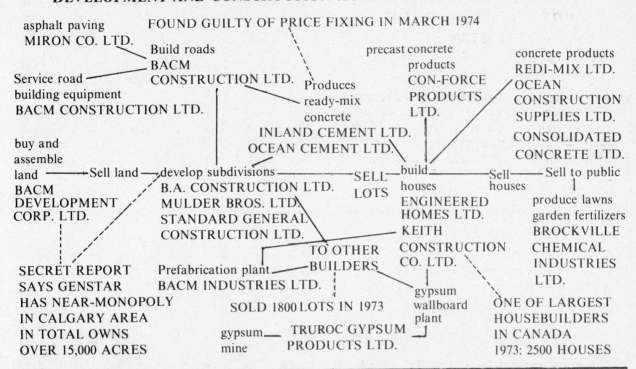

asphalt paving
MIRON CO. LTD.

FOUND GUILTY OF PRICE FIXING IN MARCH 1974

Build roads
BACM
CONSTRUCTION LTD.

Service road
building equipment
BACM CONSTRUCTION LTD.

Produces
ready-mix
concrete
INLAND CEMENT LTD.
OCEAN CEMENT LTD.

precast concrete
products
CON-FORCE
PRODUCTS
LTD.

concrete products
REDI-MIX LTD.
OCEAN
CONSTRUCTION
SUPPLIES LTD.

CONSOLIDATED
CONCRETE LTD.

buy and
assemble
land
BACM
DEVELOPMENT
CORP. LTD.

Sell land — develop subdivisions
B.A. CONSTRUCTION LTD.
MULDER BROS. LTD.
STANDARD GENERAL
CONSTRUCTION LTD.

SELL
LOTS

build
houses
ENGINEERED
HOMES LTD.
KEITH
CONSTRUCTION
CO. LTD.

Sell
houses

Sell to public

produce lawns
garden fertilizers
BROCKVILLE
CHEMICAL
INDUSTRIES
LTD.

SECRET REPORT
SAYS GENSTAR
HAS NEAR-MONOPOLY
IN CALGARY AREA
IN TOTAL OWNS
OVER 15,000 ACRES

Prefabrication plant
BACM INDUSTRIES LTD.

TO OTHER
BUILDERS

SOLD 1800 LOTS IN 1973

gypsum
mine

TRUROC GYPSUM
PRODUCTS LTD.

gypsum
wallboard
plant

ONE OF LARGEST
HOUSEBUILDERS
IN CANADA
1973: 2500 HOUSES

---

tion firm which in 1974 was integrated into the Genstar complex. The Sogemines group had good political connections all along. Louis St. Laurent, ex-Prime Minister of Canada, was appointed chairman of the Miron Co. in 1959 after his humiliating defeat in 1957.

Along with its Liberal party connections, Sogemines is intimately tied in with the Royal Bank of Canada complex. The head of the company is usually a director of the bank, and the president of the bank, currently Earle McLaughlin, in turn is a director of the company. The two are further tied together through F. Campbell Cope, a senior partner in the Royal's law firm, Ogilvy, Cope, Porteous, Hansard, Marler, Montgomery & Renault.

This connection has tangible results for Genstar. When in 1973 Genstar took over Ocean Cement — the largest cement company in western Canada — it was with the aid of a $2.4 million loan from the Royal Bank of Canada.

Genstar's profits have been increasing astronomically. Its earnings in 1971 surpassed the previous year's by 35%. The 1972 income was another 37% above that of 1971. And 1973 was the best year ever, with net profits of $25 million. And these are only stated profits, not the real profits which include appreciation of all the land owned by Genstar; and the deferred income taxes and depreciation and depletion allowances, which are like interest-free loans granted by the government to allow Genstar to further increase its domination of the Canadian development industry.

Genstar subsidiaries are scattered throughout the lower mainland area.

Genstar subsidiary Ocean Construction's office for Vancouver.

Genstar has this gypsum products plant under construction (by a Genstar subsidiary) on Annacis Island.

There are three Genstar ready-mix and concrete depots in the area: this Granville Island depot, one in Westminster, and one in Marpole.

Genstar's concrete products plant in Richmond. Workers were on strike when this photo was taken.

Genstar has been doing just that. In 1969 it took over BACM Industries, a Winnipeg-based construction and building material supplies conglomerate active in the prairie provinces. Over the years it picked up other companies along the way, such as Keith Construction Co., a large Calgary-based house-builder, and Ocean Cement.

Genstar buys companies very shrewdly, according to a carefully-conceived strategy of gaining total control over all aspects of development. Genstar owns over 15,000 acres of raw land, giving it one of largest landbanks in Canada. It dominates the concrete industry in western Canada. It is one of the largest house-builders in Canada. Its two house-building subsidiaries, Engineered Homes and Keith Construction Co., are both active in the Calgary area.

Here's how the Genstar group can operate. BACM Development Corp. buys and assembles the land. Let's say it has put together enough land for a subdivision in Coquitlam. Next it hires Standard-General Construc-

Genstar has recently acquired Seaspan International and Vancouver Shipyards Co., which is one of the largest landowners and employers in North Vancouver.

Genstar's gravel pit in Langley, operated by the Construction Aggregates subsidiary.

tion to service and subdivide the land — put in the sewers, sidewalks, water mains, streets, and other services. If the subdivision has poor accessibility, the BACM Construction Co. may be hired to build road access, using ready-mix concrete and asphalt from Ocean Cement, and concrete products such as pipe from Ocean Construction Supplies. On each transaction one subsidiary makes a profit.

BACM Development Corp. then sells the lots to other builders with whom it has contracts or to Engineered Homes. In either case it charges market price for the lots. In 1973 it sold 1,800 lots to other builders and the rest to Engineered Homes. Engineered Homes then does the actual building of the houses. But it gets all its building materials from other subsidiaries. There is a prefabricating plant which supplies all the pre-cut lumber, a gypsum wallboard plant that supplies the drywall, and of course all the concrete products come from one or another subsidiary. Each transaction here, too, involves a separate profit for the company.

Engineered Homes then sells the houses to the public. It is one of the largest house-builders in Canada, with 1973 sales of 2,500 houses. Finally, one more subsidiary, Brockville Chemical Industries, sells lawn and garden fertilizers to the people who have just bought the Engineered Homes houses.

And of course, Genstar is helped along the way by the government. Writes David Lewis in *Louder Voices: The Corporate welfare Bums:*

Through its wholly-owned subsidiary BACM Industries Ltd., the company, as of December 31, 1971, held land for sale valued at $32,218,000, land located in every major western city. This represents 11,400 acres, over 2,000 of which are in Metropolitan Winnipeg, BACM's home base. Genstar's rate of taxation, at 18.1 percent in the period 1966-1971, was higher than many other companies. But in this period

Genstar subsidiary Engineered Homes' subdivision in suburban Coquitlam about an hour's drive from downtown Vancouver. Genstar subsidiaries are involved in every aspect of the operation — from subdividing and servicing the land, using products of other subsidiaries (such as asphalt, cement products and concrete pipe) to building and marketing the houses. Prices for the houses range from $63,610 to $77,950.

it had deferred tax payments of $8,199,000, more than enough to pay the interest on its $32 million worth of land. Like other land developers, it received an interest-free loan to acquire land and other assets. Of course the ordinary taxpayers have to pick up the tab for these handouts. There is also the fact that should one of these taxpayers buy land from BACM-Genstar (and in some cities he would have very little choice if he wanted a home there), he can expect to pay interest on his own mortgage, interest which is not tax deductible.

By keeping the price of housing high, and by taking advantage of all the corporate tax concessions offered by the federal government, a foreign-owned conglomerate like Genstar benefits enormously from the continuing housing crisis.

Part IV City Hall

26 The politicians: TEAM and the NPA

In earlier chapters we have seen a pattern emerging of extremely close ties between the corporate interests involved in Vancouver and political power at every level. Large corporations like the Royal Bank of Canada, Canadian Pacific Railway and Power Corp. of Canada are tightly tied to federal politicians, especially to the powerful federal Liberal party. The powerful local families have their own ties to national politics. The British Columbia Liberal party is a maze of connections between business and government at all levels. Similarly in looking at housing and the housing industry we found high-level ties to the federal cabinet and to the federal government's housing agency Central Mortgage and Housing Corp., and a tangle of similar business-political connections at the local level in the various authorities and public bodies involved in housing in the Vancouver area.

When it comes to the day-to-day decisions about greater Vancouver and its future, the power lies in the hands of the ten aldermen and the mayor of Vancouver and with the local politicians on neighbouring municipal councils. Obviously no city government is an independent power unto itself, able to act apart from the policies and actions of other more powerful governments or to separate itself from the general conditions of the economy. Yet city hall does have a measure of power in governing Vancouver, power which many citizens have encountered in controversies over urban renewal projects, freeway schemes, downtown demolition and development, parks, roads, zoning, and planning.

In this part we examine Vancouver city politics in some detail in order to discover who really controls city council and city hall, and whose interests the city politicians are protecting and promoting. In this chapter, we look at the politicians. In the next, we turn to the bureaucrats hired by politicians. In the third chapter we look briefly at the politics of The Elector's Action Movement (TEAM) administration.

The Non-Partisan Association (NPA) dominated Vancouver city government for an unbroken 35 years. It was formed by a group of wealthy Liberals and Conservatives in 1937 to keep the Co-operative Commonwealth Federation (CCF) out of power. This came at the height of the depression and the CCF had improved its civic electoral position to the point where it could have won power at the next civic election. A CCFer, Dr. Lyle Telford, had been elected mayor, and the CCF had made strong inroads on city council, the

Vancouver city hall

parks board, and the school board.

The local business establishment, together with their provincial Liberal and Conservative allies, organized to fight off the socialist threat. Brenton Brown senior, insurance executive and Liberal party fund-raiser, and F. Drewe Pratt, Conservative party secretary, were two of the originators of the idea of forming a new civic party. Others who joined in included Straits Towing boss and Liberal MLA Stanley S. McKeen, mining magnate Austin Taylor, department store owners Col. Victor Spencer and William Culham Woodward (a Liberal MLA at one time), and grocery store owner and former mayor W.H. Malkin.

The NPA won the first election it entered, and never looked back. With extensive funds provided by the members and their sympathizers, the NPA was able to mount effective large-scale campaigns. At about the same time, the NPA interests successfully pushed for the abolition of the ward system, making it necessary for every aldermanic candidate to run on a city-wide basis. This required far more costly campaigns that only the NPA-backed candidates could afford, and the CCF was soon wiped out as a civic force.

The NPA always supported real estate promoters and big business interests, believing that what was good for the real estate industry was good for Vancouver. Many NPA executives were themselves developers, property insurance or real estate agents, developer's lawyers or directors of the large corporations. Many were members of the Vancouver Club, whose self-appointed task was to run the city. NPA

It was over a secret deal made by NPA mayor Tom Campbell concerning the land on which the Bow Mac auto centre sits which lost the NPA much of its establishment business support. Surrounded on all sides by high-rise office towers, city planners and neighbouring property owners agreed that this land should be a park. The city expropriated in January 1971. Surrounding owners — including Clark Bentall and J.V. Clyne — agreed to pay part of the cost of the land. And B.C. Telephone decided to move to a proposed fourth tower in the neighbouring Bentall Centre.

After arbitration had awarded the owner of the property, Peter Birks, the sum of $1.8 million as the expropriation price, NPA mayor Campbell and Birks got together and made a deal. They agreed on a complicated land exchange which left Birks in possession of most of his property — and which killed the proposed park. The deal was pushed through the NPA-dominated council in a secret session in December 1971. On December 20, 1971, Peter Birks was elected president of the NPA. Four days later, as *Vancouver Sun* columnist Allan Fotheringham reported in his exposé of this deal, Birks and Campbell signed the deal for the property.

members dominated the board of governors of the universities, the civic boards, and the cultural institutions. In short, the NPA and its supporters ran Vancouver.

In spite of this long history of unquestioned domination of Vancouver city politics, the NPA was decimated in the 1972 civic election. The apparent cause of the defeat was the blatant conflict of interest involving the NPA's mayoralty candidate that year, Bill Street.

Bill Street was the developer's lawyer and paid lobbyist at city hall. Bill Street was also the fund-raiser for the NPA. He collected the money from the developers to pay the election expenses of the NPA aldermen. He would then appear before those alder-

men to plead the cause of those same developers. Bill Street served a two-year term on city council in the early 1960s, presumably to learn the ins and outs of city hall, and hence serve better his clients.

Every developer dealt with his own law firm on most matters. But whenever the developer had to go to city hall to get a rezoning, or a higher density for his development, or some other special consideration, he would retain Bill Street to do the job.

The shock raised by these revelations caused Street to resign from the mayoralty race and left the NPA in a state of confusion.

But the NPA had been in trouble in the early 1970s even without the Street affair. Many NPA supporters were becoming dissatisfied with the NPA's perform-ance. The NPA had been in power for so long that it seemed to be losing touch with reality. The inanity of nominating Bill Street for its mayoralty candidate was just one example.

A secret deal made between NPA mayor Tom Campbell and Bowell McLean Motors head (and NPA president) Peter Birks, which would have allowed Birks to build a high-rise office building on his property after Campbell had announced that the property would be acquired for open space, infuriated many of the most powerful NPA supporters, including B.C. Telephone Co. president Ernie Richardson, who cut off his financial support of the NPA.

The Chinatown freeway proposal, the Arbutus Shopping Centre controversy, and the Block 42/52 giveaway all aroused strong hostility from many of the NPA's middle-class supporters, and split the usually solid pro-NPA business community. These elements, while pro-development in outlook, felt that develop-ment should be carried out in an orderly way so that property owners and business interests could make their plans in a more stable investment and political environment.

They feared that the NPA might be losing its popular base of support. At the rate they were going, it was not inconceivable that the NPA might lose out to the socialists and other progressive elements that had been successfully kept off city council for 35 years. It was time to set up a new civic political party to per-petuate control of city council by the business esta-blishment. That new political party was The Elector's Action Movement.

Though TEAM was to take over the reins of pow-er at city council from the NPA, the NPA did not fade away as many had expected. After the rout in 1972 when only a single NPA alderman was elected, the party regrouped its forces and put together a "new" look for the 1974 election, renaming themselves the New Non-Partisans. It was, however, hard to tell that there was anything new about the NPA from the names who appeared on the 1974 NPA slate. The successful NPA candidates in 1974 were four tired old faces: ex-fire chief, former alderman for ten years, and arch-reactionary Hugh Bird; board of trade executive and architect Warnett Kennedy; former parks board commissioner and NPA city planning commission appointee Helen Boyce; and former alderman, False Creek property owner, and unofficial CPR representative at city hall, Ed Sweeney. Those who didn't make it included Carol Young, daughter of developer Ben Wosk; and Barry Dryvynsyde, law partner in the firm of Bull, Houser & Tupper, local lawyers for the Royal Bank of Canada; and Patrick Graham, insurance executive with North America Life and Casualty Co.

The new NPA president, epitomizing the New Non-Partisans, was 34-year-old Michael Francis, sporting sideburns to mid-earlobe and dark horn-rimmed glasses. Michael Francis had all the right connections for Vancouver political parties. He was treasurer of the provincial Progressive Conservative party, and a chartered accountant with the big corporate chartered accountant firm of Deloitte, Haskins and Sells. Francis is married to one of the daughters of Walter S. Owen, corporate lawyer and lieutenant-governor of the province of B.C.

There are two other parties in the sweepstakes for power at city hall: the Committee of Progressive Electors (COPE) and the New Democratic Party (NDP), both parties of the left and defenders of citizen interests. COPE was formed the same year as TEAM to help dispel the impression that TEAM was a reform party. COPE support came from the Vancouver and District Labour Council, the left wing of the NDP, and the Communist Party. Unlike TEAM which had a preponderance of lawyers, university professors and corporate executives, COPE was stacked with school teachers and union officials. COPE ran a partial slate of candidates in the 1968 election, but only Harry Rankin was elected. Rankin had been elected to council for the first time in 1966 after running unsuccessfully many times before.

In 1970 the NDP entered civic politics and COPE and the NDP ran five aldermanic candidates each, but again only Rankin was elected. In 1972, the year that it really counted because of the disarray in the NPA, each group ran a full slate, and split the remaining reform vote that hadn't swung to TEAM. Thus TEAM swept into power.

The lesson learned, each group again ran partial slates in 1974, but a provincial government backlash, among other things, reduced the reform elements again, with only the perennial alderman Rankin being re-elected. During his eight years on council, alderman Harry Rankin has been the only consistent pro-citizen voice, although he was joined by TEAM alderman Walter Hardwick in the opposition role from 1968 to 1972, and alderman Darlene Marzari in 1973 and

REAL ESTATE BOSSES BARRED AS CANDIDATES

ELECTORS ACTION MOVEMENT

The interim president of TEAM—The Electors Action Movement—said Friday his group will not field any council candidates who have real estate interests. SUN APR 27 1968

Art Phillips told 40 members of the Building Owners and Managers Association that TEAM has established a policy prohibiting persons whose primary business interest is in real estate or building management from running for the organization.

"We felt that in many people's minds there is the idea of a conflict of interests between real estate and civic government," Phillips said.

He added that TEAM also does not plan to have directors with real estate interests.

TEAM president clarifies policy

ELECTORS ACTION MOVEMENT

Real estate people are welcome to join TEAM, says Art Phillips, president of The Electors' Action Movement.

He told the Apartment and Lodging House Association on Thursday night that previous remarks he had made about the role of real estate people in TEAM had been exaggerated.

"It is important for people in public affairs not only to do what is right but to appear to do what is right," Phillips said. "For this reason, in making up the slate of nominees for the board of directors, we wanted to demonstrate that TEAM is not controlled by any groups who are major real estate interests."

He said he referred only to the makeup of the board and not to possible TEAM civic election candidates.

"Anyone in the real estate business is free to come before our membership for backing as a candidate," he said.

Many real estate people are involved in TEAM's policy committees, he said. Those in the field of property development have special knowledge which would enable them to make an important contribution to policy.

"Anyone who joins TEAM can automatically participate in the policy sub-committees of his choice," Phillips said.

As these 1968 clippings indicate, the question of TEAM's relationship to real estate interests came up right at the beginning of the party's history. When founder Art Phillips said that real estate people have a constant conflict of interest in city government, it took him only a few days to clarify TEAM's position to be one of keeping real estate people in the background, not keeping them out.

1974. Rankin has consistently voted against giveaways to developers, and for low-income housing and the interests of tenants and working-class people.

TEAM is a younger, more vigorous and flexible group than the NPA but there is no question that *TEAM represents exactly the same interests as the NPA,* with two minor differences: TEAM is much more closely tied to the Liberal party; and TEAM has a preponderance of professional and middle management types, whereas the NPA executive was top-heavy with the speculators and entrepreneurs for whom the TEAM people work.

For example, *Bob Henderson,* Mayor Art Phillips' handpicked choice for 1974-75 TEAM president (he was narrowly defeated) is director of management information services for B.C. Telephone Co., that bastion of NPA support. In 1972, five members of the board of directors were active members of the NPA. For many years, B.C Telephone was the main source of funding for the NPA.

Another active TEAM member is a supervisor for Crown Life Insurance Co. For many years, Crown Life was headed by Brenton Brown senior, one of the original founders of the NPA. Two of Brown's sons are still influential in the company.

The wives of middle management personnel are also active in TEAM. One TEAM executive member's husband is a vice-president, marketing for Cominco. Cominco president Gerald Hobbs was an NPA vice-president, and Cominco was reputed to be the NPA's second largest source of funds. Elsje Armstrong, a member of Phillips' campaign committee and TEAM's 'girl Friday', is the wife of Bill Armstrong, University of British Columbia deputy president and front man for the NPA-loaded UBC board of governors. Former UBC chancellor Allan McGavin was an NPA executive member, and his firm, McGavin Toastmaster, another large source of NPA funding.

As well as the corporate and professorial types, TEAM included the consultants to big business, architects such as Geoff Massey and Harald Weinreich, engineers such as Tom Ingledow, accountants such as George Wiginton, manager for McDonald Currie & Co., and J.C. Clapham, resident partner for Kates Peat Marwick & Co., and finance consultants such as Phillips himself and Dennis Diebel of Geoffrey A. Higgins & Associates.

But there are other even stronger, more intimate connections between TEAM and the local and national business establishments, and these connections also often lead directly to the NPA. Many local law firms and corporate boards included both NPA and TEAM members. Mayor Art Phillips himself has strong business connections with the NPA through Grouse Mountain Resorts and Bude Holdings, and his former association with Seaboard Life Insurance Co.

Since TEAM and the NPA are so closely aligned the crossing of party lines should not be unusual. Jack Volrich, a current TEAM alderman and past president, was unsuccessful in his bid to get NPA endorsement as a parks board candidate in 1966. Harald Weinreich, another TEAM founder, had tried unsuccessfully to get NPA backing as a city council candidate in 1964. Theo DuMoulin, NPA parks board commissioner, 1960-66, tried to run as a TEAM candidate for council in 1972.

There is a clear merging of interests between TEAM and NPA, but TEAM is much more closely aligned with the Liberal party. Mayor Phillips was onetime campaign manager for Jack Davis, his neighbour on Bowen Island. Phillips himself ran, and lost, as the Liberal candidate for West Point Grey in the 1963 provincial election. Alderman Jack Volrich is a law partner of Liberal MLA Garde Gardom. Another founding member of TEAM, Peter Oberlander, formerly head of the UBC School of Planning and after that Ron Basford's right-hand man at urban affairs in Ottawa, was an unsuccessful Liberal candidate in the 1974 federal election. Ed Lawson, another TEAM founder and president of the Teamsters' Union (he was always held up as TEAM's labour connection), is a Liberal Senator in Ottawa. Architect-developer Rand Iredale, a TEAM fund-raiser, is president of the West Point Grey Liberal Association. Former TEAM director, developer's lawyer Isidore Wolfe, is closely associated with Liberal MP Ron Basford's campaign fund-raising efforts.

But the strongest Liberal party/big business connection of all is through Haig Farris, the fund-raiser for Art Phillips' costly election campaign in 1972, and one of the originators of TEAM in 1968. Through his family and his business, venture capital financing, Farris has contact with many of the powerful political and corporate figures, and, presumably, access to the necessary funds.

All of the TEAM connections are epitomized in Art Phillips, and it is appropriate that he should be TEAM mayor. Phillips is a millionaire like the two previous NPA mayors, Tom Campbell and Bill Rathie, that preceded him. Phillips is a Liberal, as we have already noted. And Phillips' business activities tie him in directly to the centres of business power and indirectly to the NPA.

There were a number of conservative NPDers and liberal social workers associated with TEAM but these never formed more than a very small minority and their influence has declined further as they have gradually drifted out of the organization over the years. The main thrust of TEAM has been to replace the NPA as the business party that controls city council. TEAM has been so tied in with business interests and through them to the NPA that it is impossible to separate the two.

The plum that TEAM captured for the first time in 1972 is power at city council. Basically, power at city council means controlling development and regulating land use. Almost everything city council does, in one way or another, deals with real estate. The city owns it, plans it, protects it, services it, and gets most of its money from it.

The list of services starts with roads, sidewalks, sewers, water (GVRD), and utilities (provincial government). It includes maintaining these facilities and providing garbage collection, fire protection, traffic control, public transportation (GVRD), and public health measures.

Besides servicing urban property, the other main function of city hall is regulating urban property, controlling (usually in minute detail) every aspect of the way every piece of land can be used: what sort of building can be erected, how big it can be, how it must be constructed, and how its occupants may use it. Regulating urban property includes city planning, of course, but it also involves the system of zoning by-laws, by-laws regulating construction of new buildings, by-laws about minimum standards, fire standards of existing buildings, and so on.

The agenda of a typical city council meeting shows about 75% of the time being spent on real estate-related matters. Two of the four standing committees of council — housing and environment, and planning and development — deal exclusively with real estate-related matters. A third — finance and administration — deals with internal city hall operations, and the fourth — community services — deals with 'people' problems. City hall departments and boards can be divided in the same way.

Even parks serve real estate interests. For example, downtown property owners were allowed to cram 20,000 people into the Georgia-Burrard-Pender-Thurlow superblock only because the city was providing a park on the Bowell-Maclean property. By providing a certain proportion of its property as parkland, Marathon Realty Co. was allowed to build a higher density development on its False Creek lands.

With so much of its time and so many of its powers concentrated on real estate — on regulating it, or providing services for it — it is perhaps no surprise that so many of the businessmen who are involved in Vancouver city politics are in some aspect of the real estate and development industry. A very large number of NPA aldermen, often a majority, have been in the real estate business. In 1972, the last year of NPA rule, seven out of the eleven city council members were tied in to the real estate industry: mayor Tom Campbell, developer; Earle Adams, credit agency; Ernie Broome, property insurance agent; Brian Calder, real estate agent; Marianne Linnell, real estate agent; Art Phillips, investment broker; Halford Wilson, former building contractor.

Nor was 1972 an unusual year for real estate representation on city council. The make-up of the 1962 council showed exactly the same trend. Four of the 1972 real estate city council members were on the council that year: Campbell, Adams, Broome and Linnell. Four other aldermen were active in real estate: Orson Banfield, property insurance agent; Aeneas McB. Bell-Irving, steel construction; Frank Fredrickson, insurance agent; Phillip Lipp, real estate agent. Thus in that year, eight out of eleven city council members were in real estate.

In 1972, with TEAM's victory, there was some change. TEAM was very sensitive about its image. As then alderman Art Phillips had put it in a talk to the Building Owners and Managers Association, 'It is important in public affairs not only to do what is right, but to appear to do what is right.' Appearances have always been important to TEAM planners who didn't want any out-and-out developers among their aldermanic hopefuls, so these elements in TEAM were kept in the background. The TEAM strategists sought out the professionals and the experts who work for the developers.

Thus in the 1975-76 city council, only two out of six TEAM council members and one out of four NPA council members are directly involved in real estate: investment counsellor Art Phillips and planner and landscape architect Art Cowie of TEAM; and planner and architect Warnett Kennedy of NPA. But TEAM was top heavy with the professionals who normally act as consultants to the developers and government agencies. According to TEAM backroom planner Paul Tennant, speaking about the TEAM members of the 1973-1974 council:

The nine TEAM members are the cream of the cream. All of them are university graduates; eight of them have post-graduate degrees; and of these eight, four are UBC professors with Ph.Ds or equivalents. What is even more significant is that, with one or two partial exceptions, each of them is a professional expert in an area of direct concern to urban policy-making.

An analysis of the TEAM voting record for 1974, however, shows that these experts had a remarkably similar outlook to the developers and their allies that had run city council for so many years.

27 City Hall bureaucrats and planners

In theory, the elected politicians make the decisions in city council, and the bureaucrats at city hall carry them out. If people don't like those decisions, they can vote the politicians out at the next elections. The bureaucrats, as the official version of city government goes, remain outside the political process and merely carry out the council's orders.

In Vancouver as in every other city, the reality is quite different. For years, Vancouver city hall was run by the city's chief administrator Gerald Sutton-Brown, an English planner who had come to Vancouver in the early 1950s when the city planning department was being set up. Sutton-Brown was the first director of planning and in 1956 was appointed a commissioner on the newly established two-man board of administration, along with John Oliver (Oliver retired in 1964 and was replaced by the present commissioner Lorne Ryan). The city hall bureaucracy was organized into a hierarchical structure, and at the top of the structure was the board of administration, and in particular Gerald Sutton-Brown.

Sutton-Brown's power permeated city hall. He controlled the flow of information from the city hall staff to city council and from council back down to the staff. No report from any department could reach council without going through his hands. Often he rejected reports, sending them back to the author for rewriting to meet his approval. Even then, every report needed a recommendation from the board of administration. Requests or orders from council would be routed by Sutton-Brown to whatever departments he considered relevant.

Sutton-Brown had the power of hiring and firing of staff — a power which extended up to department head level, those immediately below him and with whom he had the most contact. He prepared the annual budget for submission to city council. With this power he could keep departments in line by threatening to cut their departmental allocations for the year. He also had the power to recommend changes in the structure of the way that city hall operated — he could add to or take away power from departments as he wished.

Sutton-Brown or Ryan dealt personally with the outside boards such as the board of parks and public recreation or the city planning commission — and was also the channel from them to city council and to city hall staff. He also played an important role in development decisions. A developer with big plans would first go to the mayor's office and second to

Sutton-Brown. And Sutton-Brown kept close contacts with many local developers.

In effect, Sutton-Brown together with the senior staff made the city's policies. The city's longstanding plans for a freeway system were an illustration of this. As early as 1954 Sutton-Brown and a committee of technical experts had concluded that Vancouver would need a freeway system and developed a comprehensive freeway plan. Over the next 15 years, the members of city council with their varying ideas about transportation came and went, but the freeway plans lived on under Sutton-Brown's careful nurturing. When TEAM came to power in 1972 with its policy for rapid transit, it was necessary to sack Sutton-Brown in order to get rid of the freeway plans. Nowhere was Sutton-Brown's control more complete than in the area of planning.

A complicated structure had been set up in which planning was done at city hall, which involved a city planning department, a technical planning board, a design panel of outside architects and engineers, a city planning commission, and the board of variance which had the power to permit 'minor' variances from zoning by-laws. At the *technical planning board,* representatives of all relevant city departments and outside bodies like the school board and parks board came together to comment on planning proposals. Officially the city's director of planning was the chairman of the technical planning board, but in practice Sutton-Brown and Ryan, who as the board of administration had veto power over every technical planning board decision, dominated its decision-making.

The *design panel* was a group of architects and planners appointed by council to advise the technical planning board on matters of 'public amenity'. The panel should have played an important role in assessing the quality of development proposals, but its terms of reference and scope were so limited as to make it totally ineffectual. It could only deal with matters passed to it by the technical planning board. Even then, it was a purely advisory body, so that more often than not its recommendations were vetoed by the director of planning, the technical planning board or the board of administration. Finally, it was not allowed to address itself to major matters such as the traffic implications or overall impact of a project, but was restricted to matters of cosmetics and facades.

The *city planning commission* had originally been established in 1926 by provincial act as the city's first planning body. Formed at the height of the 1920s building boom, it had been promoted by businessmen concerned about stabilizing property values through planning. When the planning department was set up in 1952, the city planning commission was supposed to become a body of laymen presenting to city council the point of view of the general public in development matters. This did not occur. The members of the commission, appointed by city council, almost always turned out to be defeated Non-Partisan Association aldermanic candidates, more often than not builders, developers or planners. Obviously it was pro-development in outlook, but there were occasions when it took its mandate seriously and opposed objectionable projects. If its opposition got in the way of city council's plans it was conveniently ignored.

The *board of variance,* formerly the zoning board of appeal, had the power, under the Vancouver city charter, to allow relaxations of the city's zoning by-law if strict enforcement would cause undue hardship to an applicant. It was composed of five members, two appointed by the provincial government, two appointed by city council, the four then appointing a chairman. Twenty years of provincial Social Credit rule and 35 years of municipal Non-Partisan Association rule had resulted in a board of variance loaded with pro-development interests that allowed relaxations for favoured developers enabling them to increase the densities of their developments beyond the limits set down in the zoning by-laws.

Normally it was the *city planning department's* position that got watered down because of the lack of leadership exhibited by the director of planning. For ten years, the planning department was headed by Bill Graham, an architect from Saskatoon. In the first place, the director of planning was susceptible to control from the board of administration because of that board's veto power over any planning department recommendation. Secondly, Bill Graham himself was dominated by the strong-willed Sutton-Brown. Sutton-Brown had been the director of planning before Graham, knew the position inside out, and quickly beat down any attempts by Graham at independence. Further, Sutton-Brown was an engineer by training, and was more likely to relate to the city engineer's position than to the planner's.

It seemed that the city planning department gave the developers everything they wanted. All large-scale development proposals were dealt with on a highly confidential basis behind closed doors. Secret meetings would be held between the mayor, senior city council members, the board of administration, the director of planning, and the developer, setting the rules to be followed in their negotiations. Often these decisions were politically tainted. Throughout the process of arriving at a solution acceptable to both parties, Graham would keep in very close contact with the developer and at meetings with his staff seemed to become an advocate for the developer.

Inside the city planning department there was tremendous dissatisfaction, and a steady stream of planners left their jobs and voiced their concern in

City planner said to face trouble

By HARVEY OBERFELD

City planning director Ray Spaxman will be under extreme pressure when he meets city council Aug 1 to iron out problems on local area planning.

A council source told The Vancouver Sun that there are behind-the-scenes indications that at least six aldermen are unhappy with the planner.

Spaxman was hired by city council last fall after it fired former planning director Bill Graham.

Earlier this month, the new

director clashed openly at a city council meeting with ideas put forward by Mayor Art Phillips regarding the department's operation and staffing.

The mayor had suggested substantial changes in the department's setup and local area planning programs.

He had also recommended that council turn down Spaxman's request for 33 more staff members in his 84-member department.

"He (Spaxman) is quite aggressive and to a large degree he is a political person," the council source said.

Vancouver Sun 22 July 1974

Mayor tries to soothe ruffled city planner

Mayor Art Phillips moved today to smooth the ruffled feathers of city planning director Ray Spaxman.

Spaxman had expressed "shock" Tuesday in city council after the mayor released a report over the weekend calling for substantial changes in

the planning department setup and local area planning programs.

Phillips had also recommedned that council turn down Spaxman's request for 33 more in his 84-member department.

Vancouver Sun 10 July 1974

public about the way that both planning principles and the public interest often got lost in the race to give developers everything they asked for.

When TEAM came to power, a partial restructuring of the bureaucracy took place. First to go were Gerald Sutton-Brown and Bill Graham. The board of administration was emasculated to deal with purely internal housekeeping matters such as personnel, budget, legal matters, and other city business of a minor nature, such as property acquisitions and sewer installations. Commissioner Lorne Ryan remained the sole member of the board, and eventually his title was changed to city manager.

To some extent policy-making was taken out of the hands of the administrators and put back into the hands of the elected aldermen. Heads of major departments dealt directly with city council, so that aldermen could hear the various opinions on an issue before making a decision.

The TEAM majority in September 1973 hired a new director of planning, Ray Spaxman, a strong, politically aware, ambitious planner from Toronto. Spaxman proceeded to reshuffle the planning department staff. In February 1974, three of the assistant planning directors lost their titles and administrative duties (without any cutback in salary) and were made 'consultants'. There were further resignations at the same time and the press suggested that Ray Spaxman was in trouble. However mayor Art Phillips stepped in to back up Spaxman. He said that city council was 'extremely pleased' with Spaxman. The planning department had run downhill in recent years and drastic steps were needed.'

Phillips had supported enthusiastically Spaxman's plans for local area planning, one of TEAM's 1972 campaign promises. But Phillips, as late as March 1974 an ardent supporter of Spaxman, soon began to have second thoughts when the consequences of local area planning became apparent. In April Spaxman asked to increase his staff from 81 to 114, with an increase in budget of $500,000 (in 1972, the total budget had been $640,000).

Commissioner Lorne Ryan, representing the old guard in city hall, refused to recommend approval, passing the buck to city council for action. This issue dragged on until July 1974, by which time mayor Art Phillips had become even more disenchanted with planning and refused to approve Ray Spaxman's request. His staff would be kept at its present level of 81. It was further brought out that at the time of Spaxman's request for 33 new positions, there were 16 unfilled positions in the city planning department.

Gerald Sutton-Brown's departure from city hall had left a vacuum, and Spaxman, once settled into his new position, had been looking for more power. For instance, he got more authority to deal with development permit applications. But the social planning and the engineering departments refused to endorse Spaxman's staff enlargement requests. Lorne Ryan pushed the attack home with a recommendation that the social planning department should expand into space then occupied by the planning department, a move strongly resisted by Spaxman.

Spaxman was more successful on another front in his continuing war with the old-line bureaucrats. In December 1974, the technical planning board was abolished. Under the old system, the technical planning board had the final say over many conditional uses in the zoning by-law. These were all transferred to the planning department which now reports directly to city council on all rezoning amendments without the intervention of another body. A development permit advisory council was established composed of the city engineer, the medical officer of health, the director of permits and licences, and others where appropriate, to advise the director of planning.

These changes in the structure of the bureaucracy were a product of the shift in style from the NPA to TEAM. Yet in both cases the bureaucrats were implementing programs and policies consistent with what the city council majority wanted. The bureaucrats and planners do have their independent spheres of action, but only so long as they recognize and respond to the real interests of the city hall majority.

Despite the restructuring of the bureaucracy, an underlying consistency is clearly discernible. In 1967, under the old regime, the CPR came out with a proposal to erect a huge regional shopping centre in the midst of the upper middle-class Arbutus district. In preparing its application for rezoning the property from residential to comprehensive, the developer for the CPR required the use of a number of transportation and economic consultants to prove the need for the shopping centre and to demonstrate that traffic would not be a problem. It was then the job of the planning department to assess the application and to recommend approval or rejection. Many people were extremely upset when the planning department came out in favour of the project. However, it turned out later that the planning department had relied heavily on figures provided by the developers' own consultants in assessing the proposal, rather than undertaking its own independent analysis. A more favourable report could hardly have been done by the CPR itself.

Seven years later, under the new regime, the planning department was engaged in a study of long-range planning for the downtown area. In January 1975, the Downtown Study Team presented its thinking on what the downtown should become. It assumed that the downtown employment population would double from the present 95,000 to about 180,000 in the year 2000. The planning department calls this *controlled growth,* but clearly it is *continued rampant growth.*

To accommodate this growth, the planners recommended putting limits on the existing high-density office core stretching west from Georgia and Granville streets and instituting three new high-density office cores. These would be located: (a) on the Burrard Inlet waterfront, at the foot of Granville St.; (b) on the north end of the Granville St. Bridge; and (c) on the north end of the Cambie St. Bridge. Associated with each would be a major rapid transit stop, intensive retail activity, and adjacent high-density residential accommodation. As it turns out, each of the three high-rise cores happens to be next door to CPR property; the Granville St. and Cambie St. centres

CITY'S DOWNTOWN AREA

Doubling of population projected

By HALL LEIREN
Sun City Hall Reporter

Doubling of both the working and residential populations of Vancouver's downtown area is projected for the year 2000 by a city planning department report going to council Tuesday.

The preliminary report by the department's downtown study team, entitled Future Scenarios for Downtown Vancouver, states that such a growth rate would preserve and enhance downtown livability.

The scenario assumes the employee population in the downtown peninsula would increase to 180,000 in 2000 from about 100,000 this year. The residential population on the peninsula is projected to rise too 105,000, from the present 47,000.

The preferred s c e n a r i o takes what the report calls the "useful middle ground" between two extremes.

The extremes consist of a no-growth policy that would be achievable only if very s t r o n g inter-governmental controls were applied immediately, and the u n l i m i t e d growth that would occur if only minimal controls were applied.

Vancouver Sun 27 July 1974

flank the CPR's False Creek holdings, and the foot-of-Granville St. centre flanks the CPR's waterfront property.

The astronomical increase in value of land located near rapid transit stops is well-known. Usually the windfall profits go to a considerable number of developers and owners; this time most of the increase will accrue to just one company — the CPR. And even the CPR could not have envisioned a more favourable plan.

And TEAM's new-look city planning commission was remarkably similar in composition to the commission of the old Non-Partisan Association days. The members of the 1975 city planning commission, appointed by city council are:

George Brekalo: defeated NPA aldermanic candidate 1974, president of the Pacific Northwest Automotive Dealers Association; lives in West Vancouver.

Margaret Pigott: defeated NPA parks board candidate 1974, housewife; vice-chairman, Save the Entrance to Stanley Park Committee; secretary, Save Our Parkland Association; was on city planning commission before.

Stan Hamilton: real estate consultant and professor of commerce and business administration, University of B.C.

Jim Lowden: senior planner with the GVRD
Marlene Hier: Ph.D., instructor in planning, University of B.C., and TEAM director.

John MacD. Lecky: member of the city planning commission since 1966 and its past chairman; a director of Sun Publishing Co., publishers of the Vancouver *Sun;* former director of Cunningham Drug Stores.

Geoff Massey: developer-architect, former TEAM alderman, lives in West Vancouver.

Joseph Segall: president of Fields Stores; his board of directors is a hornet's nest of development interests; there are interlocking directorships with Block Bros. Industries (two in common), First City Financial Corp., Pemberton Securities, Grouse Mountain Resorts, Blue Boy Motor Hotel, Wakely Insurance Agencies, Garibaldi Olympic Developments Association.

King Ganong: a senior bureaucrat with Central Mortgage and Housing Corp.

VOTING RECORD SUMMARY

	Planning and Development	Tenants	Citizen power	Relations with property industry	TOTAL
GOVERNMENT GROUP					
Hard-line					
Fritz Bowers TEAM	1-5	0-4	0-3	0-2	1-14
Art Phillips TEAM	1-5	0-3	0-3	0-3	1-14
Walter Hardwick TEAM	1-5	1-2	0-3	0-3	2-13
Marianne Linnell NPA	2-4	1-3	0-3	0-1	3-11
John Volrich TEAM	2-4	0-4	2-1	0-3	4-12
Setty Pendakur TEAM	2-3	1-1	1-2	0-2	4-8
Soft-line					
Geoff Massey TEAM	6-0	0-4	1-2	0-3	7-9
Bill Gibson TEAM	4-2	2-0	1-1	1-2	8-5
Michael Harcourt TEAM	4-2	2-2	3-0	2-1	11-5
OPPOSITION GROUP					
Harry Rankin COPE	6-0	4-0	3-0	3-0	16-0
Darlene Marzari TEAM	6-0	4-0	3-0	3-0	16-0

Development & planning issues

1. Requiring Ben Wosk, owner of the Sheraton Landmark Hotel, to turn off his outside yellow night-time lights, as they did not conform with the terms of the development permit and were upsetting many people (Jan. 15/74).

2. Negotiating a compromise design solution with United Equities Ltd., who were proposing a 23-storey addition to their West End Sands Motor Hotel (Jan. 15/74).

3. Down-zoning the highrise areas of Kitsilano to a 3-storey maximum for a one year period (Jan. 31/74).

4. Asking the provincial government to buy the Birks Building since the Vancouver City Council lacked the power to prevent the demolition of any historical building (March 19/74).

5. Allowing Ben Wosk to put an addition on his Sheraton 500 Hotel over the objections of neighbouring residents (approval in principle (July 23/74).

6. Allowing the Canadian Legion to change its funding arrangements with CMHC, so that it could go ahead with a high rise for senior citizens over the objections of the residents of the area (March 12/74).

Tenant's issues

7. Urging the provincial government to tie rent increases to the cost of living index for the previous year (Jan. 22/74).

8. Asking Block Bros. to agree to mediation of a dispute with Century House Tenants' Association who organized after Block Bros. raised their rents from 20-30 per cent (Feb. 5/74).

9. Limiting rent increases in city-owned Englesea Lodge to 9.3% (March 12/74).

10. Passing a by-law which would give the city discretionary power to prevent the demolition of housing which was affording accommodation for low income tenants (June 25/74).

Citizen Involvement

11. Reimbursing the West Broadway Citizens' Committee $275 for expenses incurred in publicizing the down-zoning of Kitsilano hearing after the director of Planning had noted that the West Broadway Citizens activities "contributed significantly to the high degree of community involvement" (April 23/74).

12. Chopping 1/3 from a grant request by the Community Development Unit of Neighbourhood Services Association for funds to pay its community development workers (April 9/74).

13. Agreeing to a request for a further down-zoning of Kitsilano made by the Kitsilano Planning Committee, representing the citizens of Kitsilano (July 9/75)

Relations with property industry

14. Setting up a committee to examine the problem of the speculative buying of buildings, rent raising and remortgaging which was driving up rentals and housing prices (April 9/74).

15. Asking the provincial government to water down its Public Officials and Employees Disclosure Act so that information on only a portion of an official's holdings would be available to the public (May 28/74).

16. In a by-law to regulate street vending, leaving to city hall control so that "incompatible goods and displays in poor taste would not be detrimental to adjacent property owners" (June 11/74).

28 TEAM in power

With a TEAM majority and the personnel changes in the city hall bureaucracy after the 1972 election, some changes were made in the mindlessly pro-developer, pro-freeway policies of the previous NPA administration. But even though some TEAM decisions moderated the conflict between citizen groups and city hall that had been so strong during mayor Tom Campbell's term of office, there was no major shift in direction by TEAM. And on the few matters where TEAM promised to make major reforms, their election victory was quickly followed by a retreat from those promises.

The best overall picture of TEAM's performance in power comes from an analysis of the city council voting record. The period from January to August 1974 was selected as a reasonably representative one for the TEAM majority. It came after 1973, during which time TEAM aldermen often claimed they were dealing with the unfinished business of the previous administration. And it ended before the pre-election period of 1974, when the city politicians might have been paying more attention than usual to the concerns of the electorate.

Sixteen major issues came to a vote between January and August 1974. Pro-citizen interests received a majority on four. Three of these were development and planning issues: downzoning the high-rise areas of Kitsilano for one year; requiring hotel owner Ben Wosk to turn off his yellow night-time lights; and asking the provincial government to buy the Birks Building. The fourth pro-people vote was on a tenant issue, limiting rent increases in city-owned Englesea Lodge to 9.3%.

Of the remaining 12 votes, 11 went against the people and in favour of developers and business interests. The twelfth issue, on cutting the grant to the community development unit of the Neighbourhood Services Association, had a pro-developer outcome because even though a majority of aldermen voted *not* to cut the grant, a two-thirds majority of council was required to approve the funds.

The TEAM city council voted against citizen involvement on all three issues which came up during the period, and voted for the property industry on all occasions.

In terms of their voting record, there is no doubt that TEAM was continuing the pattern of city government, friendly to the real estate and development industry, which had so long been maintained by the NPA. The image was different, but the votes went

much the same way.

A younger version of the NPA was certainly not the way TEAM billed itself in its election campaigns. And in fact there were some relatively strong reform measures which were part of TEAM's platform. Immediately after the 1972 election, however, TEAM began to forget their campaign promises.

One of the important changes promised by TEAM was a return to a ward system in Vancouver. This would be an important step in reducing links between corporate business and property industry with city hall, and would make it easier for people to elect aldermen who supported their interests. TEAM did hold a referendum on the issue in October 1973, but by that time the TEAM city council members were split, with some wanting a full ward system and others wanting only a partial ward system. The public was inevitably confused by this, and mayor Art Phillips avoided playing any part in the public discussion or coming out strongly in favour of TEAM's original commitment to a full ward system. The media launched a vehement attack on any kind of ward system, and TEAM did nothing to counteract this propaganda. The outcome of the referendum was a foregone conclusion — defeat for the ward system.

Another area where TEAM backed quickly away from its policies was on neighbourhood and city planning. TEAM proposed decentralized planning, with community planners assigned to neighbourhoods to work with local groups. Ray Spaxman, the director of planning hired by TEAM, was chosen especially for his experience in this method of operation. But when he set to work in earnest, establishing planning offices in several parts of the city, TEAM began to back-pedal furiously. The problem was that local people were getting involved and were coming up with recommendations that city council did not want to hear: controlling growth, downzoning, local control over development. The newspapers weighed in against Spaxman's approach, and TEAM cut back. The very first recommendation that came from the Kitsilano Citizens' Planning Committee — to downzone areas of Kitsilano temporarily until a plan for the area had been completed — was slapped down by the TEAM majority at city council.

On the key issue of growth, TEAM's approach did differ from that of the NPA, but only in detail. The NPA attitude was that what was good for the developer was good for the city as a whole. Art Phillips claimed to want to adopt a 'selective approach' toward development, saying 'I'm not one of those who believes that all growth is good.'

What Phillips and his TEAM colleagues meant by statements like these was that they weren't against more high-rises; they simply wanted them to be more attractive and more spread out. As Phillips told the

Downtown Business Association: 'Downtown is the executive centre of western Canada. There is a great deal of room for expansion in the core area. But I believe basic densities should be reduced.'

TEAM did downzone the downtown commercial areas, but this merely spread the development out. If anything, the pace of downtown development increased after TEAM took office. One reason for this was that downtown business interests were happier about a TEAM administration than the NPA, and considered TEAM a more stable group. The other reason was TEAM's promotion of rapid transit oriented toward the downtown core. Even before TEAM won the 1972 election, downtown business interests had seen the wisdom of rapid transit access to downtown rather than a spaghetti-maze of freeways with half the core area given over to parking. A rapid transit system would make downtown more accessible to people, make the limited supply of downtown land more desirable for development, and hence increase its already inflated value.

The real issue for downtown was how to control the total growth of population in the Vancouver area and the continuing concentration of office workers. TEAM did not deal with this.

Perhaps the most telling example of the TEAM approach to city government came in the False Creek development issue. Land ownership around False Creek (really a bay that separates the downtown Vancouver peninsula from the inner residential neighbourhoods), was divided between the province and the CPR. When the CPR decided that it would be profitable to use the land for high-density residential and commercial uses, the city obligingly rezoned it from heavy industrial to residential-commercial-recreational. Following a complex series of land swaps, the city ended up owning 85 acres on the south side of the creek, and the CPR ended up owning the north side. Early in 1972, as a gesture to the TEAM minority on the 1971-72 city council, NPA mayor Tom Campbell set up a special False Creek committee under TEAM alderman Walter Hardwick to oversee the total False Creek development, and to plan for the city's 85 acres.

Harwick hired a private developer, E.D. Sutcliffe, to act as liaison with private developers and to set up controls to ensure a quality development. Attempts by citizen groups to have some influence over the planning of the project were nipped in the bud by Hardwick. When Fairview slopes residents — next door to the city's land — found out that the city had almost finished its detailed plan, they set up an organization of all concerned groups in Fairview to deal with city hall. Hardwick first responded by questioning the validity of the organization and refusing to deal with it. A series of meetings were then organized to tell residents about the city's plans, but no channels were set up to enable residents to respond to these proposals. A community worker was hired to promote the city's plans, and when she began organizing real citizen input she was quickly fired. To avoid the genuine citizen groups, Hardwick set up two advisory committees on housing and open space, composed of developers, academics, and professionals. Even these committees came up with recommendations which Hardwick found unacceptable, so he scrapped them.

One of the crucial issues about the project was the mix of the housing which would be built on the city's land. Originally there had been talk about providing housing for low-income families, those with the greatest need. But these ideas gradually disappeared from the discussions between politicians and planners. TEAM argued that the land was too valuable for subsidized low-income housing, and besides that the poor do not need to live close to downtown. The outcome was a decision that only a third of the housing should be for families earning below $9,600, and two-thirds for those above.

The False Creek project clearly illustrated the reality of TEAM in power in Vancouver, running roughshod over the needs and wishes of the citizens to serve downtown business interests and large corporate interests. Its actions revealed TEAM for what it was, the old business establishment with a new face.

Part V Citizen Opposition: The Record

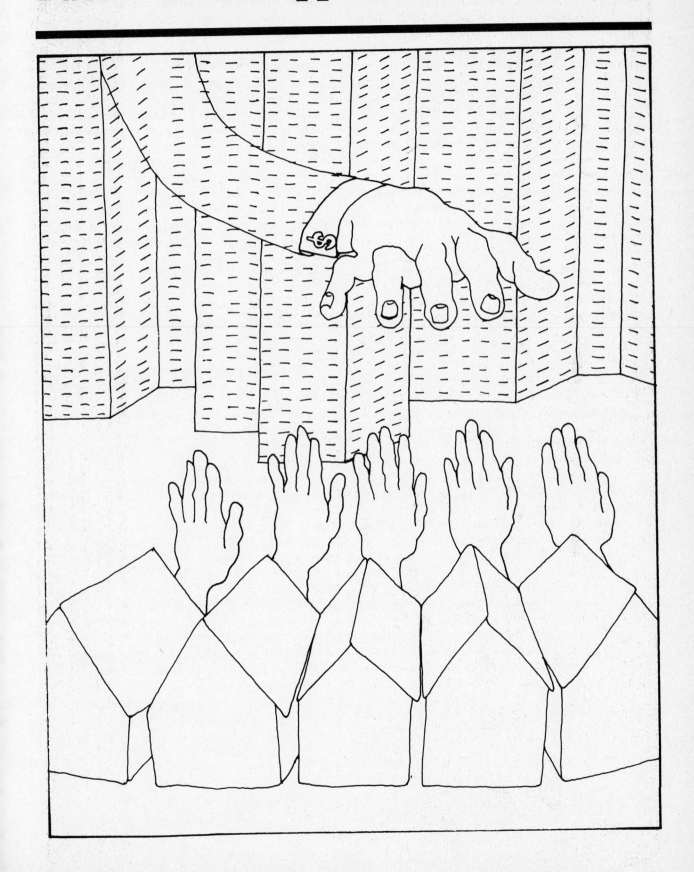

Up to now, in our description of the way development occurs in Vancouver, things have looked pretty grim. Developers and multi-national and national corporations, in alliance with the financiers, are changing Vancouver into a regional executive and administrative centre. Through the local business establishment and its dominance in the local political parties, they have been able to exert strong control over the direction of Vancouver's development. Both the Non-Partisan Association (NPA) and The Elector's Action Movement (TEAM) seem dedicated to accommodating their every wish. The parties' handling of the major issues for Vancouver — control of growth and citizen participation — shows that they have little dedication to the interests of the present residents of Vancouver. Even the city hall bureaucracy seems structured to accommodate developers and is little able to preserve and maintain existing neighbourhoods or current value systems.

Vancouver's destiny has been in the grip of profit-hungry developers and speculators ever since there was a Vancouver — and even before.

But it hasn't been all bad. Time after time, average Vancouver residents have come to the rescue, to stop developments when they were seen to be harmful to the interests of the citizens or destructive to the environment. The recent history of Vancouver is rich in such actions, ranging from the big freeway controversies — the Cassiar St. connection, the third crossing of Burrard Inlet, the Chinatown freeway — to the massive public and private redevelopment schemes — the gigantic Arbutus Shopping Centre, urban redevelopment in Strathcona, Four Seasons site — to the park and beach issues — Adanac on the east side, Jericho and Wreck Beach on the west side — to more local controversies — Shannon estate, Broadway beautification. As well as the big-name fights, there have been the innumerable confrontations with bulldozers and unscrupulous landlords, unsympathetic city council, and the indifferent bureaucracy at city hall. These actions demonstrate that the citizens of Vancouver *are* deeply concerned about their environment and their living conditions.

Nor is citizen action in Vancouver a new thing. As early as 1906, residents in both Grandview and Kitsilano areas were organizing to protest poor conditions. Both areas were in the midst of their biggest building booms, after being opened up in 1905 with the construction of streetcar lines, to Grandview along Park Dr. (now Commercial St.), and to Kitsilano over the Kitsilano Trestle Bridge and along the waterfront. Both areas were rapidly filled with single-family homes, but the city was unable to keep up with the need for services — the roads, sewers, water, sidewalks. The residents had houses, but that was about all. Most of Grandview was without

sidewalks. Children had to walk to school along the electric railway tracks, thus endangering their lives. Their mothers were virtual prisoners in their own homes. In 1907, Grandview residents formed the Grandview Progress Association to make their demands heard at an unsympathetic city hall.

In Kitsilano as well, the city dragged its feet in installing essential services. The same year residents had formed the Kitsilano Ratepayers Association 'to promote and advance the financial and social interests of the body of ratepayers within, and the physical welfare of, the Kitsilano district.' Although in the midst of a long period of decline, with a very reactionary outlook toward urban issues, this ratepayers group exists today, making it one of the oldest continually active such groups in Canada.

The Kitsilano Ratepayers Association rose to prominence during the hungry thirties, fighting for reduced property taxes and for conservative spending policies, such as lowering the salaries of aldermen. They also fought a number of issues that threatened to destroy the residential nature of Kitsilano. In 1929, Harland Bartholomew, an American planner, had prepared a plan for Vancouver. One of Bartholomew's proposals was to build a Burrard St. Bridge to link the downtown peninsula to Kitsilano and then to connect the bridge to the corner of Arbutus St. and Broadway with an elevated freeway which would then proceed up Arbutus St. to Kerrisdale and the outer suburbs. In Bartholomew's plan, the freeway would have required the destruction of many Kitsilano homes. The ratepayers association fought the scheme, but they lost the Burrard St. Bridge part of it; the bridge was built and there was a drastic increase in the amount of traffic through the area; but they were able to fight off the Burrard-Arbutus connector. Once something is on the books at city hall it never dies. Forty years later, the city is still trying to build the connector although this time the ratepayers association is in favour of it. Other citizen groups have organized to carry on the fight.

Citizens organized again in 1937 to oppose the construction of the Lions Gate Bridge over the First Narrows of Burrard Inlet, and the causeway through Stanley Park which led from downtown to the bridge. The construction of the causeway would mean the destruction of many stately Douglas firs. However, the interests promoting the bridge and causeway, the Guinness family's British Properties, were far too influential, and the trees were felled and the causeway built.

The greatest flowering of citizen opposition occured during 1967 and 1968, when a number of separate concerns and issues coalesced to cause the first questioning of the old value, that whatever was good for the developers must be good for the city. The major issues which just seemed to arise one after the

other included the urban renewal of Strathcona, the freeway through Chinatown, the Arbutus Shopping Centre, the Four Seasons Hotels project, and the third crossing of Burrard Inlet. Because of massive and prolonged opposition, not one of those projects went ahead in its original form. At the same time, it was becoming clear to many people in the Vancouver establishment that the Non-Partisan Association (NPA) was losing its base of support, and a new political party would have to be set up. That party, The Electors Action Movement (TEAM), came as a direct response to one issue in particular, the great freeway debate, in late 1967 and early 1968.

We have already seen the real meaning behind the rise of TEAM to power in city council, but what about the protests themselves? Was anything more substantial gained by the citizens of Vancouver? As we will see, there have been gains — but there have been losses as well.

29 The Chinatown Freeway fight

For many years, the City of Vancouver together with business interests had been trying to build a network of freeways through and around Vancouver, but had been frustrated in every attempt both by unco-operative federal and provincial governments and hostile public reaction. As early as 1954, a committee of North Shore and Vancouver politicians and bureaucrats, and real estate interests, had recommended a third crossing of Burrard Inlet. They were worried that a congested Lions Gate Bridge might slow down development on the North Shore. Provincial premier Wacky Bennett's response was to buy the Lions Gate Bridge from the Guinness family interests that had owned it. But the committee's recommendation to build an additional crossing became a basic assumption in every succeeding report and study.

A long chain of reports on reports and studies of studies followed, each building on the previous ones, the number and location of freeways becoming more and more fixed in the minds of the city and its hired consultants. Rail rapid transit was rejected in a 1961 provincial study which had concluded that there just was not enough demand to justify the expense. But that study had been based on a 1959 study which had been based on data collected in 1956.

The 1959 study had assumed that there would be an east-west freeway by 1980, and that most people would be travelling by car, so that the cheapest form of rapid transit would be express buses on the freeway. The assumption that the freeway would be built clearly biased the estimates of demand for other kinds of transportation. Nevertheless, the conclusions of this study, that there was insufficient demand for rapid transit, became another built-in assumption on every succeeding study.

The city made its freeway decisions on the basis of who would pay for the parts of the freeway system rather than on the need. Thus a third crossing of Burrard Inlet was seen to be a good idea because Burrard Inlet was a national port, and the federal government would contribute toward the cost. Another decision made in 1965 was to build a waterfront freeway to connect to the new crossing and to service the proposed $300 million Project 200. It seems that this decision was made because the Canadian Pacific Railway, owner of most of the waterfront, had tentatively agreed to donate the right-of-way. This surprising largesse becomes understandable when you realize that the CPR was one of the major owners of Project 200, and a third Burrard Inlet crossing and waterfront freeway were considered essential for the economic viability of the development. This decision, too, became built into the freeway jigsaw

Two more pieces were added the same year. The 1964 amendments to the National Housing Act had authorized the federal government to contribute to the transportation aspects of urban renewal projects. The city immediately set to work planning an east-west freeway as part of the Strathcona urban renewal project. The plan the city produced required the demolition of 600 houses. In 1965 Vancouver ratepayers were asked to vote on a $10 million money by-law authorizing city council to replace the 'structurally unsound' Georgia Viaduct. Assuming this meant simply putting up a new viaduct, voters passed the by-law. There was no indication that the viaduct would be part of a freeway system, since Vancouver at that time had no overall transportation plan (as far as the public was aware).

In late 1965, the city hired engineering consultants Phillips, Barratt and Partners to study a new alignment for the Georgia Viaduct and to advise city council on street planning in the Strathcona urban renewal area near the viaduct. The consultants were asked to 'consider' certain freeway components when designing the new viaduct — an east-west freeway along Venables and/or Prior streets; a waterfront freeway, and a third crossing; and a north-south freeway along Main St. 'Consider' turned out to mean 'assume that these freeways would be built.' Yet none of the 'components' were officially adopted by city council, except for the waterfront freeway which had been approved in principle. But by setting these guidelines, council was committing $10 million of the taxpayers money to a project which was expected to fix Vancouver's transportation system permanently in the direction of this freeway system without any public discussion.

Encouraged by the smoothness of the process, city council hired another firm of consultants, Parsons, Brinkerhoff, Quade and Douglas (PBQ&D) of San Francisco in August 1966, to evolve a general transportation plan for Vancouver. This was to be done in conjunction with the Georgia Viaduct study being undertaken by Phillips, Barratt and Partners.

On June 1, 1967, city council was presented with the Vancouver Transportation Study (VTS) by PBQ&D, Phillips, Barratt and Partners, and Erickson-Massey, architectural consultants. Not surprisingly, the $212,000 study recommended a waterfront freeway connected to the Georgia Viaduct via a Carrall St. connection cutting through Chinatown, and thence to a north-south freeway and an east-west freeway extending to the city boundaries. Council

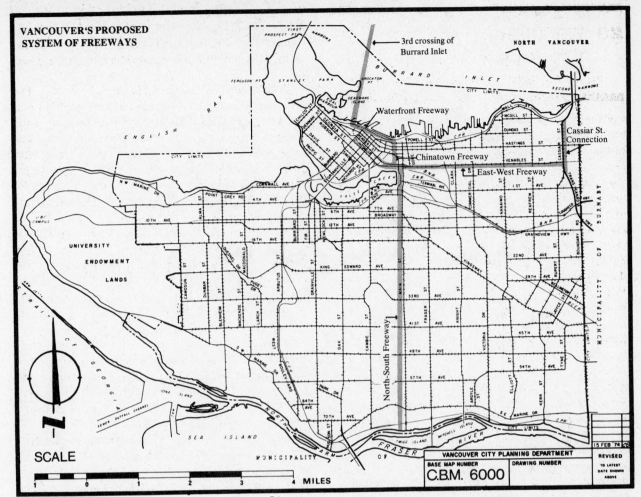

3rd crossing of
Burrard Inlet

NORTH VANCOUVER

Waterfront Freeway

Cassiar St.
Connection

Chinatown Freeway

East-West Freeway

North-South Freeway

UNIVERSITY
ENDOWMENT
LANDS

MUNICIPALITY OF SUBURBY

SCALE

1   0   1   2   3   4   MILES

VANCOUVER CITY PLANNING DEPARTMENT		REVISED
BASE MAP NUMBER	DRAWING NUMBER	TO LATEST DATE SHOWN ABOVE
C.B.M. 6000		15 FEB '74

was to consider and vote on the VTS in two weeks' time.

City council's intention to accept the recommendations of the VTS sparked the strongest public protest Vancouver had ever experienced. The freeway connection between the waterfront freeway and the Georgia Viaduct was to be an eight lane, 200-foot wide, 30-foot high wall cutting into the western edge of Chinatown. A campaign to save Chinatown was immediately launched by Chinese businessmen (led by the Chinese Benevolent Society) and local architects. The businessmen claimed that the freeway would suffocate the business life of Chinatown; the architects that it would kill chances for revitalization of the historic Chinatown; and the Chinatown Property Owners Association that it would result in the loss of one of Vancouver's foremost tourist attractions. At the June 15 meeting when council was to make its decision, it was shocked to discover the narrow terms of reference that had been given to the consultants by city hall staff — the consultants had not been authorized to consider any alternative to the Chinatown freeway.

It was further revealed that the consultants were taking instructions from a group called the trans-portation steering committee which included representatives from the National Harbours Board, the CPR, and B.C. Hydro & Power Authority. One alignment which would have skirted Chinatown on the west had been rejected by this committee because it would have interfered with the Project 200 proposal and the offices of the CPR. Another alignment to the east was rejected because the National Harbours Board did not want the freeway running over its property. Thus Chinatown was the only answer. After hearing these revelations council bowed to public pressure and decided to have a public hearing in three weeks time.

At the July 5 meeting, 17 delegations voiced opposition to the consultants' proposals. City council further bowed to public pressure and agreed to authorize the consultants to undertake a further study with extended terms of reference — to study all possible connections. This study took several months to complete and served to hold off public pressure temporarily.

The consultants reported back in October that the Carrall St. alignment was the least expensive. City council endorsed the consultants' report on October 17. However it was revealed under renewed public

155

If the Chinatown freeway had been built, this photo would have been taken from a spot directly underneath the middle of the 30-foot high 200-foot wide structure. In contrast, Carrall St. (centre of the photo) is only 50 feet wide.

protest that the consultants 'free hand' had been limited to a study of Gore St. two blocks further east, a single alternative.

City council's decision to reconfirm its Carrall St. motion caused even stronger public reaction which eventually forced council to hold another public meeting. The November 23, 1967 meeting was explosive. The arrogance of some city politicians, especially mayor Tom Campbell, sparked angry response from the audience. Over 500 people crammed into Vancouver's city hall. After three and a half hours, only one of 20 delegations had been heard, and council was forced to schedule another meeting to hear the rest of the briefs.

The following meeting two weeks later which 800 people attended was more orderly but still almost unanimous in its condemnation of the consultants' proposals and city council's actions in relation to the study. Even such traditionally strong council supporters as the Board of Trade, the Building Owners and Managers Association, the Architectural Institute of B.C., and the Downtown Business Association stressed the need for proper long-range planning. The only group that supported the freeway proposals was the city-appointed city planning commission. The commission chairman presented the brief, then resigned from the commission on the spot because he couldn't agree with the stand taken by the other members.

City council debated the matter over the next few meetings but postponed a decision until after Christmas. City officials strongly recommended that council approve the consultants' report and continue with the current studies. But on January 9, 1968, council rescinded its previous motion and scrapped the Carrall St. alignment plan, thus saving Chinatown from the 'concrete knife'. At the same meeting council voted to proceed with the Georgia Viaduct, which was completed in 1971.

The citizens of Vancouver were thus able to stop one element of the ubiquitous plans for freeways, but in so doing they let another part slip through, a part which was designed to fit into the very transportation system that the protests were aimed at stopping. So, Chinatown was saved from immediate demolition, but this method of reactive protest could at best only buy time.

At the second public meeting discussing Vancouver's freeway system in 1967, the Vancouver Board of Trade and the Communist Party of Canada were allied in opposing the Chinatown freeway.

PUBLIC MEETING BECOMES SHOUTING MATCH
Freeway Foes Heap Scorn on Campbell

By GEORGE PELOQUIN
Sun City Hall Reporter

A public meeting on freeways was turned into a shouting, arm-waving melee and was adjourned by Mayor Tom Campbell Thursday night when he felt it had reached near-riot proportions.

Campbell, who looked calm through it all, cut the meeting off after three hours and said another would be held in the next two weeks at a location at to be announced.

A crowd of 500 jamming the council chamber and overflowing into two adjacent committee rooms heaped scorn on members of council and hurled abuse at city officials.

Seasoned observers at city hall said it was the most disorderly meeting they could recall.

Campbell later summed it up as a "near-riot."

At one point it became unclear who was running the meeting — Campbell, or the critics of the city's planned freeway network.

Campbell was called a coward by someone in the crowd when he called for a coffee break adjournment and Alderman Ernie Broome and Peter Graham were booed off the floor.

Some individuals called for the firing of city traffic engineer Kenneth Vaughan-Birch and Ald. Broome called for the ejection of principal freeway critic and University of B.C. professor Walter Hardwick.

Minutes after the meeting started Campbell announced there was a sell-out crowd.

"It was a sell-out before it started," someone shouted back.

Campbell urged speakers to come to the microphone so those in the committee rooms could hear.

Someone mentioned the closest one was behind Campbell's desk and he suggested the person come up and use it.

"I can't get in there until after the election," the person shot back.

Vancouver Sun 24 November 1967

30 The Strathcona urban renewal fight

Strathcona is city hall's name for the residential area bounded by Gore, Hastings, Raymur, and Prior streets. To the east is Grandview-Woodlands, to the north of Hastings St. the mixed residential-commercial area of Japantown, to the south the Canadian National Railway tracks, and to the west the commercial, visible parts of Chinatown. Most people know this area as the residential part of Chinatown; in fact just over 50% of the population was Chinese. There were substantial Russian and other caucasian minorities living in the area, but it was the Chinese community that led the long fight against urban renewal.

Chinese immigration to Vancouver started in 1858 and continued until the completion of the Canadian Pacific Railway in 1885. At that time, no longer needing the cheap Chinese labour, the federal government levied a head tax of $50 on new immigrants. This was subsequently increased to $500 in 1903. A few years later white pressure groups staged a number of violent labour riots and the British Columbia government barred Chinese from public schools. A ban on all Chinese immigration was instituted in 1923 and lasted until 1947.

Ten years later, in 1957, Strathcona, the home of many Chinese Canadians, was selected for an urban renewal project sponsored by the federal, provincial and city governments. The plan was based on superficial data and followed the usual lines of proposals for urban renewal areas: expropriation, demolition, and a combination of new public housing, private development, and new industrial uses.

City officials liked the project, but the home owners and small businessmen who would be displaced by the program did not look too kindly upon it. Similar programs elsewhere such as Regent Park in Toronto had been dismal failures, and residents felt that the proposed redevelopment could destroy their neighbourhood. Strathcona had been a good residential area for 40 to 50 years, and already had many of the amenities essential to viable neighbourhoods — schools, churches, social centres. True the area was run-down in places, but it could be easily repaired. However, once the city designated the area for urban renewal, deterioration became rampant. The city stopped putting any money in for repairs and maintenance — it stopped fixing the roads and sidewalks, didn't clean the streets, and so on. Residents often followed the city's lead.

City council approved the Vancouver Redevelopment Study in principle on February 4, 1958. In April, the city invited citizens to attend meetings at City Hall to view and discuss these plans for Strathcona urban renewal.

On hearing the news, 300 Chinese residents met to establish the Chinatown Property Owners Association. Their first decision was to send a delegation to the city council meeting to 'fight against demolition' and save their homes. In April 1958, council heard their protests and pleas. Council advised the citizens that the 1957 study was really only 'preliminary' and that the proposed redevelopment program was 'tentative and approximate'. The citizens went home. Eight days later, city council rezoned about 90 acres from commercial and industrial uses in the area to residential, the first step in the program. Council then began making plans for Urban Renewal Project No. 1.

Final plans for the area were completed a year later and formally adopted by city council on March 10, 1960, with little publicity. A public meeting was held in October of that year. A delegation of 50 persons representing 68 Chinese societies, seven Chinese Christian churches, and four language schools, and led by the Chinatown Property Owners Association appeared before council and made their objections known. This time, council simply voted to acknowledge the delegation, and told the residents that the city was already committed to the urban renewal plans.

This first urban renewal project in Strathcona was carried out between 1961 and 1967. It displaced 1,600 people and cleared 28 acres of land (most of which had been single-family homes) for public housing and industrial lots. In addition, one block was acquired for a new park to replace the former McLean Park (which had been used as the site for the first McLean Park housing project).

Numerous delays in the project resulted in major problems for the residents of the area. A squabble developed among all three levels of government over who had jurisdiction and who had to pay for what. This caused undue delays and inter-governmental recriminations. Some of the expropriated land lay barren for four years until redeveloped as public housing.

In July 1961, just as it began to buy the properties for Urban Renewal Project No. 1, council voted to prepare a second urban renewal plan covering another part of Strathcona. This took one year to complete. The Chinatown Property Owners Association — now reorganized as many of the original members had been forced to move out after their properties had been expropriated — presented a brief to city council in January 1963, opposing the project.

From that time until September 1963, when city council approved Urban Renewal Project No. 2, the briefs poured in objecting to the plan. The city had set up a redevelopment consultative committee to involve the area residents in the planning but in 1963, Foon Sien, president of the Chinatown Property Owners Association, resigned because he felt that his position on the committee was mere tokenism.

Nevertheless, city council approved the second project in September 1963, and in 1965 began clearing the land. It displaced 1,730 people and cleared 29 acres for industrial lots, private and public housing, and a school and recreation site.

Prior to 1964, city governments had to pay for roads and services in urban renewal projects. However in that year the federal government decided to share in the cost of these items. This prompted Vancouver to prepare a third, far more extensive scheme under the new provisions. What really was happening was that the city was desperate to find sources of funding for its proposed freeway system. In 1965, the electorate voted funds for a replacement for the Georgia Viaduct (without realizing that it was going to be part of an extensive freeway system). The city next wanted an east-west freeway to link the viaduct with the Trans-Canada Highway at Cassiar St. Part of the costs for the freeway and access roads could be paid for out of urban renewal funds, especially where it sliced by Strathcona. The east-west freeway could then link up with the proposed waterfront freeway by the Chinatown freeway connection going up Carrall St. or Gore St.

This time around, resident protests were stronger, better organized, and achieved far greater success. In May 1965, the Strathcona Area Council, a voluntary organization, had been set up under the auspices of the United Community Services, in an attempt to coordinate services in the Strathcona area. The area council was typical of most area councils that had sprung up over the past few years: it was composed of well-meaning professionals who had little connection with the people who actually lived in th area. It was prepared to write briefs, but not to take any stronger actions.

After the preliminary report for Urban Renewal Project No. 3 had been submitted to city council, it was referred to the United Community Services and from there to the Strathcona Area Council. During late 1967 and early 1968 the area council sponsored a number of meetings to determine the community's reaction to the report and to present briefs to city council. The briefs accepted the need for demolition of homes and dwelt on the council's proposed policies for relocating people displaced by the demolitions. However, very few people actually threatened by displacement attended these meetings.

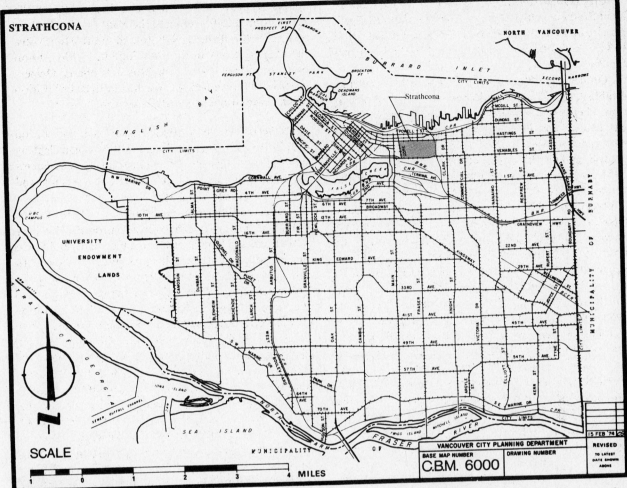

STRATHCONA

VANCOUVER CITY PLANNING DEPARTMENT
BASE MAP NUMBER | DRAWING NUMBER
C.B.M. 6000

REVISED
TO LATEST
DATE SHOWN
ABOVE

15 FEB '74

SCALE

MILES

But at a meeting held by the Strathcona Area Council on October 17, 1968, Chinese residents turned up in very large numbers to voice their bitter opposition to the urban renewal scheme and demanded the right to stay in Strathcona. The situation was becoming desperate: the city had just approved the clearing of 424 properties in 22 blocks which would displace 3,000 people.

After the meeting the Strathcona Area Council prepared a brief to city council. But the brief failed to reflect the outright hostility of the residents to the renewal project and, instead, concentrated on asking for fairer prices for houses and for more effective assistance in relocating people. It was this weak brief that led the residents to realize that the area council could not represent their interests adequately.

With the help of community development workers, the residents began to organize among themselves to get what they wanted. On November 7, 1968, Paul Hellyer, the federal minister responsible for housing, and his task force on housing and urban development, held meetings in Vancouver. They heard appeals against the demolition of houses in Strathcona. Having heard similar pleas from residents' groups in urban renewal areas across Canada — and faced with

exploding budgets to cover the federal government's open-ended commitment to share urban renewal costs — the task force led quickly to a freeze on funding for urban renewal.

In the meantime, the Strathcona residents carried on their organizing on a block-by-block basis and at a meeting held on December 14, 1968, the overflow audience agreed to form the Strathcona Property Owners and Tenants Association (SPOTA) 'to ensure that the people who live in this area will be fully informed and that their interests and their community will be protected.'

SPOTA began an intensive lobbying campaign aimed at all three levels of government. Its basic demands were: the right for local residents to continue to live in Strathcona; a fair exchange value if their homes were expropriated; priority for local people who wished to build on certain blocks; and a chance for small businesses in the area. Although Paul Hellyer resigned in April 1969, his successor, Robert Andras, was also favourably disposed toward SPOTA's demands. At the provincial level, municipal affairs minister Dan Campbell publicly supported SPOTA. It was only the city council who foot-dragged its way through eight months of 1969. Finally, in August 1969,

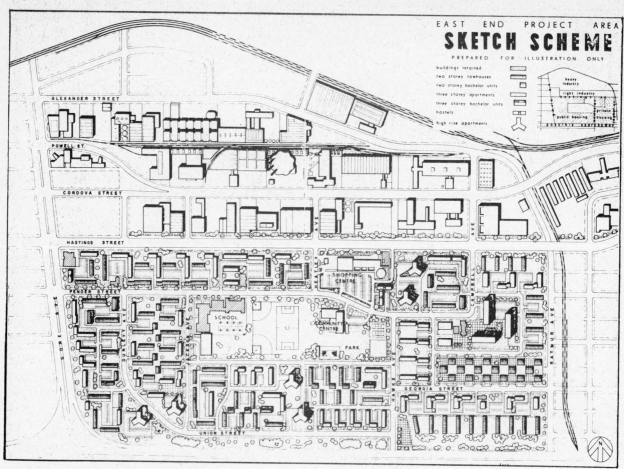

An urban renewal plan for Strathcona. As early as 1951 planners were anxious to see the area torn down. One scheme published by UBC and the Vancouver Housing Association called for an enormous swath of demolition in the area.

The plan for Strathcona drawn up by the Working Committee called for rehabilitating and upgrading area houses like these...

FUTURE PROSPECT

Image versus reality: above, an architect's sketch of what a 'renewed' Strathcona would look like. Below, a photograph of what it turned out to be. The federal government finally halted its funding for demolition-style urban renewal in 1969.

the federal government informed the city that federal funds would no longer be available for the Strathcona urban renewal project unless residents were involved, and further, that the government supported renewal, not demolition.

The city, faced with a cutoff of federal funds, was forced to agree, and in September 1969, set up the Strathcona Working Committee to develop a rehabilitation program for the area. The committee was composed of representatives from all three levels of government and an equal number of representatives from SPOTA. It was the first time that a citizen organization had equal power with a government to take part in planning decision-making.

The result was a completely different kind of plan for Strathcona, one which expropriated no home owners, protected the rights of small businesses, stressed repairs and renovations, and avoided the wholesale neighbourhood destruction of the two previous plans. Strathcona 1974 is a far better place than it would have been under urban renewal, but Strathcona residents have had to fight all the way to hold city council to its commitments.

...and SPOTA embarked on a program of building houses like these on the many vacant lots in the area.

31 The Third Crossing

A third crossing of Burrard Inlet at the First Narrows to the North Shore municipalities had been in the freeway plans as early as 1954. Although premier Bennett nipped the plans in the bud at the time, the idea of another crossing remained deeply etched in the minds of Vancouver and North Shore politicians and bureaucrats.

In the 1959 report which proposed a $340 million freeway system, a third crossing played a key role. In 1964, another report proposed a third crossing paralleling the existing Lions Gate Bridge. Each time the plans were scotched by the rurally-dominated Social Credit provincial government who refused to contribute to metropolitan roads. The provincial government's priority was to build highways in strong Socred ridings, not in the big city where many voted Liberal or New Democrat.

The 1967 Vancouver Transportation Study, which also recommended a network of freeways with a Carrall St. connector to link a waterfront freeway with the new Georgia Viaduct, sparked one of the strongest public protests Vancouver had ever experienced. But even as the public was dealing a death-blow to the Carrall St. connector, plans were under way for two more links in the freeway jigsaw, the waterfront freeway and the third crossing.

Both proposals were ultimately revoked, the one because the needs of business interests had changed, the other because of even more massive public opposition than that caused by the Chinatown freeway.

The main purpose of the waterfront freeway was to service Project 200, a $200 to $300 million commercial-residential development proposed for the Vancouver waterfront, a consortium of CPR (which owned the land), Grosvenor-Laing (an English firm which was doing developing) and Simpson-Sears and Woodward Stores (which were going to build large department stores in the development).

After planning the project for five years, and pressuring the freeway consultants to make automobile access to Project 200 a top priority, the partnership began to fall apart because of internal disagreements. With the rescinding of the Carrall St. connector decision, Project 200 further bogged down. Alternative plans for a waterfront distributor from the third crossing were put forward, but the Project 200 partners found them unsatisfactory because the eastern end of the project would not be served adequately. Meanwhile downtown business interests

Here's YOUR Bill for a 3rd Crossing-Freeway

$75* A YEAR FOR 20 YEARS!

ESTIMATED COSTS

	MILLIONS OF $
1. North Shore approaches	12
2. Burrard Inlet Tunnel	120
3. Waterfront distributor	12
4. Thurlow Tunnel - Drake Street cut	32
5. False Creek tie-in to Georgia Viaduct	18
6. Georgia Viaduct to 401 Freeway	65
7. Columbia - Quebec connector	?
	259
add 10% inflation to 1972	26
MINIMUM TOTAL	**$285**

POSSIBLE REVENUES

	MILLIONS OF $
Federal government 7% loan	120
Provincial government grant	41
North Shore municipalities	1
	162
Leaving a minimum of	123*
to come from Vancouver property taxes and tenants' rents.	
*($123 million ÷ 20 years ÷ 80,000 households = $75)	
TOTAL	**$285**

PROGRAM

The Citizens Co-ordinating Committee for Public Transit wants a modern, fast, cheap, public transit system for the Greater Vancouver Regional District.

Our program calls for 37½% federal, 37½% provincial, and 25% municipal financing to obtain:
- More frequent bus service over more routes.
- Light rail rapid transit—example: Central Park, Arbutus - Marpole interurban lines.
- Heavy rail rapid transit (subways and surface) to the east and southeast.

The massive financial costs of the Third Crossing-Freeway would "kill" the above program.

We need your help to conduct the petition - education campaign for a plebiscite.

Send a financial contribution to our office at Room 7, 199 East 8th. Phone 876-4919.

The opposition had done its homework. This was one of the leaflets produced by the Citizens Co-ordinating Committee for Public Transit.

generally began to favour the idea of rapid transit access to the downtown core. When one building of Project 200 was constructed at the foot of Granville St., provision was made for a rapid transit stop in the development. The idea of a waterfront freeway gradually faded. Thus it was not surprising when, in February 1972, at the height of the third crossing debate, Phil Boname, general manager of the B.C. region of Marathon Realty Co., CPR's development arm, came out strongly against the crossing, saying it would actually be bad for business. He was planning a rapid transit station somewhere in Project 200, saying that it would present 'phenomenal possibilities for real estate development.'

In certain circles the desire for the third crossing was becoming stronger. During 1968 the federal government, acting through the National Harbours Board, had hired two consultants, Swan Wooster Engineering Co. and CBA Engineering, to design the crossing and the necessary approaches and freeway links. Up to this time, the new crossing was to be merely part of the downtown freeway system. With the lack of decision on the part of city council, the emphasis was shifted to the crossing design as top priority. The rest of the system could be designed later to accommodate the crossing.

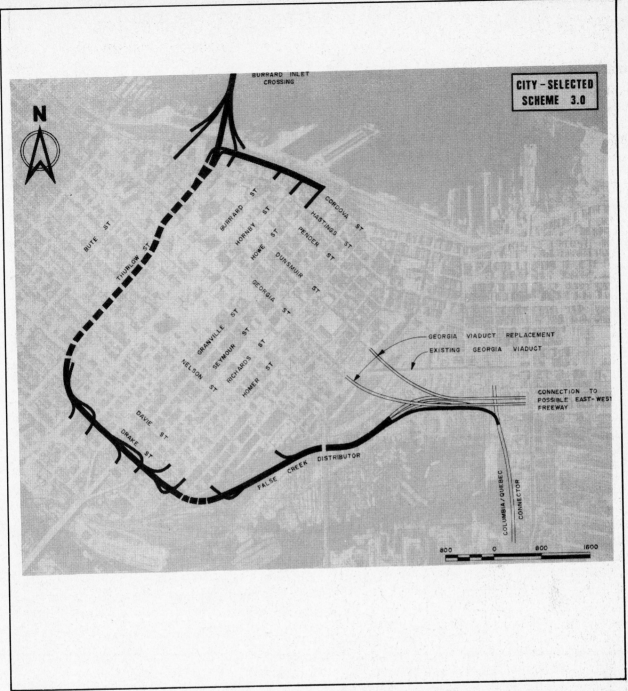

In July 1968, city council's transportation committee was presented with a new waterfront distributor plan. Although the meeting was secret, it was revealed that the proposal depended heavily on the co-operation of the National Harbours Board, and the CPR and the federal and provincial governments which would do the financing. At this time, the proposal involved a connection to Project 200.

The National Harbours Board had included in its directives that the consultants obtain a final decision from city council on the location of at least the first stage of a link between the third crossing and the

This is the third crossing as it was designed in 1971. The Chinatown freeway was dead by this time — killed by the public opposition described in chapter 29 — so the planners had devised a more complicated downtown by-pass route that went under Thurlow St. and then along the north side of False Creek where it joined up with the new Georgia Viaduct and with the previously-proposed north-south and east-west freeways. The strategy this time was to get a commitment on the third crossing, and then use it as a lever to get the remaining components of the system built.

Third crossing opponents marching on the B.C. Legislature in February 1972 presenting a 21,000-signature petition to premier W.A.C. Bennett. *Andy Garner photo*

eastern edge of the city. Thus the crossing was being used as a lever to force from city hall a decision on a route for a downtown freeway. In order to make this decision, city council hired N.D. Lea & Associates (which was already a sub-consultant on the third crossing study) to study the best way for linking the crossing with the Trans-Canada Highway. And council further hired Swan Wooster Engineering Co. (the main third crossing consultants) to come up with plans for the downtown freeway. Further studies were done during 1969 and 1970, tying the crossing proposal more closely to the proposed freeway net. So, if the crossing were ever built, it would be much easier to get further pieces added, because one piece was already there.

From 1968 to 1971 there was little publicity given to the third crossing proposal. In late 1971, the pro-crossing side began gearing up for a major push. Bill Rathie, former Vancouver mayor (who had been the most rabid proponent of freeways), had recently been appointed chairman of the Port of Vancouver Authority by his patron, North Shore Liberal MP Jack Davis. Rathie had the further job of pushing the crossing.

Vancouver's then-mayor Tom Campbell struck the first blow on October 21 when he announced that construction would begin the following spring. Campbell said he met with the three North Shore mayors and had arranged the financing.

On November 24, premier Wacky Bennett, who was not against the crossing as long as he didn't have to pay for it, announced that he had reached agreement with the federal government to share costs after extracting $14 million more from the feds. That same day Bill Rathie announced that he had been given the job of co-ordinating the construction of the crossing, by federal transport minister Don Jamieson (minister responsible for the National Harbours Board). The opponents of the third crossing began to mobilize their forces. Two groups were set up, the Citizens Committee for Public Transit in Vancouver, and the North Shore Transportation Committee for North Shore residents, to oppose the crossing and push for better public transit.

Who was behind this third crossing push? In fact the ranks supporting a third crossing were rather thin. First and foremost, there were the North Shore real estate interests, and their political allies. A University of British Columbia study released in February 1972 demonstrated that property values in downtown Vancouver and on the North Shore would jump $163 million within one year of the opening of a new crossing. Second, there were the North Shore residents who, every morning and evening, were faced with the crawl across the Lions Gate Bridge. Amongst these North Shore residents were some of the city's more affluent and influential citizens. Many media personalities lived on the North Shore, and it was the media that was doing much of the promoting for the third crossing.

Third, and perhaps most important, at this time in late 1971 the federal government was faced with waning popularity and increasing unemployment in the west. An election was likely within the next six months, and a big make-work project like a third crossing would look good. North Shore residents happened to be represented in Ottawa by ambitious Jack Davis, who had clawed his way into the federal cabinet as environment minister. His Coast-Capilano constituents were watching him closely, and he was coming out very strongly *for* the crossing. Bill Rathie had been hand-picked by Davis to head the Port of Vancouver Authority, and to push for the crossing. The other two Vancouver federal cabinet ministers, Ron Basford (whose riding included the Vancouver end of the crossing) and Art Laing, were not as strongly in favour of the crossing, preferring to leave it to a public plebiscite to decide.

Davis didn't want a plebiscite, nor did Vancouver mayor Tom Campbell, who was well aware of how it would turn out. The City of Vancouver had to put up $12 million as its share of the costs. Normally, a money by-law plebiscite would have to be held, but Campbell wanted to pay it out of general revenues, by-passing the normal process. However, Campbell was having trouble even with his usually solid majority. On December 23, 1971, city council squeaked out a 6-5 vote to pay $3.2 million of the third crossing costs out of general revenues and not hold a plebiscite or a public hearing on the matter. The TEAM members of council were not against the third crossing but wanted more money and emphasis put on the transit aspects of the proposal.

Undaunted by the setback caused by city council's vote, the opponents of the third crossing pushed on with their drive to get a plebiscite. A public meeting was held on January 16, 1972. Seven hundred people turned up, but none of the politicians who favoured the crossing were there. Alderman Harry Rankin, one of the three Vancouver aldermen who did attend, clearly stated the issue. Once Vancouver embarks on a freeway system, he said, there will be no chance for decades of introducing rapid transit. 'This is the watershed. It must be stopped now.' The meeting decided to continue pushing for a plebiscite by getting a huge petition to all levels of government.

The crossing opposition kept up the pressure.

MAYOR FINGERS CROSSING-SABOTEURS:

'Maoists, pinkos, hamburgers'

By HALL LEIREN
Sun City Hall Reporter

The proposed new Burrard Inlet crossing is on the verge of being sabotaged by "Maoists, Communists, pinkos, left-wingers and hamburgers," Mayor Tom Campbell said today.

He defined hamburgers as persons without university degrees.

Campbell said the crossing will founder unless the entire city council rallies to support it.

That would be a victory for the Communist Party of Canada, he said.

The highlight of former Vancouver mayor Tom Campbell's career: the night his strategy failed on the third crossing, when he red-baited its opponents outrageously.

There were signs of splits among the Liberal MP's. Vancouver South MP Arthur Laing's view was that there was not enough public support to justify the spending of such a large amount of money. Bill Rathie said that there would have to be a plebiscite before the federal government would commit the funds, although Jack Davis immediately denied this. Ron Basford, the third Vancouver cabinet member, came out in favour of a vote, thus tipping the balance in favour of the opponents. At the city level, Harry Rankin and Walter Hardwick introduced motions to have evening public meetings on the issue, and to decide about the plebiscite. But the next day Davis reiterated his stand that no vote was necessary. The following Tuesday, NPA alderman Ernie Broome broke ranks and voted *for* Hardwick's motion 'to have an evening meeting at which substantive information on the question would be presented by the National Harbours Board consultants and professional planning and engineering groups.' Suffering from the pressure, mayor Campbell helped torpedo the whole third crossing project with verbal overkill when he said that the Burrard Inlet crossing was being sabotaged by Maoists, Communists, pinkos, left-wingers and hamburgers.

The meeting, held March 15, was a marathon six-hour session. Eric Hamber School auditorium was jammed with 1,000 people. Almost unanimously, the briefs condemned the third crossing. Opponents argued that the tremendous outlay of funds for this one facility would prevent Vancouver from building any other facilities for years to come. This would mean that rapid transit could not possibly be considered. They suggested that the Swan Wooster Engineering Co. report was technically inadequate and they pointed out that by assuming that the crossing would be paid for by tolls, the consultants were committing Vancouver to build a freeway system to provide the necessary traffic.

In spite of some unscrupulous tactics tried by mayor Campbell, the meeting had its effect. So much opposition was demonstrated — and opposition from traditionally strong NPA supporters such as the Downtown Business Association who came out strongly in favour of rapid transit — that action on the third crossing was stalled.

On April 4, the federal government announced that it was shelving the third crossing until after the next federal election. A minority government was returned and the Liberals were almost wiped out in B.C. At the same time, the push for rapid transit was on the upswing. Within a week of the March 15 meeting, consultants Wilbur Smith & Associates presented their report on Downtown Vancouver Transit Concepts to the Greater Vancouver Regional District. Freeways were disappearing from the talks of government officials, and public transit — improved bus systems, streetcars, and rapid transit — was becoming the highest priority item on the election platter. A provincial government and a city council dedicated to rapid transit were elected within three months of each other. There still may be a third crossing of Burrard Inlet, but it will be only for public transit. That much is now certain. Or is it?

32 The Four Seasons issue: Victory and defeat

If anything is sacred to Vancouverites, it is Stanley Park. They may allow views of the water and mountains to be blocked; they may allow Vancouver's fine old homes to be destroyed; they may allow the English Bay waters to be polluted; they may allow the North Shore hillsides to be ravaged; but Stanley Park cannot be touched. Located at the westernmost end of the downtown peninsula, the area was declared a park soon after Vancouver was incorporated in 1886, and it immediately became Vancouver's pride.

Next door to the park is the waterfront area known as Coal Harbour. Until the early 1960s it was a lively vital area, filled with many interesting waterfront and harbour activities. Now it is a desolate bleak area. Coal Harbour has been a battleground, as wave after wave of developers have attempted to make enormous profits from public land, and have been opposed all the way by the citizens of Vancouver, fighting to retain the inviolate sanctity of Stanley Park. The battle raged for over ten years. Finally, the moment of total victory apparently at hand, the citizens were betrayed by the very politicians they had just elected to office to ensure that their demands were heard.

Four times in 11 years, four different developers proposed four very similar schemes for Coal Harbour. The four have been William Zeckendorf with his Coal Harbour Investments; Harbour Park Developments; Four Seasons Hotels; and Daon Development Corp. Each proposal was bitterly fought by the citizens of Vancouver.

William Zeckendorf came forward with the first proposal in 1963. The city's own planning department was strongly against the scheme, but this didn't deter the politicians. Mayor Bill Rathie called a public hearing for the rezoning in June 1963. The hearing, attended by 600 people, was explosive. Harry Rankin, at that time president of the Central Council of Rate-payers and a perennial candidate for alderman, was the champion of the opponents to the scheme.

Opposition seemed futile. Even though everyone except Zeckendorf and his consultants was against the scheme, city council called a special meeting three days later and, with few members of the public present, approved the rezoning. Thus the public lost round one.

Two years later they lost round two. Zeckendorf had folded, and the properties had been sold to the Harbour Park Developments consortium. A second public hearing was held in April 1965, with the same groups presenting their same arguments. These were

Stanley Park Entrance?

Study the diagram below. Area A represents about 10 acres - the block nearest Stanley Park and the water front.

Area B represents about 4 acres of land furthest from the park entrance, along Georgia Street between Guildford and Denman Street. There are some buildings standing on this Area B land now and if it is not purchased, it would continue to have some low profile buildings.

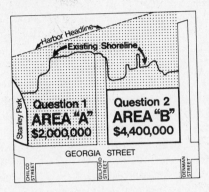

NOW STUDY THE QUESTIONS BELOW:
If you are in favour of acquiring Area A for $2,000,000.00, vote "Yes" on Question 1.
If you are in favour of acquiring both areas (A & B), for a total of $6,400,000.00, vote "Yes" on both Questions 1 and 2.

THE QUESTIONS:
1. Are you in favour of the Council having the power to pass by-laws without the assent of the electors in any of the years 1973-1983 inclusive to borrow from time to time, by the issue of debentures, sums not to exceed over the said period $2,000,000.00 in the aggregate?

The following, in brief and general terms, sets out the proposed project:

The acquisition of all of the privately-held interests in and to an area the approximate boundaries of which are indicated on the map below and marked as "A" for public use.
Amount allocated - $2,000,000.00

2. Are you in favour of the Council having power to pass by-laws without the assent of the electors in any of the years 1973-1983 inclusive to borrow from time to time, by the issue of debentures, sums not to exceed over the said period $4,400,000.00 in the aggregate?

The following, in brief and general terms, sets out the proposed project:

The acquisition of all of the privately-held interests in and to an area the approximate boundaries of which are indicated on the map below and marked as "B" for public use.
Amount allocated - $4,400,000.00

A New School Trustee?

Concerning the resignation of school trustee, Olive Johnson, and the balance of term 1973-74, one candidate has to be elected.

At this writing, nominations are still being received and candidates are not yet announced.

However, full details and candidates' names will be announced by newspaper advertisements, well in advance of the election date.

---

much more clear-cut than previously. The Harbour Park scheme was so gross that even a development-hungry city council couldn't approve its current form. The scheme was referred to the city design panel in the hopes of some improvements, but the panel came out strongly against the overall concept. As a way out, Harbour Park asked the city to approve only a 'first stage' of the scheme for the first block east from Stanley Park. Council happily agreed and passed the rezoning the next day. Thus the public lost round two.

Round three didn't get under way for another four years. In the interim, Harbour Park Developments had unloaded the third block to the Bayshore Inn people, and then leased the remaining two blocks to Four Seasons Hotels of Toronto. Four Seasons proposal was the same as the previous two, except that it was now for two blocks only. Mayor Tom Campbell was ecstatic. 'I like the proposal. It will put $40 million on the tax roll,' he announced. The planning department didn't share Campbell's opinion and called for a completely revised scheme, complaining about the hotel which totally shut out the view of the harbour. The third public hearing was held on August 28, 1969. Again, many of the same groups presented their cases, but city council, without even a pretense of listening to

Within a year of the final defeat of the Four Seasons proposal for the property, Dawson Developments (now Daon) had taken over and made its own $50 million proposal. This was rejected, and the question of whether the city should acquire the land for a park was put to a plebiscite. But the plebiscite was worded to get the result TEAM politicians wanted: to buy one block for park, and allow development on the second block. The outcome was a foregone conclusion.

---

them, approved the rezoning the same day.

Legal technicalities prevented the passing of the amendment to the zoning by-law until May 1, 1970. During that time the board of parks and public recreation, concerned about any encroachment on Stanley Park, began to take a more active role in fighting the project. It stirred up public opinion at home. It went to see Four Seasons Hotels president Isadore Sharp in Toronto and got him to pull back the hotel a few feet further from the park. It lobbied effectively the B.C. cabinet ministers in Ottawa. On December 1, 1970, environment minister Jack Davis announced that he was holding up the signing of a sublease by the National Harbours Board required to transfer the lease from Harbour Park Developments to Four Seasons Hotels.

A group of prominent women (including Mrs. J.V. Clyne, wife of the MacMillan Bloedel head, and Mrs.

Frank Ross, mother of justice minister John Turner) and environmentalists kept up the pressure on city council. The National Harbours Board announced that it was re-examining the terms of the leases. In March, eight of the organizations fighting the project joined together in the Save the Entrance to Stanley Park Committee (SESPC), but at the same time city council reaffirmed its approval of the Four Seasons project and sent a telegram to transport minister Don Jamieson (minister resonsible for the National Harbours Board). The vote was 6 to 4, and the minority of three TEAM members and Harry Rankin sent their own telegram.

As a concession to the opponents, city council agreed to hold a public 'information' meeting on March 31, 1971. Twenty-seven briefs were presented to city council, all of them opposing the project, and urging council to buy the land for public use. Council finally gave in to the pressure and agreed to have a plebiscite on June 23. An appraisal had to be done for the plebiscite, and mayor Tom Campbell artificially inflated the price the voters would have to pay for the land. The vote was open only to property owners, and had to receive a 60% majority to pass. It seemed hardly likely that the opponents could win.

Before the plebiscite took place, things began to happen thick and fast. On May 27, SESPC took the City of Vancouver to court challenging on a legal technicality the validity of the original rezoning and all subsequent rezonings. The following weekend a group of young people occupied the site and turned it into a park and campground called 'All Seasons Park'. The developer was reluctant to remove them by police force since one of the development firm's partners, Graham Dawson, was a member of the police commission. The 'All Seasons Park' flourished all summer, and at one point there were over 200 people camping on the property.

In spite of an inflated price tag of $10 million on the land, and with only property owners being allowed to vote, 51.2% of the voters voted to buy the site. It was not the required 60%, but it was a majority.

During the summer and fall of 1971, Four Seasons Hotels proposed a series of trivial changes in its proposal, moving the hotel back another 80 feet, reducing its height by 10 feet, and reducing the overall density by something less than 3%. City council promptly approved it. The parks board kept on the pressure, especially in Ottawa. Finally, on February 10, 1972, Vancouver *Sun* columnist Allan Fothering-ham announced that the Four Seasons project was dead. There was still one waterlot that had not been leased to the developer, and the government finally decided not to sign the lease. The cabinet decision was the result of pressure from urban affairs minister Ron Basford, whose Vancouver Centre riding contained the Coal Harbour property.

The development proposal was dead. On August 22, Four Seasons Hotels quietly pulled out of the development after the lease with Harbour Park Developments expired. The Save the Entrance to Stanley Park Committee and the parks board continued to pressure city council to acquire the land for park and other public purposes. But the lure of lucrative development was not dead. In May 1973, the owners of Harbour Park Developments sold the company and its assets to Dawson Developments for $6 million.

Dawson Developments immediately proposed a $50 million project. The plan, including a hotel, office tower, and four apartment buildings totalled 1.35 million square feet compared with 1.8 million in the rejected Four Seasons Hotels project.

Now, however, things at city hall were different. There was a new city council supposedly dedicated to promoting the wishes of the people who had finally swept the developer's party out of office. TEAM, in fact, was opposed to private development only on the first block from Stanley Park. The special committee of city council on the Burrard Inlet waterfront proposed that the first block be acquired for public open space, and set down guidelines for development of the second block. Yet at a public meeting held on August 2, 1973, 17 briefs were presented, almost unanimously in favour of public acquisition of *both* blocks.

City council ignored the results of this meeting and decided to put the question on the plebiscite held October 24, 1973. The voters were asked whether the city should buy one block for $2.4 million, or both blocks for $6.4 million. The people were confused enough by the TEAM rhetoric to settle for buying only the first block. The second block will be developed privately under generous guidelines set down by the waterfront committee, which allows hotel-office-apartment-type uses.

Thus the final curtain rang down on the Coal Harbour drama. It was a partial victory for the citizens of Vancouver, ten years in the making, but it was also a loss.

Part VI Challenging the Developers

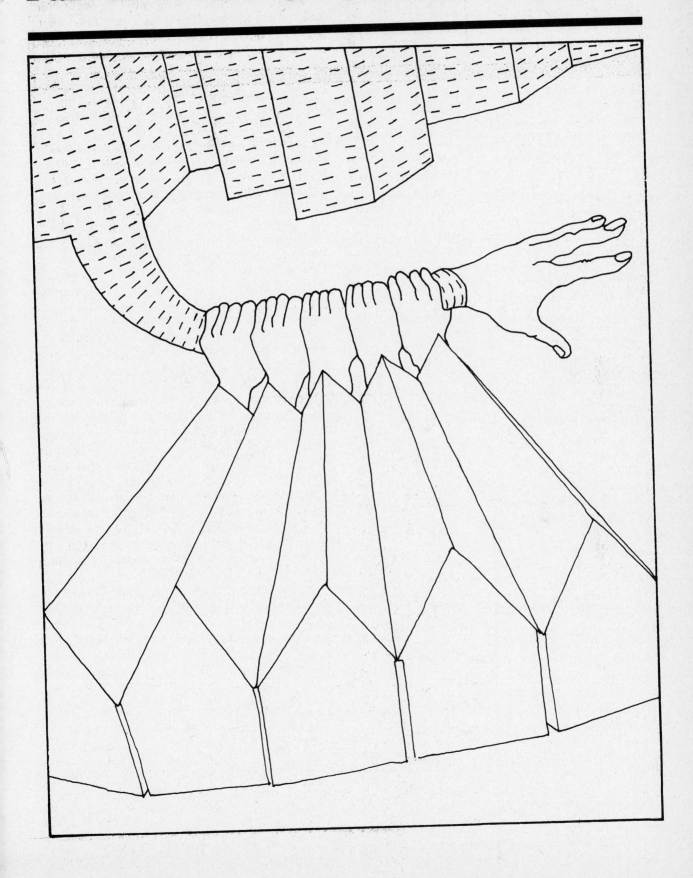

It should now be clear that the interests of the land development industry are different from those who live in the city. Those who develop the city:

— want to see property values as high as possible and continually rising;

— want to see high building costs in order to protect the value of existing buildings;

— want to be able to demolish buildings without any regulation;

— want to see continued population growth and business expansion;

— want to see continual upzoning of land to higher densities and more profitable uses;

— want to continue to grow and dominate the development industry, and to see continued growth in assets, revenues, and profits;

— want to preserve the status quo, to maintain their control over city government, and to strongly resist any efforts to change the present system.

Those who live in the city want to see exactly the opposite of everything desired by the development industry. They:

— want to see housing costs and consequently land values as low as possible;

— want to see old buildings capable of providing adequate accommodation preserved;

— want to see a limit put on population growth and redevelopment;

— want to see downzoning of land to lower densities, with strict controls on development which should be based on *need*, not *profit;*

— want to have more say in planning and development decisions, eventually coming to a position of control;

— want to see the phasing out of the huge development corporations and their replacement by locally-controlled neighbourhood housing and building societies;

— want to have a city government that listens to their requirements and acts strongly and positively to meet them.

On many occasions citizen protests have stopped destructive projects or at least modified them. But given the structure of governments which always seem to operate to promote the interests of property owners and developers, citizens of Vancouver have to maintain an eternal vigilance against new atrocities, or older ones rearing their ugly heads. The third crossing may not be dead at all, but just marking time for a few years until a younger generation of Vancouverites is not quite so set against the destruction of Vancouver's amenities. Large developers such as Marathon Realty Co. can afford to wait years until things cool down before proceeding with their grandiose developments. Citizens have to be continually on guard to stop this... change that.

Clearly, this approach by citizens, necessary as it is, will not by itself produce the humane environment and adequate housing that most of us want. It is too negative and reactive; it only stops the things we don't want. A further step is necessary: people themselves must take the initiative for housing and development into their own hands. In fact they have begun to do so in a number of ways.

In this part we look at some of the possibilities for citizen action aimed at getting more control over development decisions. Four general areas are explored:

1 Co-operative enterprise: producing developments and institutions owned neither by government agency nor by private developer, but by the people who occupy or make use of them; the two most well-established forms in B.C. being co-operative housing and credit unions.

2 Organizing: dealing with the issues that affect your neighbourhood or your way of life, by building up strong locally-based citizen groups and tenant unions; educating neighbours to the realities of redevelopment; promoting the common interests among neighbours or tenants; building common bonds among resident homeowners, tenants and local merchants.

3 Direct actions: challenging the stranglehold of developers over planning and development and passing the initiative into the hands of those who are directly affected by those decisions. The possibilities in this area are limited only by the imagination of the people involved. One of the most effective actions would be the systematic occupation of vacant land and buildings by well-co-ordinated groups of people now lacking proper accommodation.

4 Political action: taking control of the city government by citizen and tenant groups, removing from office those politicians who support the interests of developers, and electing citizen representatives. Ultimately this will involve the establishment of a ward system, so that the people elected to office will be more directly accountable to those who elected them.

33 Co-op housing

Most Canadians would still like to own their own single-family home on its own separate lot. But home ownership involves a high down payment as well as high monthly payments; and both of these costs have escalated so dramatically that only relatively high-income people can now afford to own their own home. Elsewhere in this book we have seen a major cause of the housing crisis in the profit-hungry private sector — the developers, banks and loan companies, building material suppliers, builders — with the co-operation of all levels of government who were unwilling to step in and upset the existing system. Governments, in fact, have taken action only in crisis situations where there weren't enough profits to be reaped by the developers. But even in the public housing field, the governments have built so little that they have made hardly a dent in the problem.

Neither developers nor governments, acting on their own, are at present going to provide the necessary housing for the increasing number of low and moderate-income people who require it. So people themselves must take the initiative — to push governments to provide more public housing, to ensure that developers' profits are kept within reasonable limits, and to organize themselves together to meet their own needs through *co-operative housing projects.*

A co-operative enterprise is one which is owned by the people who use its services; control rests equally with all its members, and the gains are distributed to the members in proportion to the use they make of its services. This contrasts significantly with a private enterprise which is owned by the shareholders where both control and gains are distributed in proportion to the number of shares held.

The co-operative movement began in Europe in the 1840s. Money lenders and merchants were charging exorbitant interest rates which kept the farmers in perpetual debt. So farmers banded together and pooled their resources to form people's banks which provided credit to buy seed and equipment. Artisans and craftsmen did the same to be able to buy materials. From its beginning in England, Germany, and France, the co-operative movement has spread throughout the world, into many different types of activities. One of these was the establishment of *caisses populaires* or credit unions, in which the members pooled their financial resources. Other major types of co-operative enterprise included: producer co-ops, such as farmers organizations in Europe and Japan; consumer co-ops, such as the rural electricity co-ops in the U.S.A.; and housing co-ops, in which an individual *leases* his dwelling unit from a co-operative society in which he is a joint *owner.* Co-op housing has been a way of living in many countries throughout the world. In Sweden, almost a third of all housing is owned co-operatively. In New York City, a large development called appropriately enough Co-op City, sponsored by some labour unions, has about 15,000 families.

Many types of producer co-ops are well-established in Canada. Almost 65% of Canada's wheat crop is marketed through the co-operatively owned wheat pools. Other examples of producer co-ops are an oil refinery in Regina, the Prince Rupert Fisherman's Co-op, which processes and markets its own products, and the Fraser Valley Milk Producers Association with annual sales of over $50 million.

Consumer co-ops are also well-established in Canada. In B.C. over 50 consumer co-ops range in size from the very small group that buys its groceries together, to the very large association like the Surrey Co-op with three stores and over 15,000 members. The Sointula Co-op Store Association on Malcolm Island is over 60 years old. And the B.C. credit unions are the fastest growing financial institutions in Canada.

Yet there have been very few housing co-ops in Canada. Only once, in Nova Scotia, during the depression years, has extensive use been made of co-operative housing, and then it was a different type, the so-called building co-op. In a building co-op, a group of people join together to pool their resources and build their own single-family homes, using what is called 'sweat equity' (i.e., using their own labour as capital). This system was used in smaller towns; it never spread beyond Nova Scotia, and even there it is gradually being phased out.

Why hasn't co-op housing become more popular in Canada? It might be that the ideal of owning your own home on a separate lot is so deeply ingrained in the Canadian mentality that co-op ownership just seems too foreign. In urban areas, where the pressure on land is so great that some form of multiple housing becomes necessary, many people have decided on the condominium form of ownership, because you still 'own your own home'.

Yet only a few years ago, condominiums were also unacceptable to most Canadians. Builders and developers launched massive advertising and promotional campaigns to market this new type of housing. There have been no such massive funds available to promote the positive features of co-operative ownership. And no one in the private sector is enthusiastic about co-operatives. Real estate agents and lawyers don't like them because there are no real estate commissions or legal fees to be made when a share in a co-operative development changes hands. Banks and other sources of mortgage funds are not interested

Two examples of co-op housing: This older house in Kitsilano was sold to a co-op group by its previous owner for $20,000 less than he was offered by a developer who was trying to assemble property on the block.

This co-op project, De Cosmos Village, is a newly-built townhouse development in the Champlain Heights area of Vancouver. The land is leased from the City of Vancouver. Payments for residents are $152 for a two-bedroom, $164 for a three and $172 for a four.

because there are no profits to be made for them. And the developers who own most of the land around cities are not interested, because of the lack of profits for them too. Since most governments favour private developers, they too suffer from a lack of enthusiasm.

This disinterest of the private development industry in co-op housing points out the basic difference between the co-operative and other forms of owner-occupied housing. Co-op housing is for *use,* not investment.

Co-op housing is non-profit. The individual member of the co-op leases his particular unit in the development from a co-operative society of which he is a joint owner. He is thus a tenant, but he is completely secure, and cannot be evicted on the whim of the landlord. His monthly payments are stable; the only increases are for taxes and maintenance, not because of profits skimmed off by the landlord. He has a voice in how the development is run. The members themselves set policy and elect their own directors who are responsible for general operations and carrying out policies.

There are also distinct financial advantages. Initial capital requirements are usually kept to 5% of the cost of the unit; the rest may be provided by a low-interest loan from Central Mortgage and Housing Corp. The member's equity, together with increases due to inflation and any improvements he may have made to his unit, are refunded if he leaves. Co-ops can be a real alternative for all income ranges. For example, a certain percentage of the units in a development can be set aside for low-income occupants, who could be receiving provincial public housing allowances, so that their units would be indistinguishable in the total project.

In spite of the disinterest of private developers and governments, co-op housing is becoming more popular. A number of successful projects have been completed over the past ten years, with many more on the way. The first major project in Canada was Willow Park in Winnipeg, begun in 1964, providing 200 townhouses. Sarcee Meadows in Calgary, built by the Co-op Association of Calgary, provided 380 cluster units in a medium-density development. Then there is also Solidarity Tower in Windsor, Ontario, a 26-storey high-rise of 300 units.

Co-op housing was slower in getting started in B.C. The first major project, De Cosmos Village, comprised of 110 two, three, and four-bedroom townhouse units is located at 49th Ave. and Boundary Rd. in southeast Vancouver. The development has been extremely successful, and a long list of people are waiting to get in.

In De Cosmos Village each member of the co-op had to put up a 5% share as his downpayment, roughly $1,700, but $500 of this could be covered by the B.C. government's Home Acquisition grant. The remaining 95% was covered by a National Housing Act mortgage at a low interest rate of 7¼%. The land was leased from the City of Vancouver at 80% of market value, for 50 years. Monthly payments for residents thus worked out to $152 for a two-bedroom, $164 for three, and $172 for four.

The project was initiated in 1968 by some members of the United Church, unionists, and other concerned individuals. Interim funding was provided by the church, the B.C. Federation of Labour, and Local 452 of the Carpenters Union. Because of the success of the project, a permanent organization — the United Housing Foundation (UHF) — was formed to promote further co-op projects. UHF assembled a core group with the necessary expertise to help co-op groups get their projects built. Some other projects which have been completed with the help of UHF include: Azalea Gardens, a 65-unit apartment in Coquitlam, a project in Haney for senior citizens, and a townhouse development in Victoria. UHF has many more projects in various stages of preparation. And hundreds of other groups are forming with the intention of building co-op housing.

A further impetus to the co-operative form of housing was provided by the NDP provincial government. Large-scale production of housing on a co-operative basis was seen by housing minister Lorne Nicolson as one way of easing the situation in B.C. Nicolson was prepared to channel substantial funds into the area. But Nicolson was going to require the participation of United Housing Foundation in all projects using provincial money. Nicolson was proposing to make UHF the sole agency for co-operative housing in B.C.

Now, all housing co-ops need to have access to planning and organizational experts to get their housing built. Average groups of citizens probably do not have the necessary knowledge of law, of planning and architecture, of building and specification-writing, of real estate, of how to deal with governments, and a thousand and one other things. This situation leads to the notion of the 'mother co-op,' an on-going organization that has all of this information and to which groups just starting up could turn to for advice and help. Sweden, for example, has a very elaborate system of mother co-ops.

Nicolson was proposing to make UHF the mother co-op for all co-operatively-built housing in B.C.

UHF does indeed have much of the required expertise. Its board of directors included many people from the development industry, property lawyers, real estate agents, insurance agents, mortgage managers, and builders. The question was whether UHF would act in the interests of the groups of individuals who had turned to it for help, or whether it would become part of the development industry — another bureaucracy, forcing each group into the same mould, turning out a standard product, making itself indispensible, and becoming a powerful lobby.

One of the major advantages of co-ops is that the members are supposed to be involved right from the beginning in the planning and design of the project. This method stands in stark contrast to housing produced by the private sector, where the potential resident has absolutely no say about what the developer builds. All he can say is yes or no.

Penta Group Encounters Opposition

Recent announcement by the "Pente Group" of home-seeking citizens that they want to erect co-op housing on City-owned property between 20th and 21st Avenues next to the Camosun Bog in the Dunbar District has brought quick reaction from residents in the surrounding area.

Story of the Penta project was broken in last week's edition of the Western News.

The plan calls for the building of six clusters of 2-storey residences containing a total of 26 units.

The Penta Group consists of 44 adults and 23 children.

Last Saturday, the Group placed a model of the project on display at Dunbar-West Point Grey Information Centre, and fielded questions by a steady stream of visitors who passed through the Centre during the day.

Since then, a protest committee of residents has been put together, and a mimeographed flyer has been circulated, outlining the Penta plan, what action has been taken to prevent its fruition, and reasons for the action.

Listed as members of the Committee are Hal Robertson, Steve Brewster, Fred Nears, Gerry De Carmo and Mike Potter.

Main point of contention is that the construction of co-op housing on the site chosen by Penta will mean placing the equivalent of two houses on every 33-foot lot, resulting in a higher density than at present and a consequent lowering of residential quality.

It's not all smooth sailing for co-op housing, as this story from a local newspaper in the West Point Grey area illustrates. *Western News 27 March 1975*

The UHF seemed to be taking on the role of the private developer and omitting the co-op groups altogether. Dissatisfaction with UHF became more widespread among co-op groups during 1974, and a move was started to make the UHF board more representative of the actual users.

At the 1974 annual general meeting of the United Housing Foundation, representatives of the co-ops were able to get a clear majority — 10 of 16 — on the board of directors. Most of the old board resigned; lawyer William Wright remained as the only direct representative of the property industry. There were also two representatives from the provincial government, one a bureaucrat, the other a politician, and two representatives from the credit unions, plus the executive director of the UHF. However, even with a clear majority of co-op representatives on the board, change has come slowly to UHF. There has been some loosening of the rigid control held by UHF over co-op groups. Adanac Co-op, for example, a group of almost 90 working people in the east end of Vancouver, with one representative on the UHF board, has done the bulk of the organizing and preliminary design work

The B.C. provincial government, in its continuing struggle with the big eastern-dominated banks, sees the credit union movement as a potential ally. *B.C. Teachers Credit Union November 1973*

itself, using UHF only when necessary, for example, in negotiating the mortgage or in calculating project costs.

Co-operative housing is not a large force on its own, but it does demonstrate the fact that there are alternatives to the private developers and government-built public housing. It could grow to the point where, because of its non-profit nature, it would begin to force down the cost of all other housing.

34 Credit unions

Did you ever wonder what happened to the money you deposited in your bank account? Some of it may have been loaned to a foreign government to build better roads, so that its troops could be moved around the country more quickly. Another part of it may have been loaned to a multi-national oil corporation for oil exploration in the North Sea. Another part of it may have been loaned to a foreign corporation to buy up Canadian companies as, for example, when the Royal Bank of Canada made a $2.4 million loan to Belgian-owned Genstar so that it could acquire Ocean Cement.

What about the money that you pay in the form of life insurance premiums or trust company deposit certificates? Is it used in a better way? Well, a large part of it may have been used to finance the Pacific Centres and Royal Centres that are destroying our cities. Or another part of it may have been invested in the stocks and bonds of American-based companies such as ITT or INCO.

Even your pension dollars aid in the destruction of the environment. After all, it was the Canadian National Railway Co. pension fund that was bank-rolling the Four Seasons Hotels development on Coal Harbour.

Where then, can you put your hard-earned dollars, aside from under your mattress?

At the present time, credit unions, or *caisses populaires* (as they are known in Quebec) provide an alternative. By putting your money into a credit union, you are at least certain that it will not be used to support foreign governments or American corporations. And you do get a slightly better interest rate than you would at the banks or trust companies, since credit unions are non-profit.

But the credit union movement has not become the powerful social and economic force that it might have. At a local level, credit unions could have become much more involved in community affairs. One way would be by acquiring key pieces of property in a neighbourhood, thereby preventing developers from completing assemblies for unpopular projects. Or credit unions could take the initiative in providing housing for low-income people.

At a national level, the considerable financial weight of credit unions could be used to prevent companies from being bought out by foreigners, or to buy back Canadian resources for the general public welfare.

Over 5.5 million Canadians belong to credit unions or *caisses populaires*. In B.C., 450,000 people have deposited over $675 million and borrowed $625 million from their credit unions.

A credit union is owned by its members, not by the shareholders as in a bank. Membership must be based on some common *bond:* occupation — Gulf and Fraser Fishermen's Credit Union; association — Greater Vancouver Catholic Credit Union; or identifiable community — Surrey Credit Union.

The credit union movement has grown astronomically in both membership and assets over the past few years. On the other hand, the actual number of credit unions in B.C. has diminished. In 1961 there were 328 credit unions; by 1972 this had decreased to 202. What this means is that the existing credit unions are becoming larger, and many are being merged into others. Credit unionism is becoming big business. Vancouver City Savings Credit Union is now the largest credit union in Canada, with 46,000 members and $200 million in assets.

Credit unions are pushing to become more like banks and other large corporations. They now allocate large budgets for advertising and public relations. Is this what the members want?

Certainly credit unions were not always this way. From the first farmers and artisans co-ops of the 1850s developed people's banks or co-operative credit unions which were completely owned by the members and thus by-passed the usurious interest rates charged by banks. The first *caisse populaire* was founded by Alphonse Desjardins, a journalist, in Levis, Quebec, in 1901. As Desjardins described it in *The Co-operative People's Bank, La Caisse Populaire:*

It was the deplorable revelations brought about by law suits in Montreal and elsewhere, where poor borrowers had been obliged to pay to infamous usurers rates of interests amounting to several hundred per cent for most significant loans, that induced the writer to study carefully this problem with a view to finding out the best possible solution ...

After 15 long years of constant study, at last believing that he had acquired the necessary theoretical knowledge and being induced to do so by many of the leaders of the movement in Europe, he undertook the establishment of the new system. Aided by the devoted zeal of a certain number of citizens — the parish priest and several members of the Catholic clergy of the locality — he succeeded in founding in Levis, Canada, the first bank of this type ever organized on this continent.

The Levis Co-operative People's Bank was organized on December 6, 1900, but for one reason or another did not begin its business until January 23, 1901.

The first instalment paid was a dime and the total of the first collection amounted to only $26.40 ...

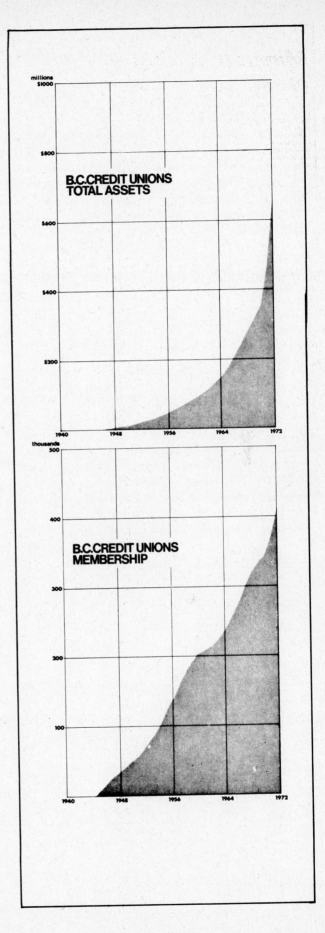

The movement has always had its biggest impact in Quebec. By 1970 there were over 1300 *caisses populaires,* over 2½ million members, and assets of over $2,600 million.

In British Columbia, credit unions are governed by the Credit Unions Act, first passed in 1938. They are under the authority of the attorney-general, who appoints a chief inspector of credit unions. The provincial government has been very sticky in allowing changes in the act. They don't want to tread on the toes of the financial community.

As presently constituted, credit unions have one major function, to make personal or mortgage loans to their members; they may also develop, own, or operate housing for their members. However, they have seen fit to co-ordinate their housing activities with the private development market, or to act as traditional developers themselves.

Credit unions need to become a much more positive force in the desperate housing situation we all now face. To start a credit union, you need only ten people, but you must demonstrate a need for a new organization. This may prove difficult, given the present trend to bigness and consolidation. A better strategy may lie in trying to influence the policies of existing credit unions such as Vancouver City Savings Credit Union, or the B.C. Teachers Credit Union. Any member of the credit union may run for the board of directors. Many people are beginning to see this as a means of implementing change at a local level. If this interest expands, the credit union movement could become an alternate financial system, owned by the people of a locality, and promoting genuinely Canadian interests.

35 VanCity: Portrait of Canada's largest credit union

The challenge faced by our whole society today is to properly utilize the great potential we have to satisfy human need. We can meet this challenge only by directing our economic capacities, administrative abilities, and tremendous technological knowledge toward this end. As a viable financial institution, VanCity can play its part by focussing on:
— improving the quality of life — from the quality of our services to the quality of our environment.
— demonstrating impatience with economic hardship by continually striving to assist people in sound money management.
— continually reminding ourselves of our credit union's basic values — social and moral as well as economic.
(from the directors' report to the membership, Van City *Working Dollars*)

In early 1974, it was revealed that the British Columbia government's attorney-general's department was conducting an investigation into possible breaches of the B.C. Real Estate Act by real estate salesmen Stanley Silverman and Edward Walmsley. Their operations are described earlier in Chapter 19.

What possible connection could there be between the actions of Silverman and Walmsley and the goals of a credit union? One of S&W's favourite tactics was to buy a revenue house, drive up the rents, then get the house reappraised and remortgaged, the increase in value being skimmed off in profit. The investigation revealed that it was Vancouver City Savings Credit Union that was providing Silverman and Walmsley with a substantial proportion of their mortgage money, and was thus directly implicated in the most blatant blockbusting tactics.

John Iseli, manager of the Broadway and Waterloo streets branch of the credit union admitted that VanCity had provided the mortgage loans for some of the transactions. He said the loans had stopped a few weeks before the investigation was made public. According to Iseli: 'We're in the business of providing mortgage money, when we have such money available that can get a high rate of return and if it is a good risk.'

How did this situation come about in which VanCity has been diverted from its original ideals? Why did VanCity get caught up in the growth and bigness syndrome? Why has VanCity tried through every means possible to become more like the existing banks

One of VanCity's eight branches. It was this branch from which real estate salesmen Silverman and Walmsley borrowed some of the money for their 'dizzying' deals buying and selling houses.

and other establishment financial institutions?

Right from the beginning Vancouver City Savings Credit Union was growth-oriented. It started modestly enough after World War II when 11 people pooled $22 in 1946. The next year saw its first merger, with the University Employees Credit Union, followed by another in 1949 with the Hastings East Veterans Credit Union. By 1952, VanCity had 2,500 members and assets of $500,000. The growth curves for both membership and assets over the next 20 years tell the story.

VanCity spurred its growth campaign through two methods: (1) by extensive advertising and promotion through the mass media; (2) by continuing to take over smaller credit unions. Several taken over in 1973 included the Glad Tidings Temple and the Gorbel credit unions, and in 1974 the Dillingham, B.C. Ice and Cold Storage, and the Filipino credit unions. According to its charter, any person who lives in the City of Vancouver or in the municipality of West Vancouver may join VanCity (other municipalities have already established credit unions such as North Vancouver, Surrey and Richmond). But the VanCity management has been lobbying the provincial government to broaden its membership to include anyone who lives in south-western B.C. If granted, this would effectively force most of the remaining credit unions in the area to merge with VanCity.

There are at least two major reasons for the drive for bigness: (1) that since 1972, credit unions have had to pay income tax and this could amount to about 2% of revenues. VanCity has argued that only a very large credit union can afford this added expense and still maintain its financial viability; and (2) the belief that only by growing very large can you achieve an efficient operation. The directors explain their heavy growth policy thus:

Large size does not necessarily bring a maximum efficiency but it does provide the opportunities for economies of scale and volume needed to help minimize the spread between the savings and lending rates. VanCity's present size is not optimum for such economies but to find optimal size is difficult because it is a moving target. VanCity should continue to grow therefore, because steadily increasing assets indicate that more and more needs of more and more members are being met.

While VanCity is undoubtedly Canada's largest credit union and likely among the four or five largest credit unions in the world, it is not large when compared to the financial giants such as chartered banks and trust companies. Your credit union is not large enough to have much influence in the money market but must operate in the financial climate of government policies and huge financial corporations. (from the directors' report to the membership; VanCity *Working Dollars.*)

Recognizing the unfortunate direction in which VanCity was heading, a number of people from active citizen groups in 1973 stood for election to the board of directors. However, the election procedure almost precludes any significant change. Three directors of a total board of nine stand for election each year for three-year terms. A nominating committee of the board recommends the people it thinks should be elected, usually the former directors standing for re-election. And the members who turn out for the annual meeting usually follow the advice of the directors. Thus, the challenge was beaten back.

The present board is composed mainly of lower middle-class supervisory and sales people, and semi-professionals such as general accountants. Some of the directors in 1974 were:

Stanley Parsons, president, member since 1950, Vancouver regional sales manager, Western Supplies, plumbing and heating wholesalers.
Mike Betts, vice-president, sales representative, Alcock, Downing & Wright.
James Forbes, professor of economics, University of B.C.
Sandra Sutherland (new board member) partner,

Campney & Murphy, lawyers — at one time one of Vancouver's most powerful law firms, now in a state of decline; both her parents were active in credit unions.
Rolf S. Perry, member and director since 1947, retired, was assistant to superintendent of forest products research, University of B.C.
Herbert McConnell, distribution manager, Michelin Tire Co., member since 1951.

While VanCity may be now imitating some of the less desirable practices of large privately-owned financial institutions, it is still accessible to control by its member-users especially if they are well organized, and its large resources offer the potential for creative and effective policies.

Informational meetings: one way of raising community awareness.

36 Organizing

There is, of course, no secret behind successful citizen groups. It is a long hard process, an uphill fight to protect existing neighbourhhoods and to stop bad developments. But there do seem to be some general steps followed by most groups.
1) They build up membership by taking on smaller issues that people relate to and that can be won by the group.
2) They gain knowledge about how the system works and what they must do to win their issues.
3) They build up a structure that ensures that natural leadership will continue to develop from the community.
4) They move to broader issues that affect larger segments of the community and strike closer to the roots of the problems.
5) They engage in a continuing program of community education and awareness raising, which develops bonds among people.
6) They engage in positive actions that demonstrate that people can make a significant contribution to the life of the community.
Countless groups of people are continually organizing for one thing or another — to stop houses from being expropriated, to prevent a supermarket from expanding its parking lot, to stop construction of a high-rise apartment building in a low-rise area, to get a traffic light at a busy intersection where children are constantly crossing. Most of them pass into oblivion. Either they lose their fight and feel the situation to be hopeless, or they win and feel no further need to continue.

For whatever reason, some groups do continue to exist after the initial issue has been dealt with. There is a necessity for assistance in this from organizers with a feeling for the political realities of the day. One goal is to expand the base of the groups to contain as many elements of the community as possible. Further issues have to be selected carefully — they have to be at least potentially winnable — from a broad spectrum of possible issues that continually threaten neighbourhoods.

As the group builds up its membership, a number of other things may happen. By coming up against the system time after time, the group gains valuable first-hand knowledge of the system in operation: city by-laws which protect absentee owners, provincial and federal agencies which co-ordinate their efforts with the private developers and discourage and frustrate the efforts of citizens to compete in getting their needs met, the high-priced developers' lawyers, the politicans who present an image of public concern yet somehow always vote in favour of the developers. The group begins to understand how the whole system works and learns its way around city and provincial governments.

The group must also build up a structure of people who have worked and fought together. Through careful analysis of their successes and failures they gain an invaluable political education in the realities of the modern-day corporate world. Some groups seem to develop an inner elite, with this knowledge and power concentrated in a few perpetually-visible hands. But to become broadly representative of a community, it is essential that leadership continues to develop from the bottom by involving as many members as possible in making decisions. As the originators of the group get 'burned out' they often can move on to other areas of endeavour, carrying their knowledge with them.

Eventually the organization moves on to broader and more difficult issues that affect larger segments of the community, and get closer to the basic forces behind development. Vancouver has a classic example of such an issue in the wide-scale demolition of lower-cost housing accommodation to make way for more profitable development. This might then involve the organization of a tenants union to put a stop to these needless demolitions without the provision of alternate low-cost accommodation. This issue gets much closer to the economics of development, deterioration, demolition, and redevelopment, a process so wide-spread in most cities that the urban experts have come to look upon it as a 'natural process', when in fact it merely represents the power that real estate interests wield in our society. The process can be stopped, but it means that people affected by it have to work together to build up a strong enough voice so that their needs will be listened to as well.

As part of broad-scale organizing, almost as a 'fall-out' from the process, the level of awareness in the community rises. People begin to understand what is happening to their community and why, and what interests are being served. They see the whole process and not just a series of apparently isolated incidents. Hopefully they begin to see the common interests they share in the community. By publicizing the area's history, landmarks and people, residents begin to build a common *bond*, becoming aware that they share a common fate, and that if they want to improve or protect their neighbourhood they must act together.

Finally, at this stage, groups may become involved with more positive actions, producing alternatives that satisfy the needs of the residents. Some such actions might be the establishment of a housing society to buy up older homes capable of being renovated, and preventing developers from completing their land assemblies (reverse blockbusting), or building housing

Focussing on the developers: an example from the West Broadway Citizens Committee.

projects for senior citizens or other deprived members of the community. Such projects have at least three results: they produce better accommodation than existed before; they demonstrate to the community that the organization is made up of responsible concerned citizens willing to engage in hard work for the good of the community, not just a mob of negative rabble rousers; and they begin to loosen the stranglehold that blockbusters and speculators have over the neighbourhood.

SOME ORGANIZING TACTICS

One of the most effective tactics open to residents in their attempt to build a strong organization is to focus directly on the developers who are engaging in blockbusting, evicting tenants, and building poor projects, and to bring their actions under public scrutiny. Who are the owners, directors, and lawyers? What are their political affiliations? What are the sources of capital and mortgage money? Are there related or interlocked organizations engaged in similar activities? Can we build a picture of land assemblies through a systematic survey of all property in a given area?

As an extension to this tactic, citizen groups can buy shares in development companies, attend the annual general meetings and demand that management account for their actions, or try to elect citizen representatives to the boards of directors. Unfortunately, too many local developers are privately owned and thus inaccessible to this kind of effort. Even some of the large national corporations such as the Imperial Ventures or Dominion Construction Co. are privately held by a few individuals.

A related tactic is to focus on the inadequacies of existing government legislation and institutions in protecting the rights of tenants and resident home owners. In B.C. the recently-enacted landlord and tenant legislation and the establishment of a rentalsman is one such example. The *rentalsman* is based on the ombudsman concept, an office to which people experiencing difficulty in their dealings with government bureaucracy can go for satisfaction. One would expect, then, that the purpose of the rentalsman is to help both landlords and tenants with their difficulties over the landlord-tenant legislation. Yet the office soon became partisan in its dealings and quickly came to favour landlords more often than not. In fact, it seemed that tenants had been better off under the old legislation when disputes were resolved through the small claims court.

In most successful citizen groups both types of organizing tactics are usually combined. A tenants

An example of the value of good research: in the struggle to prevent Imperial Ventures from building a luxury high-rise condominium building, the developer and his associates were carefully researched. Thus at this demonstration it was possible to identify two people present (centre, speaking to each other) as associates of the developer. They were photographing people at the demonstration and taking notes of what was said.

WEST BROADWAY TTTTT CITIZENS COMMITTEE
– Speaking for the people of Kitsilano and its future development –
2865 WEST 4th AVENUE, VANCOUVER, BRITISH COLUMBIA V6K 1R3, TELEPHONE 736-2944

OUR HOME IS KITSILANO

Will YOU be kicked out next? ? ?

EVERY WEEK MORE AND MORE TENANTS AND RESIDENT HOMEOWNERS ARE BEING PUSHED OUT OF THEIR HOMES, UPROOTING THE WHOLE COMMUNITY!!

WHY???

GREEDY DEVELOPERS AND LAND SPECULATORS WANT KITSILANO PROPERTIES FOR HIGH PRICED CONDOMINIUM DEVELOPMENTS –– THEY EVICT TENANTS ON SHORT NOTICE AND HARRASS AND INTIMIDATE MANY RESIDENT HOMEOWNERS TO SELL. FAMILIES WITH CHILDREN, SENIORS, PEOPLE WITH LOWER INCOMES ARE SLOWLY BEING SQUEEZED OUT.

ALL LEVELS OF GOVERNMENT HAVE SAID THEY WILL DO NOTHING---Apparently they support developers in making Kitsilano a playground for the wealthy elite.

WHAT CAN "AVERAGE CITIZENS" DO?

Recently in Kitsilano, ORGANIZED CITIZENS HAVE:

(1) Exposed Real Estate corruption leading to Provincial investigation and pending Legislation.

(2) Forced City Council to pass a motion saying that private homes would never be expropriated for private developments.

(3) Saved residential land from being used for parking.

(4) Forced developers to sell and clean-up houses that were being used to "BLOCKBUST".

(5) Forced developers to put parking underground.

(6) Fought for local residents to get traffic signal – Vine & Broadway.

(7) Helped Homeowners fight Lies, Intimidation, Harrassment, and other tactics by Real Estate Companies to get their homes.

(8) Forced the City of Vancouver to DOWNZONE the area – NO MORE HIGHRISES.

(9) Forced developers at 7th and Maple to reduce 13 storey building to 3 storeys. This, after the project was legally approved and endorsed by all the politicians.

(10) Set up SENIORS NON-PROFIT HOUSING – the Government has not met the need.

(11) Pressured the City to set up immediately, a Citizens Planning Programme – At some point, Local Residents will determine what developments come into the area.

Developers are moving very quickly. YOU may be NEXT to go. Our only protection is strong organized neighbourhoods and people who are willing to help each other

KEEP KITSILANO OUR HOME.

IT CAN BE DONE, but not by leaving it to someone else. HELP YOUR NEIGHBOUR HELP YOURSELF. FIGHT BACK WHILE THERE IS STILL A CHANCE.

CALL US 736–2944

Building awareness, getting results: a West Broadway Citizens Committee leaflet.

---

union might be formed around the blatant actions of some landlords and the inequities in the existing landlord-tenant legislation. Tenants, propertyless, and, in a time of housing scarcity at a distant disadvantage in the market, may be more willing to join together to protect their rights.

WEST BROADWAY CITIZENS COMMITTEE.

The West Broadway Citizens Committee, a citizen group in the Kitsilano area of Vancouver, by the end of 1974 had grown to a membership of 500 people drawn from the many elements of Kitsilano. It was formed in the fall of 1972 when a number of Kitsilano home owners discovered that their properties were included in the city's plans for a large-scale 'beautification' (i.e. redevelopment) project for the area's main street, West Broadway. The citizens asked the city planners what would happen if they didn't wish to sell their houses to the city. The answer came back, 'Well, I guess the city would have to expropriate.'

It was at this precise moment that the West Broadway Citizens Committee (WBCC) was formed. The home owners got together and, with the help of some local planners and a community development worker, they were able to halt the project after an eight-month struggle. Many of these original WBCC members have remained in the group for over two years, because they have been able to do something to preserve and maintain their neighbourhoods.

The WBCC membership also includes a large number of senior citizens who joined the group as a result of the area's second issue, a 13-storey senior citizen high-rise in an area of Kitsilano where there were no high-rises. The area was, in fact, zoned to allow them, but none had so far been built. Thus the approved building conformed to the zoning. All three levels of government were contributing funds or land

When all else fails, it is sometimes necessary for citizen groups to take direct action. In these three photos West Broadway Citizens Committee members are attempting to stop an excavation for a high-rise building by Imperial Ventures.

to the developers, a non-profit service group, which would then have to maintain its rents below a certain level. The issue for WBCC was to get the governments to require that the building be scaled down to a height in keeping with the rest of the neighbourhood before the funds would be granted. Area residents felt that this high-rise was the thin edge of the wedge, that once one high-rise went up, others would be close behind. They believed that the developer was merely using senior citizens as a way of getting the first high-rise

in. To support this contention it was pointed out that the man who had assembled the land for the service club, a business associate of the club's president, had tried his hand at developing before. His project had also been a high-rise for an area of Kitsilano in which all the existing structures were no more than three storeys. That too was successfully opposed by many Kitsilano residents.

The WBCC and the area residents won the fight — the building was eventually redesigned to four storeys, still providing the same number of suites. As a result of the positive role played by the senior citizens who came into the WBCC, a separate group, the Kitsilano Seniors Housing Association, was set up to plan and build senior citizen housing for those on the lowest incomes.

A major weakness in the WBCC membership is the lack of representation from local merchants and businessmen. In fact, many of these people are faced by the same threat as the resident home owners and tenants: escalating commercial rents are forcing out many of the established merchants, and replacing them with large national chains and franchises. However, the merchants have traditionally acted through their own organization, the Kitsilano Chamber of Commerce, and WBCC members see the necessity of maintaining friendly relations between the two groups.

The majority of WBCC members are tenants, because the vast majority of Kitsilano residents are tenants. Gradually most WBCC activities have become centred around the problems of tenants as these become more desperate. At first the members tried to deal with the issues as they arose — fighting another high-rise for which six perfectly good houses were demolished; helping other residents to get a traffic light put in at a corner where two people had been killed; and taking on tenants rights cases in small claims court. Yet this one-at-a-time reactive approach must inevitably fail. The time, energy, and financial resources of citizen groups are severely limited, while, on the other side, there is no end to the legal, political, financial and technical pressure that can be brought to bear when developers move in to an area. Thus the WBCC embarked on a more ambitious venture, the organization of a tenants union. The initial organizing was being done in the apartment area of Kitsilano where many lower income tenants were being forced out of the area as their houses were demolished to make way for more profitable developments. Only by having a strong tenants union could these Kitsilano residents try to stop the demolitions and rent increases which were driving them out of the area, since city council refused to take any action.

OBSTACLES TO SUCCESSFUL ORGANIZING

There are three major obstacles standing in the way of

a group's continuation after its initial successes. Two of these originate outside the community, in attempts to discredit the group by the media and the politicians and in attempts to co-opt the group by the bureaucracy. But the obstacle from within the community — attempts to liberalize the group — may be more difficult to deal with.

OBSTACLE ONE: LIBERALIZING A GROUP

Frequently a tough stand is necessary to get the desired results. The group has written the briefs, it has collected the petitions, it has appeared before city council, it has done all the right things, and yet it has gotten absolutely no results beyond the inevitable promises. Yet the group is determined to get action. Therefore it is forced to take a stronger stand. Group members picket the government office; they confront the officers, they stop the bulldozers. Somehow the group ends up getting what it wanted. But during the process the group may have alienated others in the community, especially a middle-class community such as Kitsilano.

Too often people of middle-class background will agree with the group's goals but abhor its tactics. Many of these are professionals, the architects and social workers, the ones who usually become involved in 'community affairs'. Tough actions will eventually drive the liberals from the group. This may be a necessary step, because the alternative is the liberalization of the group from one that took strong action to solve real problems in the community to one that, after its initial successes, took a more 'responsible' position (as it is called) vis-a-vis the powers-that-be and settle into a comfortable period of decline.

Thus it may be necessary to force the liberals to commit themselves anew to the ideals of the group or to ask for their resignations. This is not so much of a problem as it seems. You still share the same concerns: (1) that government and developers should not harm your community; (2) that they should not make your community a worse place to live in than it was before; and (3) that land and housing costs should be as low as possible. If you are successful in achieving your goals the liberals will eventually be won over: it is in their own interests as well.

A good example of the liberal response and the difficulties it leads to is the Kitsilano Area Resources Association. It was set up in 1966 under the auspices of United Community Services in an attempt to identify the problems facing Kitsilano and to co-ordinate the existing services in the area, as well as establish new ones where necessary. Many area councils were set up during those years, and seemed to follow the same pattern. The Kitsilano Area Council was not different, being composed of well-intentioned professional people from health, education, welfare, and recrea-

they arose — the standard pattern with citizen groups. But nothing discourages ordinary citizens more than regular monthly meetings filled with academic jargon. The reality is that people are interested primarily in things that affect them directly and immediately. Consequently, only the small group of do-gooders — the people who wanted to help others — would show up at the meetings. The Kitsilano Area Council never represented more than a handful of Kitsilano residents.

tion. The major function of the group was to 'encourage and increase the participation of local area residents in the decisions which affect the lives of the people of Kitsilano.' The vehicle to achieve this goal selected by the professionals was to be regular monthly meetings at which issues could be discussed. The council executive expected the average citizen to become involved in the long-range planning of Kitsilano, and not merely to react to crisis situations as

Given these severe limitations the area council did achieve some worthwhile efforts. In 1969, the Kitsilano Information Centre was established to provide a wide range of information on local services, programs, activities, facilities, and events. In 1972 the Kitsilano Planning Centre was set up to give people help on planning matters. But this information was given indiscriminately to all factions in the community: to the developer who was looking for a good site to develop, and to the citizen group which had organized to fight him.

The Kitsilano Area Council became a non-profit society in 1972, changing its name to the Kits Area Resources Association (KARA) to operate on a more formalized basis as a kind of shelter organization for all of Kitsilano, 'providing a strong structural framework for citizen involvement.' Immediately KARA went into a period of decline and totally ceased to exist less than two years later.

What happened was that membership in the organization would flair up whenever an issue emerged in Kitsilano. In 1970, for example, KARA was fighting the proposed Arbutus-Burrard streets freeway connection. The organization came up with a compromise solution assuming that the connector would be built, but that it would follow the B.C. Hydro right-of-way and thus require the demolition of far fewer houses. KARA also organized a group of senior citizens to participate in the planning and design of senior citizen housing in the area (this is currently under construction). Between these issues, meetings were very poorly attended and represented basically the professional planners and social workers who were desperately trying to help the people of Kitsilano.

KARA's approach to problems was to study it, hold a series of meetings, and then write briefs; it was based on the liberal view of city politics, that basically things work well, they just need some fixing up by ironing out inequalities, and getting more citizen input into the process. Thus KARA took a negative stance toward the formation of the West Broadway Citizens Committee in the fall of 1972 to oppose the Broadway beautification project.

KARA in fact supplied a community development worker and the resources of the Kitsilano Planning Centre to the group of citizens who organized to save their houses. However, it was KARA's intention that once the Broadway redevelopment issue was more or less resolved, the West Broadway Citizens Committee would cease to exist, and the planning centre staff and the organizer would move on to the next issue. This was in line with KARA's view of itself as the shelter organization representing Kitsilano. Citizens would join together to fight their issue, then when that issue was resolved, the citizens would have no further need to remain together. KARA would maintain the initiative and collect the experiences together under its leadership.

The West Broadway Citizens Committee saw the situation in a different light. They saw that the only way to get the desired results was to build up a strong organization of people who were willing to take the necessary action to get what they believed to be right. KARA's approach would never achieve this, since the only continuity remained with the paid professional staff and not the affected citizens.

Thus when the next issue emerged in September 1973, there was a struggle between KARA and WBCC over who should take the dominant role. This issue was the proposed 13-storey senior citizen high-rise in an area where the tallest buildings were three storeys.

KARA sponsored a separate group — the Kitsilano Citizens Committee — to fight the high-rise. The WBCC also became involved. The KARA-sponsored group was short-lived, not having enough focus or understanding to see this issue through to the bitter end. Most opposition to the project centred around the WBCC, which helped the senior citizens to organize themselves in their fight for better conditions. Many of those senior citizens still remain active in the WBCC membership. In fact, the current chairperson of the WBCC is a 67-year-old former nurse who took a leading role in the dispute.

It was clear that the KARA model of organizing was no longer relevant to the conditions in Kitsilano. The crunch was coming. Who was to prevail? Was it to be the absentee landlords and developers who would continue in their classic method of allowing buildings to deteriorate, evicting the tenants, demolishing the buildings, and redeveloping to more profitable and higher density uses which the previous tenants couldn't afford? Or was it to be the existing tenants and resident owners who would protect their community and

build projects that they could live in? In this struggle, which could get nasty at some points, clearly the liberal approach — the study sessions, the brief writing, the delegations to city council — was irrelevant. By the end of 1974, KARA had gone out of existence, the Kitsilano Information Centre having been separated out and still providing a necessary service to the community.

OBSTACLE TWO: DISCREDITING A GROUP

A second obstacle to organizing is the attempt — usually by politicians or the media — to discredit a group. One example of this occurred when a delegation of citizens from Kisilano appeared before Vancouver city council in the summer of 1974 asking for a temporary downzoning in the apartment area of Kitsilano. Alderman Fritz Bowers voted against the request, adding 'We should know if we're hearing from 20 kooks, or if what we're being told is representative.' Alderman Bowers knew exactly whom he was hearing from, since he had been one of the aldermen who had voted to set up the group in the first place. It represented the Greek community, the established ratepayer groups, the social service agencies, citizen groups, the community centre association, the community resources board, the chamber of commerce, and even the city planning department. There could hardly be a more representative group anywhere in the city! Clearly Bowers' remarks were meaningless, and merely served to expose the inability of elected politicians to deal with issues that go against their own political philosophy. In this case, Bowers' was reluctant about putting any obstacles in the way of developers.

It is not unusual for citizen groups such as the Downtown Eastside Residents Association (DERA) or the West Broadway Citizens Committee to receive epithets such as 'Communist, pinko, Maoist, troublemakers, or outside agitators.'

In their efforts to protect their neighbourhoods, citizens should not expect unbiased reporting on events by the Vancouver media. In fact, the established media are intimately connected with the developers, bankers and politicians who are behind the destruction of the city. In the print media, the directors of Sun Publishing Co., owners of the Vancouver *Sun*, interconnect with developers such as Block Bros. and Bramalea Wescorp Developments; other property owners such as Garibaldi Lifts and Johnston Terminals; financial institutions such as Monarch Life Assurance Co., National Trust Co. (two directors in common), Coronation Credit Corp. and IAC. They are on the executive of the Non-Partisan Association and the city planning commission. They are represented on the boards of other major corporations such as Kelly Douglas & Co., Cornat Industries, Rivtow Straits, Inland Natural Gas Co., Okanagan Helicopters, B.C.

Sugar Refining Co., Crown Zellerbach and Burns Foods. There are no citizen representatives on the board of Sun Publishing Co.

Southam Press, owner of the Vancouver *Province,* is little better. Its directors interlock with construction companies such as Pigott Construction; financial institutions such as Eagle Star Insurance (two directors in common), Metropolitan Trust Co., North American Life Assurance Co. (two in common), Canada Trust Co. (two in common), and Dominion Life Assurance Co. They interlock with utility companies such as Union Gas and Canadian Utilities, and other major corporations such as MacMillan Bloedel (two in common), American Motors Canada, Noranda Mines, and B.C. Forest Products. Not one citizen representative here either.

The two newspapers are actually published by a third company, Pacific Press. Its board of directors is made up of representatives from both Southam Press and Sun Publishing Co., plus Gerald Hobbs, one of the key Vancouver business establishment figures. Hobbs is president of Cominco, and a director of B.C. Telephone Co., Bank of Nova Scotia, MacMillan Bloedel, Okanagan Helicopters, White Pass & Yukon Corp., and a former executive member of the Non-Partisan Association.

Citizens are as poorly represented in the private television stations, channel eight in Vancouver and channel six in Victoria, both owned by B.C. Television Broadcasting System. B.C. Television is actually controlled by two companies. One is Western Broadcasting Co., which owns 44% and has interlocking connections with Campeau Corp., Harbour Park Developments and Grouse Mountain Resorts, developers; with Imperial Life Assurance Co., Canada Permanent Trust Co., National Trust Co., Coronation Credit Corp., and the Bank of British Columbia, financial institutions. It connects with other major corporations such as Cornat Industries, Monsanto Canada, East Asiatic Co., and Greyhound Lines of Canada. One of its directors is the lieutenant-governor of B.C.

The other major owner of B.C. Television Broadcasting System, Selkirk Holdings, with 36.2%, has its own strong connections with the establishment. It interlocks with Franki Canada, a major construction company; major financial institutions such as the Bank of Montreal, the Royal Bank of Canada, Mutual Life Assurance Co. of Canada, North American Life Assurance Co., and Canada Trust Co. Selkirk Holdings also interlocks with several utility companies, Alberta Gas Trunk Lines, and Canadian Utilities.

Citizens do not come out better on the radio stations. CKNW is owned by Western Broadcasting Co., part owners of B.C. Television Broadcasting Co. CKWX is owned by Selkirk Holdings, the other major

partner in B.C. Television. CKLG is owned by Moffat Communications of Winnipeg which has its own intimate connections to the property industry; to developer Allarco Developments; to financial institutions, Bank of Montreal, Great West Life Assurance Co., North West Trust Co., Canada Permanent Trust Co., and Seaboard Life Insurance Co. It interlocks with Midland Osler Securities, an investment dealer, and with other major corporations such as National Agri-Services, Trimac Transportation, Metropolitan Stores, and M. Loeb.

Radio station CFUN is owned by CHUM, of Toronto. CHUM connects with the Power Corp. of Canada, Canada Steamship Lines, Granby Mines, and Goodyear Tire; with investment dealer Nesbitt Thomson & Co., with investment companies Great Britain and Canada Investments, and Dominion Scottish Investments; with property insurance company Reed Shaw Stenhouse; with Manufacturers Life Insurance Co., and with the Canada Development Corp.

That leaves the Canadian Broadcasting Corp., operators of television channel two, radio stations CBU and CBU-FM. CBC is a crown corporation, presumably owned by the people of Canada. At least there, citizens should be able to receive a fair hearing. Yet an examination of the board of directors of the CBC reveals exactly the same pattern as the private radio and television stations and the newspapers. At least eight of the 14 board members have some connection with the development industry. The board includes people such as Yves Menard of Montreal, a vice-president of marketing for Air Canada and a director of Allied Innkeepers (Bermuda), a wholly-owned subsidiary of Holiday Inns. The board also includes James L. Palmer of Calgary, a director of Bow Valley Industries, a large oil and engineering company which was one of the backers of Village Lake Louise, a huge international jet-set ski development in the middle of Banff National Park. Nor are B.C.'s citizens any better represented on the board of CBC. Until 1974 the west coast representative on the board was Richard B. Wilson of Victoria, a retired lawyer, who nonetheless retained directorships in some of B.C.'s largest firms including B.C. Telephone Co., B.C. Forest Products, and Canada Trust Co. In 1974 Wilson was replaced by Paul S. Plant, president of Ralph S. Plant, lumber dealers, and a member of the board of governors of the University of B.C.

OBSTACLE THREE: CO-OPTING A GROUP

The third obstacle to organizing is co-optation by the powers-that-be. A group has been successful in getting some of its minor demands met; its name has been spread around; it has achived a certain notoriety at city hall. True, city hall has resisted it at every step of the way, but in spite of that the group has succeeded. The next response from the politicians is to try to neutralize its efforts by giving its leaders jobs in city hall, or by appointing them to committees set up to study the issues raised by the group.

In areas such as Strathcona and Fairview, younger citizen group leaders have been successfully neutralized by offering them jobs in the city planning and social planning departments. Once inside city hall, those people can hardly expect to have the continued confidence of the remaining members, even though they may believe that they can do effective work from within.

Another method of co-optation has been through the local area planning program. Citizen committees were set up, or are proposed for various areas of the city to participate in the planning of the community. Even if they had worked as intended, they would have been little more than a facade, since the committees had no authority for making decisions — that was still retained by city council. But city council further neutralized the role of the committees by shortening their periods of operation, by limiting their terms of reference, and by cutting back in every way possible.

City council clearly demonstrated its intention not to take seriously the citizen committees in its reaction to the West End, Fairview, and Kitsilano programs. But the programs continue. Powerless citizen groups continue their futile meetings to draw up unlistened-to recommendations. The local area planners, for their part, are committed just to keep the programs going and to use up their budgets.

In his November 1974 report to the West Broadway Citizens Committee, outgoing chairman Jacques Khouri fingered the local area planning program as 'a sham attempt to dupe citizens into being manipulated by civic bureaucrats.' Local groups have no more decision-making power than before, and must continue to direct their efforts in the most effective manner and not be side-tracked into useless efforts that waste their precious resources and valuable manpower.

37 Direct action: Pre-emption and squatting

The idea of people taking direct action to solve their housing problems is hardly new to Canada or British Columbia. Most of western Canada was settled through pre-emption — a method by which people would clear the land and build upon it as a prerequisite to claiming it as their own. This was the only way to tame the vast space of the uninhabited country. With the severity of the present housing crisis, and the demonstrated inability of governments or developers to solve it, it is time for people to move this long-standing tradition of pre-emption and squatting into the city.

Vancouver had one example of such activity in its recent past during the summer of 1971 when the Four Seasons Hotels site at the entrance to Stanley Park was occupied. It was the last weekend in May 1971 when a group of young people executed a well-planned move to take possession of the site for a park and home-stead. They immediately renamed the barren waste-land All Seasons Park. They brought in trees, flowers and topsoil, planted a garden, laid out rockery, baseball diamond, and children's playground, and proceeded to camp out. The owner of the property, Harbour Park Developments, was loathe to call in the police to have them removed because Graham Dawson, one of the partners in Harbour Park, was a member of the police commission, and it would have looked a bit peculiar. Therefore, the occupants were allowed to stay.

Thus the situation was ripe for a relatively effective and permanent squatters settlement. Over the next weeks a number of imaginative shelters were built. The overnight population swelled to 300 to 400, as young transients swarmed into town after school was out for the summer. About 50 of these were permanent residents. Many thousands of people visited the park during the summer months. Society ladies, wanting to save both blocks for a park, trooped down with their flowers for planting.

The squatters remained on the site over the summer of 1971 despite attempts to have them removed. The fire and health departments of Vancouver waged a prolonged campaign of harrassment and threats. The only sources of water and electricity were mysterious-ly cut off. The settlement did straggle over the winter of 1971, but public interest had waned to such a point that when local National Harbours Board boss Bill Rathie called in the NHB police in April 1972 to demolish the remaining houses, there was little public response.

Thus, physically, the All Seasons Park experiment failed. The issue had been to save Stanley Park from encroachment, rather than the more important one of adequate housing. Further, the organizers had failed to channel the strong public sympathy that did exist for All Seasons Park into a viable political power. And the 'concerned' professional groups — the planners and architects and social workers — were conspicuous by their absence.

But there were some very important positive aspects about All Seasons Park. One, it illustrated clearly the difference between waiting for others to act for you and taking action yourself. This strong positive direct action which challenged people's creativity and ingenuity and which promoted solidarity and under-standing among many segments of society contrasted sharply with the sorry excuse of a referendum perpetrated by the TEAM council on the Four Seasons issue.

A second important result of the take-over of the area was the educational aspect for the general public. Many people, from all segments of society supported the action, and even though most were pessimistic about the ultimate outcome, at least the potentiality for such actions was etched into the public conscious-ness.

A third implication of the exercise was the demon-stration that people are creative in supplying and *producing* their own housing, throwing into high contrast the existing market for housing where people are treated as simple-minded *consumers*.

The All Seasons Park episode suggests one direc-tion for community action. There are large tracts of unoccupied land within the Vancouver city limits. Squads of construction workers and architecture and engineering students could move in over a weekend to erect large temporary settlements. Once established, it would be difficult for the authorities to remove them without providing alternate accommodation. There are literally hundreds of unoccupied or under-utilized buildings just sitting around awaiting more profitable uses.

Such actions are far from unprecedented in the history of British Columbia. Much of the area that was to become Vancouver had been settled by the pre-emption method. The first inhabitants of the Burrard Inlet area were the so-called 'Three Greenhorns', John Morton, his cousin Samuel Brighouse, and a ship-board acquaintance, William Hailstone. After unsuc-cessfully prospecting for gold in the Cariboo, they arrived on Burrard Inlet in 1862, and were impressed by the coal seam and good clay on the banks of Coal Harbour. They made a claim for most of what is now the West End. They built a trail, cleared some of the land, built a house and planted a vegetable garden, then bought a stove and began making bricks.

Many squatters still live in the Vancouver area. These are located in a settlement on the south arm of the Fraser River.

war against squatters, the ultimate eviction has usually followed upon the taking over of the property for commercial or industrial development.

A survey done in 1937 by the city revealed that there were over 200 people living in the False Creek area in 108 houseboats and 18 houses. There were five distinct settlements ranging in character from one which the city employees described as 'the filthiest and most distressful portion of False Creek' to one described as a 'fairly bright and cheerful neighbourhood.' There were also substantial settlements along the North Arm of the Fraser River and along Burrard Inlet.

About 1940 the city declared war on the squatters. It took 30 years for most of the squatters to be cleared out. Each time a group was cleared out, they merely waited until a high tide and floated their houses to a new location.

Every five years or so, the city set up a new subcommittee to deal with the issue. There was a flurry of newspaper headlines, a little action, then everything stabilized for another few years. In 1940, 1941, 1945, 1949, 1955, 1960, and the latest episode — the Maplewood mud flats of North Vancouver in 1971 — a concerted attack was launched on the squatters. Before each campaign the city whipped up public hostility through a propaganda campaign: 'the smell was terrible', 'indescribably filthy', 'very poor and dilapidated', 'unsanitary and unhealthy conditions', were some typical descriptions.

However, there was another opinion of the squatter settlements. In 1941, K.J. Burns, Vancouver port manager of the National Harbours Board, told the city council subcommittee that squatters were respectable law-abiding citizens who should be given some consideration.

The only thing I can say about the squatters is that their shacks are unsightly. They are completely law-abiding and I have been amazed at their cleanliness I found in their cabins. Since I assumed my present position in 1924, I have never heard a complaint against them.

This was not the kind of thing the city wanted to hear. After all, the squatters were there illegally, and the city could not condone an illegal act of any kind. No building permits had been issued for the squatters' shacks. They did not meet the city requirements. They were located in industrial zones where private dwellings were not permitted.

The city politicians were always faced with one fact — Vancouver had a perpetual housing shortage. If the squatters were evicted from their homes where would they go? If we're evicted, we'll have to go on relief. If we're allowed to remain, we can make a living — not a

However, two years later they leased the land, Morton and Hailstone went to California, and Brighouse settled on Lulu Island (Richmond) where he became a prosperous dairy farmer. When the CPR extended its terminal from Port Moody to Vancouver, the Three Greenhorns were able to effect a profitable settlement.

Many other squatters had settled in Stanley Park before the incorporation of Vancouver in 1886, and remained there until they were removed by the parks board in 1918. However, two Stanley Park squatters, Tim and Agnes Cumming, were able to prove that their parents had occupied a three-acre property near Brockton Point before 1870, that they had both been born there, and had remained there continuously since. Thus they had legal title to remain on the property, and were allowed to stay paying $5 per month rent, until they passed away, Agnes in 1953, and Tim shortly thereafter.

Vancouver, being a seaport, has always been home to many squatters. One of the reasons for this is that along the shoreline property rights are very ambiguous, and the existing city by-laws more difficult to enforce. Although the city has waged a perpetual good one, but a living.'

Gradually the land became more valuable and required for other uses and gradually the squatters were removed from their settlements. A major concentration of squatters went in 1971, when the District of North Vancouver declared that the Maplewood mud flats were required for a large urban development. After lengthy court proceedings, the squatters were evicted at the end of 1971. However, it is three years later, and no sign of development work in the area has appeared.

Squatting indeed has a number of problems associated with it: the difficulty of providing adequate health, sanitary and police services; the lack of planning controls; the difficulty of collecting taxes; and the major difficulty, the fact that squatting is illegal.

But there are a number of positive lessons to be learned from the example of squatting:

1) The resident, be he squatter or owner-builder, can build exactly what he needs when he needs it, and not be forced to accept only what the private developer will provide for him.

2) He can build and make additions when he has the financial resources available, and not go into perpetual debt by taking on a long-term high-interest mortgage, which requires regular monthly payments regardless of his changing financial status.

3) The squatter or owner-builder is given the opportunity to own his own home (although not necessarily the land it is on) when the only other alternative may be as a tenant in a poorly-designed, inadequate public housing project, perhaps requiring him to go on welfare as well.

4) The squatter or owner-builder acquires highly useful skills of carpentry and building through which he may be able to receive better employment.

5) Where owner-builders pool their resources and efforts, they develop a sense of community spirit and pride, two essential sentiments if we are to preserve a high quality of life in Canadian cities.

The examples of All Seasons Park, and of squatting and pre-emption generally, show how dramatic and effective direct action can be in building a group's power, developing widespread community support, challenging the political status quo, and working to solve its members' real problems simultaneously. Of course any direct action undertaken by a group has to be considered carefully for its potential costs and benefits, and both tactical and strategic planning are necessary if the group is going to achieve any success. Direct action has major implications internally for a group as well as having obvious external effects; the tensions created by the use of direct action tactics can destroy a group if the membership as a whole has not decided collectively that this is the right course of action for the group. But the liberal

Round one to squatters

North Vancouver municipal employees refused Monday to seize the belongings of 27 squatters living on mudflats below the Dollarton Highway.

The squatters, ordered evicted by the district council, had not moved when the bulldozer arrived to knock down their shacks.

And the employees decided it was not their job to carry out the eviction order.

"We're not paid to evict people," said one worker, and the bulldozer retreated.

The municipality wants the squatters removed to make way for a shopping and marina development.

Dan Clemens, one of the squatters, said council has so far refused to grant them a hearing.

Many of the squatters paid $500 or more for their shacks and want some compensation for them, he said.

In addition, the squatters are concerned that the municipality's plans will wreck the ecology of one of the North Shore's few remaining stretches of natural waterfront.

Vancouver Province 3 August 1971

Squatters face legal action filed by North Van district

The battle of North Vancouver's Maple Wood mud flats has gone to the courts.

Squatters, victorious so far in keeping the district of North Vancouver from demolishing their homes in the area 1½ miles east of the Second Narrows bridge, will now face legal action to dispossess them.

The district issued writs Thursday in B.C. Supreme Court naming four persons as defendants and claiming they had unlawfully entered on the land and erected dwellings.

In one action the defendants are sculptor Thomas Burrows, Pat Davis and Willie Wilson, who was a spokesman for the group, which on Aug. 2 prevented the district from demolishing their homes.

Vancouver Sun 27 August 1971

approach, as we saw in the previous chapter, often condemns a citizen group to meaninglessness and slow withering away from lack of relevance and lack of results.

38 Political action

Aldermen from The Elector's Action Movement have argued that local area planning committees and other citizen groups *must remain* purely advisory in nature because a duly-elected city council cannot delegate decision-making authority to voluntary groups, even if it wished to. Under the provisions of the Vancouver city charter, council is the centre of decision-making authority. So that if citizen groups want to have some control over that decision-making, then they have to gain control of city council. That means electing a majority of pro-citizen representatives to council.

There seem to be six steps in this process:

1 Demonstrate clearly to Vancouver's citizens the true interests of the existing city council members. Who are the hardline voices on council that consistently vote for the interests of the developers? Are there any moderates on council? Which way will they vote when challenged? Who are the pro-citizen voices on council? Vancouver's residents must be given very clear answers to these questions by continuing to publicize issues, and by forcing individual council members to expose their true interests.

2 Convince the existing provincial and federal political parties to vacate the municipal political arena. In essence, this means the New Democratic Party. They must be made aware that their continued presence in civic elections can act only to lose many potential pro-citizen votes which then have no choice but to move over to TEAM. In spite of the poor showing of the NDP in the 1974 election, this will be a difficult step to accomplish, given the single-minded dedication and the long-term view of many NDP members. But without it no progress is possible.

3 Form an alliance of progressive elements: citizen groups, tenants unions, labour unions. It will not be an easy matter for citizen groups and labour unions to unite. Traditionally, labour unions, especially the labour-intensive construction unions, see citizen groups as opposed to their interests of more and more construction work providing more and more jobs. Developers and politicans help to widen the gulf by portraying citizen groups as being opposed to all construction.

And indeed when dump-truck operators are prevented from loading their trucks by a group of people standing in front of the bulldozer — and lose wages because of this — it certainly does seem that citizen groups and construction workers are in conflict.

But, of course, this not true. Citizen groups are against bad developments, developments that destroy their neighbourhoods or make things worse than they were before. Construction workers are also home owners and tenants faced with the same pressures as the citizens who have come out to stop bulldozers. They often sympathize with the issues that the citizen are fighting: the demolition of low-priced housing and its replacement by much higher-priced accommodation that neither resident nor construction worker can afford. But workers must eat!

One way to overcome this problem is for citizen groups and labour unions to collaborate on innovative housing projects, projects that put human need ahead of maximum profit. Using the financial backing of the credit unions (many of which are related to labour unions) they can emphasize renovation and rehabilitation, and seek new forms of housing and methods of construction. In the long range, residents and workers can build up confidence in each other, and work together to build up policies that benefit each other.

There are several notable examples of labor unions siding with popular protests. The British Columbia and Yukon Building Trades Council, and Vancouver and District Labour Council both supported the acquisition of the Four Seasons property for parkland, while the United Brotherhood of Carpenters and Joiners Local 452 has always been a strong supporter of citizen protests. In Australia, a strong labour movement actively opposes the construction of buildings that would harm existing neighbourhoods or damage the environment, by declaring what is called a 'green ban'. This demonstrates that the alliance proposed here is indeed feasible.

Citizen groups that have had some success must begin to forge links among themselves and to aid and encourage the many new groups that are continually forming. The major difficulty here is with the traditional fragmentation among progressive forces where an alliance is often a fragile thing indeed. Yet an ongoing analysis of the political situation can help to develop bonds of understanding and a commonality of purpose in facing the common threat. Community newspapers and other publications play an essential role in putting information into the hands of many more citizens and also help groups to become aware of each other.

4 Run a slate of citizen, tenant, and labour candidates in the 1976 elections on a city-wide basis, establishing credibility and getting names and platforms known. Because at the present time Vancouver has an at-large system of electing aldermen, their names must be well-known across the city, and the bewildered voter faced with choosing among many names, most of them unknown to him, will tend to select those with whom he is familiar. Thus the citizen candidates are not likely

Halt 'urgently needed' on Kits condominiums

A spokesman for a Kitsilano citizens' group said Wednesday he is "shocked" by city council's rejection Tuesday of a proposal to put an interim freeze on low-rise condominium and apartment construction in a 60-block area in Kitsilano.

Jacques Khouri of the West

Broadway Citizens' Committee said his group has not protested condominium development for three months after being assured by council members that action would be taken on the increasing number of expensive condominium developments being planned in the area.

On clearly-defined issues citizen groups can expose the true positions of city politicians. On the crucial issue of preventing demolition of low-income housing, Kitsilano residents now know that only three Vancouver aldermen would support them — Rankin, Marzari, and Harcourt. *Vancouver Sun 11 July 1974*

This is COPE's proposal for a ward system in Vancouver. These boundaries would produce 21 wards. The figures refer to the number of voters estimated to live in each ward.

In the short run, construction workers and citizen groups often seem to have opposite interests, but their long-term goals are the same — adequate low-cost housing based on need, not profit, and preservation of their neighbourhoods. On a major project like the third crossing, which proponents calculated would yield 4090 man-years of work for construction workers, the Vancouver and District Labour Council were nevertheless opposed on the grounds that the crossing and related freeway system would 'ruin' the city.

to elect many members the first time the slate runs.

5 Put strong pressure on the B.C. provincial government after the next provincial election to impose directly a ward system on the City of Vancouver. This means that there will finally be elected representatives directly accountable to specific constituencies.

While the property industry has an overwhelming majority on city council, as it has now, an elected politican who feels sympathies with citizen groups and their politics can support them in his votes without threatening the industry. But should his vote become crucial, the industry will bring all the pressure it can to bear, and will make it as difficult as possible for that politician to step out of line and express his personal feelings. Therefore, a ward system or some form of

area representation is essential, if citizens are to get control of city hall. As James Lorimer concluded in his book *A Citizen's Guide to City Politics:*

A politician who is not tied very tightly to local citizen groups, who does not rely on those groups for his campaign funds and campaign organization, whose social life does not revolve around friends in the groups, whose outside professional life (if he has one) does not increase his dependence on his citizen group constituency, and whose resignation is not kept in the pockets of the groups in his ward is a likely target to be picked off by the property industry should it badly need his vote.

6 Elect a majority in 1978 or 1980.

WHAT NEXT?

The four programs proposed in this section — developing more co-operative enterprise, building strong local groups, initiating direct housing actions, gaining control of city council — can begin immediately within the present economic and political structure. Granted their attainment may be years off, but many people and organizations have been hard at work in various ways to bring them about.

But what next? What will it mean for citizen groups to gain control over city council? Or for people to begin to house themselves through their own efforts? Will these actions lead automatically to a better city? Will they loosen the grip that the downtown business interests now have over development in our city? As this book has tried to demonstrate, the present model of urban development is decision-making from the top down. It is my opinion that the only way this control can be challenged is from the bottom up, through the eventual establishment of local government. Clearly the programs outlined so far are necessary prerequisites to more responsive housing and development policies, but they still do not shift the initiative for development from the profit motive to community needs. We need long-range goals that will bring the development process under community control. Some of the possibilities here are:

— the establishment of community-controlled development corporations and construction companies which plan, design, develop, and build the housing and other facilities needed by the community using the wealth of local talent and knowledge found in abundance in every part of the city.

— dismantling the large credit unions into more locally-responsive components which can provide the financing required for locally-initiated projects; private funds can also be channelled into the community through the use of limited-dividend projects.

— repatriating the land back to the community; this will be a long evolutionary process which can be aided through a number of successive tax measures. First, the provincial government should levy a tax on foreign owners of land; second, municipal government should put a tax on absentee owners; and a third tax reform measure would be to shift the basis of property tax from the improvements to the land itself. Coupled with these measures could be a series of tax incentives to promote local business and entrepreneurship.

— the ultimate goal of citizen action is community control over development in all its aspects — ownership of land, control of financial resources, planning and development, construction. A further phase is the establishment of neighbourhood governments — in which local councils are elected by the members of the community, which have the power to make by-laws and to collect local taxes.

Obviously, not all problems are local problems, not all services can be provided at a local level. Sewers, regional transportation, some commercial facilities, regional parks — these and many more apply to areas larger than the local neighbourhood, and must be dealt with at a larger-than-neighbourhood scale.

There is thus the need for some form of regional control, but a regional government more appropriate to citizen control would be quite different from the models of regional government now in operation. It could be composed of elected representatives from each of the neighbourhood governments. It would have responsibility for dealing with regional problems and processes. One of its responsibilities would be to deal with downtown development. With strong local and regional governments there is clearly no need for an intermediate level of control such as we now have in the form of the existing municipalities. The City of Vancouver as it now exists is far too large to service local needs; and it is far too small to cope with regional problems It should be superseded by a second-level city government covering the entire Vancouver area, run by politicians who would be directly accountable to the neighbourhood governments they would represent. Of course, the city politicians, elected at-large as they are now, will not be happy with this proposal, since it will put most of them out of business. Nor will the large development corporations and chartered banks take lightly the threat to their dominance; they will use their enormous economic and political muscle to attempt to crush the citizen movement. It will not be an easy struggle. Yet what alternative do we have? A future Vancouver not controlled by its citizens is a very bleak prospect indeed.